ANXIETY AND

DEPRESSION

-2 book in 1-

Get to know your problems and free yourself from:

Negative Thinking, Anger, Panic, Worry, insecurity, fear, Freeing Yourself from Chronic Unhappiness Relieve Sadness, Overthinking

By

George Brown

© Copyright 2019 by _____ - All rights reserved.

The following Book is reproduced below with the goal of providing information that is as accurate and reliable as possible. Regardless, purchasing this Book can be seen as consent to the fact that both the publisher and the author of this book are in no way experts on the topics discussed within and that any recommendations or suggestions that are made herein are for entertainment purposes only. Professionals should be consulted as needed prior to undertaking any of the action endorsed herein.

This declaration is deemed fair and valid by both the American Bar Association and the Committee of Publishers Association and is legally binding throughout the United States.

Furthermore, the transmission, duplication, or repro-duction of any of the following work including specific information will be considered an illegal act irrespective of if it is done electronically or in print. This extends to creating a secondary or tertiary copy of the work or a recorded copy and is only allowed with the express written consent from the Publisher. All additional right reserved.

The information in the following pages is broadly considered a truthful and accurate account of facts and as such, any inattention, use, or misuse of the information in question by the reader will render any resulting actions solely under their purview. There are no scenarios in which the publisher or the original author of this work can be in any fashion deemed liable for any hardship or damages that may befall them after undertaking information described herein.

Additionally, the information in the following pages is intended only for informational purposes and should thus be thought of as universal. As befitting its nature, it is presented without assurance regarding its prolonged validity or interim quality. Trademarks that are mentioned are done without written consent and can in no way be considered an endorsement from the trademark holder.

EASY NAVIGATOR

Improve your social skills and your control over panic attack

Empaths and vagus nerve

Improve your social skills and your control over panic

Improve your conversation skills, manage your insecurity, self-esteem and confidence by controlling your emotional intelligence to overcome your insecurities. Find your new self.

By

George Brown

Table of contents

Personal Interest......... **Errore. Il segnalibro non è definito.**

1. Own Interests Transformed into Public Benefits.. **Errore. Il segnalibro non è definito.**

2. Public Interest Transformed into A Personal Interest ....**Errore. Il segnalibro non è definito.**

The Opposition Between Public Interest and Personal Interest ....**Errore. Il segnalibro non è definito.**

The Conflict Between Individual Interests and Collective Interests................... **Errore. Il segnalibro non è definito.**

Contradiction and Coordination of Personal Interests and Common Interests ... **Errore. Il segnalibro non è definito.**

Common Interests ... **Errore. Il segnalibro non è definito.**

How to Reform the Toxic Social Habits? **Errore. Il segnalibro non è definito.**

You Are Embarrassed to Show Feelings................... **Errore. Il segnalibro non è definito.**

You Feel Like You're Competing. **Errore. Il segnalibro non è definito.**

Toxic Relationship Low-Income Family Relationships **Errore. Il segnalibro non è definito.**

You Are Changing.... **Errore. Il segnalibro non è definito.**

Toxic Habits in Relationship That Most People Consider Normal .... **Errore. Il segnalibro non è definito.**

1. Report Card of Your Relationship ....**Errore. Il segnalibro non è definito.**

2. Accidentally Abandoned "Hints" And Other Passive Aggression .... **Errore. Il segnalibro non è definito.**

3. Hostage Relations **Errore. Il segnalibro non è definito.**

4. Blaming A Partner for Their Own Emotions .... **Errore. Il segnalibro non è definito.**

5. The Manifestation of Jealousy "Out of Love" .... **Errore. Il segnalibro non è definito.**

6. Solving Relationship Problems **Errore. Il segnalibro non è definito.**

The First Phase Is A Protective Reaction .... **Errore. Il segnalibro non è definito.**

The Second Phase Is the Euphoria ......**Errore. Il segnalibro non è definito.**

The Third Phase Is Drug Addiction .....**Errore. Il segnalibro non è definito.**

The Fourth Phase Is A Physical Dependence on Drugs **Errore. Il segnalibro non è definito.**

The Fifth Phase Is the Psychosocial Degradation of Personality .... **Errore. Il segnalibro non è definito.**

What to Do If A Loved One Suffers from Bad Habits? **Errore. Il segnalibro non è definito.**

Killing Assumption and Mental Leap..... **Errore. Il segnalibro non è definito.**

1 Mental Development of Young Children .... **Errore. Il segnalibro non è definito.**

Young Children Are Suggestible . **Errore. Il segnalibro non è definito.**

The Primary Means of Physical Education............... **Errore. Il segnalibro non è definito.**

Tasks of Moral Education .... **Errore. Il segnalibro non è definito.**

Means of Aesthetic Education.. **Errore. Il segnalibro non è definito.**

The Functions of The Cerebral Cortex Are Improved, Memory Is Developing............ **Errore. Il segnalibro non è definito.**

Bad Listening and Effective Listening.... **Errore. Il segnalibro non è definito.**

One Ear In, The Other Out....... **Errore. Il segnalibro non è definito.**

Why Listening Is So Difficult ... **Errore. Il segnalibro non è definito.**

Heard Is Not Saved by Itself ..... **Errore. Il segnalibro non è definito.**

How Listening Can Be Better .... **Errore. Il segnalibro non è definito.**

Listen with Open Ears .... **Errore. Il segnalibro non è definito.**

1. Be A Bit of a Detective .... **Errore. Il segnalibro non è definito.**

2. Switch to Reception .... **Errore. Il segnalibro non è definito.**

3. Relaxed .... **Errore. Il segnalibro non è definito.**

4. Attunement to The Discussion, Topic and Counterpart **Errore. Il segnalibro non è definito.**

6. Show Interest .... **Errore. Il segnalibro non è definito.**

7. Do Not Listen Passively, But Actively .... **Errore. Il segnalibro non è definito.**

8. Please Remain Authentic and Do Not Let Any Ear Chew **Errore. Il segnalibro non è definito.**

Reflective Listening Techniques .. **Errore. Il segnalibro non è definito.**

1. Misunderstanding .... **Errore. Il segnalibro non è definito.**

2. Reflection (Echo) .... **Errore. Il segnalibro non è definito.**

3. Rephrasing (Paraphrase) .. **Errore. Il segnalibro non è definito.**

4. Summary............**Errore. Il segnalibro non è definito.**

Different Medicines ....**Errore. Il segnalibro non è definito.**

What Are the Manifestations of The Panic Issue? ....**Errore. Il segnalibro non è definito.**

How Is A Panic Issue Analyzed?.. **Errore. Il segnalibro non è definito.**

How Is the Panic Issue Treated? . **Errore. Il segnalibro non è definito.**

Mind Reading ....**Errore. Il segnalibro non è definito.**

Takeaway ....**Errore. Il segnalibro non è definito.**

Has an Arrangement Set Up?...... **Errore. Il segnalibro non è definito.**

Use Muscle Unwinding Systems . **Errore. Il segnalibro non è definito.**

A Nonsensical Reaction............... **Errore. Il segnalibro non è definito.**

Win Big or Bust Reasoning .... **Errore. Il segnalibro non è definito.**

Magnification..............**Errore. Il segnalibro non è definito.**

Here's A Case of How This May Function .... **Errore. Il segnalibro non è definito.**

Might It Be Able to Be Win or Bust Reasoning? .... **Errore. Il segnalibro non è definito.**

Do Panic Assault Side Effects Fluctuate? **Errore. Il segnalibro non è definito.**

Early Life Difficulty or Misuse ..... **Errore. Il segnalibro non è definito.**

What Kinds of Medications Are Available? .... **Errore. Il segnalibro non è definito.**

Panic Assault Insights. **Errore. Il segnalibro non è definito.**

Emotional Reasoning.. **Errore. Il segnalibro non è definito.**

Overseeing Anxiety ..... **Errore. Il segnalibro non è definito.**

Peruse the Full Pleasant Rules ..... **Errore. Il segnalibro non è definito.**

Ending Perfectionist Thinking ..... **Errore. Il segnalibro non è definito.**

PART 1

IMPROVE YOUR SOCIAL SKILLS

Personal Interest

Personal interest refers to the sum of various needs for individual survival and development. Particular investments are the satisfaction of their material and spiritual needs. Own interests generally include three aspects: the happiness of survival needs, the joy of development needs, and the comfort of enjoyment needs. Survival needs are the needs of individuals and their families to maintain their existence and continue their future generations. Development needs are the needs for the development and improvement of the individual's ideology, intelligence, and physical strength. The need to enjoy is the need for people to improve their quality of life.

Constraints on personal interests' Various factors constrain their interests. The level of social productivity determines the social material wealth and spiritual wealth as a whole. Material wealth and spiritual wealth are the objects of individual needs, and the amount of material wealth and spiritual wealth restricts the realization of personal interests in general. The difference in a person's status and role in society determines the difference in the way, quality, and quantity of his benefits. For example, if the ruling class occupies a dominant position in the community, they can use their power to squeeze the labour and sweat of the labourers to hold a large amount of material and cultural wealth freely. However, under the exploitation system, the majority of labourers are in a position of being exploited and oppressed. They obtain a small number of living materials by selling labour.

Public interest and personal interest Public interest and individual interest are dialectically unified, which means that on the one hand, there is no fundamental conflict between public interest and particular interest. Usually, everything that benefits the public is also suitable for individuals, and vice versa. When individual rights cannot guarantee space-time talk and obedience to the public interest, obviously it can only fall into fantasy and despair. Only based on fully respecting the rights of individuals, the boundaries of public affairs can be reasonably delineated.

Ultimately, personal interests and public interests cancel each other out and cannot achieve. On the other hand, there are inevitably some contradictions between private interests and public interests, because each individual's interests affect others and society through his actions. As the most significant public interest, the total amount of social resources is limited, and the contradiction between personal interests and public interests is inevitable.

Even so, "it should be avoided to confront" society "as abstract things against individuals", Because the purpose of protecting the public interest is only to limit personal attention moderately, it never denies its interests and own rights. Montesquieu believes that if "individual private interests should concession to public interests", it is "absurd theory." "Because public interests are always: everyone keeps the property given by civil law forever. "The dialectical and unified relationship between public interest and personal interest has fully expounded in Marxist theory. "As a general, universal and standard social interest, it is embodied as an individual, unique and individual characteristic.

Among the personal benefits, personal interests reflect the requirements of social affairs, which are the performance of social issues in unique individuals and are constrained by social interests. Social investments are general, relative reflected in personal interests Stable and repetitive things are the most potent basis of human attention. Social affairs are not merely in their interests but are realized in different forms and with varying strengths using personal interests. "

(1) Identity of public interest and private interest Public interest and individual interest should be consistent and the same. Only when the public interest is adequately safeguarded and guaranteed can personal interests be the basis for realization. If your interests are not guaranteed and satisfied, it will also jeopardize the understanding of public attention. General management only pursues public affairs, and then requires that each specific subject of general management only pursues public interests. In most cases, it is unrealistic. This way of thinking base on the simple opposition between private interests and public

interests. The interdependence and interrelation between personal interests and public interests. The identity of public interest and particular interest manifested in two aspects:

1. Own Interests Transformed into Public Benefits

As a common interest of members of society, the public interest is separated from individual attention and becomes an independent interest. This transformation has gone through a long period of development.

At first, its base on a blood relationship; later, it bases on the positional relationship; and finally, it on political ties. However, this always occurred based on the existing physical and corporal connections, language connections, larger-scale division of labour connections, and other stakes in each family or tribal Group, primarily based on the interests of all classes. However, as the general representative of the public interest subject, it is only an abstract personality subject, and cannot digest the public interest. Eventually, it still needs to be distributed to members of society to enjoy. From personal attention to the public interest, and then from general interest to particular interest, a cycle of interest transformation complete. Through this process of benefit transformation, social justice is achieved or achieved, that is, members of the society occupy the benefits on an equal basis, and the disparity between the rich and the poor in the community reverse.

China has always advocated that public interest is better than personal attention, and particular interest should obey public interest. However, under the current market economic system, whether public benefits always take priority over individual interests is debatable in our opinion. From the perspective of public interest, it has a close relationship with civil society. According to the view of the natural law school, before entering a civilized society, human beings lived in a natural state.

In the natural state, without the state, government, and laws, everyone chases their private interests, life is weak, and the relationship is cruel. The defects of the natural state make people transfer some of their rights and interests through social contracts, establish public power, and maintain public benefits and order. Therefore, the public interest is separated from personal attention and transformed from particular interest. Without their interests, there is no public interest. Although public interest exists in individual interests, it is not a simple sum of personal attention. Only this kind of universal and intelligent interest can qualify as the goal of collective behaviour and the basis of the moral value of the individual expression.

2. Public Interest Transformed into A Personal Interest

The public interest stems from private interests and based on their interests. As a holistic interest, the public interest is enjoyed by every member of society and not monopolized by one person or class of people. Since the realization of public interest creates conditions for the full understanding of personal attention, its recognition also in the awareness of the own benefits of all members of society. Therefore, public interest has become the common belief and collective choice of modern society.

By no means does it mean that we can ignore or ignore our attention. Open interest is priority based on fully respecting and protecting own interests because society is a human society, individuals are the fundamental constitution of society, and individual attention is the source and basis of any holistic benefits. That kind of public interest with no background and no premises does not exist at all, let alone priority issues. Historical experience shows that defending the so-called public interests by denying personal benefits is often an excuse for the minority power class to seek its importance and a shield to cover up its abuse of power.

The Opposition Between Public Interest and Personal Interest

The clash between public interest and private interest refers to the movement and trend of their divorce, differentiation, and restriction. Although the public interest and the individual interest are the same, there are differences after all. Once the importance separated from personal attention becomes a public interest, it is relatively independent, so it cannot be the exclusive interest of a member of society. Every member of the community always opposes the separation of public attention from his interests, and still hopes to get a share of the public interest. On the other hand, these special interests are always opposed to the imaginary common interests, and the actual struggle of these special interests makes the illusory appearance in the state's attitude.

The general's interests must interfere with and restrain special interests. "In this way, the opposition between public interest and personal interest formed. The opposition between public interest and personal interest is universal. It exists not between the ruling class as the main occupier and the members of the ruled class who have difficulty in enjoying the public interest but between the entire ruling class and the members of the ruling class; not only in the capitalist society, It also exists in a socialist society. Mao Zedong pointed out, "Our people's government is a government that truly represents the interests of the people and serves the people, but it also has certain contradictions with the people.

This contradiction includes the conflicts between national interests, collective interests, and individual interests. contradiction." In the article "German Ideology", Marx and Engels profoundly pointed out that as long as the external social division of labour still exists, the consciousness of products and people has not significantly improved, and the confrontation and struggle between public interests and personal interests will always exist. It can only eliminate in a communist society. Where civic groups are broad and include a large number of individuals, everyone has an intention to avoid performing their duties. Aristotle pointed this out very early. He believes that "all public things that belong to the majority are often the things that least cared. People care about their own and ignore public things about the public.

At most, he only pays attention to things that are somewhat related to him." He regards the collective actions of others as being determined in some way. Understand. If the public interest has produced, then his enjoyment of this interest will not be reduced because he has not contributed. If the public interest not present, then his behaviour cannot change this situation in any way—he' logic of collective action ', which is actually "the dilemma of collective action.

Personal and collective interests Individuals and collectives are both clearly distinguished and inextricably linked. First, individuals depend on organizations. The organization is a condition for individual survival. Individuals always live in a particular collective. Own growth and development are also inseparable from the organization; the organization is an essential condition for personal growth and development. The development of secret wisdom and talents is inseparable from the collective, which is the stage and conditions for the development of their knowledge and skills. The kind of "individual struggle" and "self-actualization" that leave the collective are wrong. Second, the collective depends on the individual.

Organizations are composed of individuals, and without individuals, there is no collective. The aggregate functions and functions have derived from the role of everyone in the organization. The collective power is composed of everyone's ability. Not only are there distinct differences between individual and collective interests, but they are also closely linked. They presuppose each other, depend on each other, promote each other, and develop together. First, collective interests are the source and guarantee of individual attention. Individual interests are inseparable from mutual interests. Individuals live in collectives, and collectives are the conditions for their survival and development.

Only when the organization exists and develops can individual benefits be realized. Collective interests are the foundation of collective existence. Without mutual investments, collectives cannot exist. Without the organization, the individual would have no place to live, and there would be no personal interest. Collective interests fundamentally determine and restrict individual interests. Therefore, mutual benefits are the source and guarantee of different interests. Second, individual interests are the ultimate destination of collective investments.

Just as personal attention cannot separate from mutual interests, mutual interests cannot wholly separate from different interests. Existence development collective interests are existence and development collectives, and the existence and development collectives are the survival and growth of the individual in aggregate, the individual interests of everyone in total. If the existence and development of mutual interests entirely separated from individuals and personal interests, the presence of collective interests has no meaning. Therefore, the ultimate result of the development of collective interests is individual interests, and different benefits are the final destination of mutual interests.

The Conflict Between Individual Interests and Collective Interests

Collective interests and personal interests are not always consistent, and sometimes confrontations or disputes may arise. Because, on the one hand, the level of social productivity is not high, and social products are not rich enough to fully or simultaneously meet the needs of the collective and the individual needs of each cooperative member. If the individual needs Bare met, the joint needs cannot fit; if the collective needs met, the individual needs could not reach. On the other hand, the existence of the social division of labour and the three significant differences, and the influence of wrong ideology have caused people to have unreasonable personal needs, formed individualism, and prevented people from correctly handling the relationship between private interests and collective interests.

There must be a confrontation or conflict between individual interests and mutual interests. Throughout the ages, the relationship between individual interests and collective interests has been an objective existence. As long as there are personal and collective, there is a mutual relationship between personal interests and collective interests. As long as there are private interests and collective interests, the relationship between own interests and collective interests is as explained above. However, because people have different understandings of the relationship between personal interests and mutual interests, different moral codes have emerged to deal with the relationship between individual interests and shared interests. Personal and social interests Interest itself has dual characteristics of individuality and sociality.

Particular attention refers to the individual's confirmation of the subject matter that can meet his various needs. In this sense, care is first and foremost personal, and it is the most core and fundamental part of interest. According to Weber's "ideal model", the concept of interest can be modelled from the perspective of personal interest. Due to the individuality of man, his needs and the satisfaction of needs are individualized. In this sense, any benefit is personalized. However, due to the similarity of needs between individuals, they can jointly collaboratively meet everyone's needs, and the cost reduction benefits increase; or because in social interaction, the needs of individuals may overlap, like several the intersection of planes is the same.

Although the part of this intersection comes from the needs of a single person in the most primitive sense, because it satisfies and realizes most people or all people in society in social relations, it has a relatively independent Status. As far as I understand it, social interest refers to the objects and ways of fulfilment that involve the needs of most or all members of society. This understanding can further from the concept of "public goods" in public sector economics. The social benefit of absolute sense is to meet the needs of the individual, and the enjoyment of each individual does not affect the enjoyment of other individuals.

That is non-exclusive and non-competitive goods or standard methods (such as social rules).

For example, the need for security provided by the national defence and the order provided by law is required by every individual in society. Of course, although the social interests at this level have the most extensive scope, their content is limited. The social benefits at the secondary level refer to the common parts of the investments within the secondary social group. According to tomorrow's calculations that even a very democratic decision in a very egalitarian society cannot satisfy the interests of all people in the community.

The benefits of each individual are different, so at most, the attention of most people can form. The secondary social group refers to the social community that combined due to similarity in a particular aspect or for a specific reason, and the interlinked part of the interest is the social interest. Such social benefits have a broader reality. In any sizable social system, there are various subsystems. As for the members in the subsystems, the social interests they face have different levels and therefore, different contents. The boundary of personal interests lies in the benefits of their pure satisfaction and the part of their achievement in social benefits; it is the most basic unit of benefits.

The boundary of social benefits lies in the interlinked parts of one's affairs; for social reasons, it has relative independence, and because of the hierarchical nature of social groups. Since the realization of some personal benefits can only be realized using social power or in the form of society, the social interests have possessed superior power and specific priority over the pure personal attention from the date of its creation. It makes the boundaries between the two more clear, mainly when a large community organization acts in the name of social interest.

Contradiction and Coordination of Personal Interests and Common Interests

One: -

From the perspective of historical materialism, the contradiction between private interests and common interests is a unique social and historical phenomenon, which is not always there, nor is it just the result of a vicious expansion of pure personal desires. Historically, the contradiction between private interests and common interests arises with the development of the social division of labour among people, and it is an inevitable companion to the development of the division of work at a particular stage in human history. The development of the division of labour, there are contradictory interests of a person or family and common interests of people who interact with each other. In early human society, primitive society, there was no confrontation and contradiction between personal interests and shared interests.

At that time, for each member of the community, individual interests were directly the common interests of the entire clan. What they pursued was not their private interests that were inconsistent with common interests; on the other hand, The ordinary benefits of the clan society must also be discussed, realized, and maintained by all members, and the common interests are also personal. This simple consistency of the individual attention and common interests of the primitive society determine by the primitive production methods, and its base on the division of labour in the budding state, which is not what some people think.

In the primitive society, the development level of productive social forces was shallow, and the survival of the individual depended entirely on the primitive collective, that is, the clan organization. Apart from the physiological differences, the individuals were almost wholly in the state of natural equivalence. In this case, "the division of labour was originally only the division of sexual intercourse, and then it was spontaneously or naturally generated due to talent (such as physical) needs, chance, etc." This budding division of labour does not fix at first. Even if there are some everyday things, such as sacrifice to ancestors, sharing food, directing military affairs, etc., individual members are required to take charge. These people give certain powers, but they must also engage in productive labour like other members of society and enjoy equal Social status, and living conditions are not privileged.

People produce and possess together cultural property, and joint participation in all corporate affairs shall be subject to the original public ownership. In primitive society, it is precisely because the social division of labour between people is still in its infancy; there is neither a common interest that is separated from personal interests to obtain relative independence. The benefits have not differentiated, and the individual is neither possible nor necessary to pursue a particular private investment that is different from the common interest. Therefore, in primitive societies, "criminal crimes of self-interest are rarely encountered."

The contradiction between personal interests and common interests arises at the same time when the individual benefits are separate from common interests, and the common interests are isolated from different individuals to gain some independence. In the late primitive society, with the development of social productivity, the spontaneous division of labour with fixed professional divisions gradually replaced the first division of labour. The division of labour has only become a real division of work since then, with the development of this division of labour.

On the one hand, each worker can meet his needs only by exchanging his products. It makes different activities of different individuals interdependent. "Every individual's interests, welfare, and happiness are inextricably linked to the welfare of others. Thus forming a common life and common interests among all people interacting with each other. And, "This kind of common interest does not only exist in the concept as a universal thing but also first exists in reality as the interdependence between individuals who divide each other's labour."

On the other hand, spontaneous division of labour has created clear boundaries for everyone's activities, whether he is a hunter, fisherman or shepherd, or a critical critic. Whether it is a person engaged in specific productive labour or a person holding public office in society, each realistic individual pursues particular and one-sided interests within the limits of his division of labour. Carrying out activities within the boundaries of this division of work, "Individuals always and can not start from themselves." With the development of the division of labour, personal interests and common interests have split. In the later period of primitive society, with the spontaneous division of labour gradually replacing the first natural division of work, "material and spiritual activities, enjoyment and energy, production and consumption are possible to be shared by different people and become a reality. Some people began to break away from specific and direct productive work, specialize in certain public positions, and engage in social organization and management directly related to common interests.

The vast majority of other people gradually lost their right to participate in common interests. The public social office began to separate from other occupations, and general social officials gradually became bearers, defenders, and representatives of common interests, and became the ruling class of society. The common interest, therefore, separates itself from the individual and gains a certain degree of practical independence, which becomes something external to the individual, and sometimes even opposite to their 1personal interests.

In other words, for individuals, the realization of common interests does not mean the satisfaction of personal attention, nor does the achievement of one's interests say that the common interests can realize at the same time. In this case, original consistency between individual interests and the common interests finally replace by the contradiction between the two. The development of the spontaneous division of labour is the fundamental cause of the split and contradiction of personal interests and shared interests.

When the automatic division of labour occurs, everyone has a specific range of activities that he imposes on him, and he cannot exceed this range. "He is a hunter, fisherman or shepherd, or a critical critic, as long as he does not want to lose his means of living, he should always be such a person. This spontaneous division of labour means the labour's submission to work and the labour's "alienation". It is this "alienation" that makes the common interests of all people interacting with each other formed by different activities of different individuals become a kind of alien and external force for each individual. Thus making personal interests Splits, contradictions and conflicts gradually emerge with the common interests. Some people believe that in primitive society, only the common interests of all members of the clan existed.

In the later period of primitive society, the gradual strengthening of private interests caused conflicts and even conflicts between personal interests and shared interests. This view that the contradiction between own interests and common interests is rooted in the strengthening of private interests is incomplete. It is because: First, there is no so-called common interest without personal interests; there is no so-called particular interest without common interests. "The two aspects shown in history, namely the private interests of individuals and the so-called universal interests, are always accompanied by each other." Personal interests and common interests are "two aspects of personal development, and the experience of personal life also produces these two aspects, they are just the same kind of personal development of people".

Second, common interests "always continue to arise from the other side, the side of private interests". That is to say, common interests generate during the realization of personal attention, and they develop from their interests, not the contrary. Personal care can never arise from common interests. Third, the individual always starts from his special private interests. "For each individual, the starting point is always themselves, of course, individuals in certain historical conditions and relationships, rather than" pure "individuals as understood by thinkers." The reason why an individual starts from his interests, but by the spontaneous division of labour What decide is a kind of stipulation imposed on individual activities by the autonomic division of labour. Therefore, the strengthening of personal interests is not the root cause of the conflict between their interests and shared interests.

On the contrary, logically speaking, the consolidation of private interests precisely based on the division and contradiction between it and common interests as the basis and premise. Only based on the division and opposition of personal attention and common interests will there be a vicious expansion of their interests and their damage to shared interests.

Two:-

Under the conditions of spontaneous division of labour, the common interest developed from individual interests gradually gained the form of "universal interest" in the process of gaining independence from different individuals. This form of "universal interest" makes the common interest. In reality, it manifests as an imaginary, common interest, and creates the contradiction between personal interests and common interests extremely complex in reality. The so-called imaginary common interest means that under the conditions of spontaneous division of labour when the common interest appears as the interdependence relationship between individuals who divide each other in reality, it is familiar with people.

Unreal common interest does not refer to something that does not exist at all; it is a real manifestation of common interest under the conditions of spontaneous division of labour. It is just because it takes the form of "universal interest" and does not reflect the interdependence between individuals in the division of work in the content, so we say that it is an imaginary, common interest. Under the condition of the spontaneous division of labour, the common interest as the interdependence relationship between individuals who divide each other's work must be manifest as an imaginary common interest in the process of its realization. It is because, as the spontaneous division of labour gradually replaces the original natural division of work, it becomes a reality that the common interest is separated from the individual and becomes independent.

Undoubtedly promotes the development of the common interest to a certain extent. However, under the conditions of spontaneous division of labour, since each individual is only pursuing his own, unique, and benefits that are inconsistent with their shared interests, even individuals who hold public office are no exception. At the same time, other non- public officials in the community gradually lost the right to participate in decision-making on common interests. Therefore, the common interest in the form of "universal interest" in the process of gaining independence from individual individuals will inevitably transform into the particular attention of the standard interest bearer, which becomes an illusory, common interest. In other words, under the conditions of spontaneous division of labour, the common interests declared by the ruling class in the form of "universal interests" are not entirely equivalent to the reality of the interdependence between individuals as divisions of labour.

Common Interests

In a class society, on the one hand, in the process of fighting against the ruling class, every class that seeks to gain a dominant position always appears as the representative of the whole society to win the support of the entire community, especially other ruled types. And make every effort to describe their special interests as the common interests of all members of society. On the other hand, to protect their own acquired special interests, the ruling class always declares itself as a natural representative of the benefits of the whole society, still dressing up their interests in this way as the general interests of all members of the community. It must also "give one's thoughts a universal form." For example, in a capitalist society, the bourgeoisie has always claimed that it is the representative of the whole community.

The bourgeois state is correspondingly said to be the protector of the interests of all members of society, and "actually the state is nothing more than a bourgeoisie to A form of organization that must be adopted to protect one's property and interests from the other ." What it embodies is only pretending to be of general interest. The special attention of the bourgeoisie is a kind of imaginary common interest. It can seem that under the conditions of spontaneous division of labour, the reason why common interests take the form of illusions is historically inevitable.

Under the terms of automatic division of labour, since shared interests must take the form of dreams, then personal interests and common interests in real life. The contradiction is not a flat contradiction between private interests and everyday interests, but a complex of contradictions intertwined between individual interests, real common interests, and imaginary common interests. This contradictory complex contains at least the following three aspects: First, the conflict between personal interests and real shared interests. The real common interests, as the commonality between the individual attention in the community, are mostly not contradictory to their interests. Of course, there are also confrontations between them under certain conditions, but "these confrontations are only superficial, because of one side of this opposition, the so-called 'universal' side, the side of private interests.

It is by no means opposed to exclusive benefits as an independent force with a separate history. Here, as opposed to personal attention and everyday interests, "the two aspects of personal development, these two aspects are also produced by the experience conditions of personal life".

Second, the conflict between personal interests and imaginary common interests. For individuals, the imaginary, common interests act in the name of the common interests and work in the interests of special interests. It is an alien and external force. Therefore, individuals always oppose such "common interests" not only in thought but also in action.

On the other hand, the imaginary common interests are still under the guise of safeguarding the attention of the community, and directly interfere and suppress individual care with the help of the city. The contradiction between many personal interests and common interests in real life refers to the contradiction between private interests and imaginary common interests. T

hird, the contradiction between shared interests and imaginary common interests. The imaginary common interest is the actual manifestation of the real common interest under the conditions of spontaneous division of labour. However, the imaginary common interest conceals and distorts the genuine common interest to a certain extent. Here, how to realize the real common benefits and at the same time effectively prevent the imaginary common interests from acting in the name of the common benefits to implementing the special interests becomes the key to all problems. It is particularly prominent in today's debates on human affairs and national interests. We know that various contemporary global issues such as environmental pollution, ecological imbalances, arms races, energy, and raw material crises have seriously threatened the survival and development of all humanity, and the requirement to safeguard the common interests. So urgent. However, it is not difficult to find that some countries have not given up the principle of giving priority to national importance under the guise of safeguarding the interests of all humanity by their dominant position in today's world.

Similarly, national interests also need to be defended. However, political parties in some countries rely on their status as the ruling party to protect the interests of national importance. They even ignore human benefits and desperately develop nuclear weapons. They are trying to seek party interests. Of course, this does not mean that the common interests of all humanity do not need to safeguard, and national interests need not defend. The problem is that some countries, social groups, some individuals put their special interests above national interests, or common interests of humanity, and exercise their interests in the name of common interests, so real. The common interest has destroyed again and again, and this is the real essence of the problem.

Three: -

Since the root of the conflict between personal interests and common interests lies in the spontaneous division of labour, only by eliminating the division of labour can the contradiction between private interests and common interests be fundamentally resolved? Of course, the division of labour mentioned here is not a division of work in the general sense. Still, it refers to the old-style, spontaneous division of energy with a fixed professional division. Here, "division of labour and private ownership are two synonyms, one thing is said, one is in terms of activities, and the other is in terms of products of activities." We say that to fundamentally resolve the contradiction between personal interests and everyday interests, the spontaneous division of labour must be eliminated, that is, the old-style, automatic division of work with a fixed professional division must remove.

There is the phenomenon of "alienation" of labourers' submission to work and people's introduction to things. It can only achieve in a communist society. "In a communist society, no one has a fixed range of activities, everyone can develop in any department, and society regulates the entire production so that it is possible for me to do this today as I wish, and then do that tomorrow. Things, hunting in the morning, fishing in the afternoon, animal husbandry in the evening, and criticism after dinner, but it did not make me a hunter, fisherman, or critic." So, before humans entered the communist society, especially in our real-life today, how to reconcile and resolve the conflict between personal interests and common interests? In the past historical development of humanity, the contradiction between personal interests and common interests was generally resolved on the surface by the realization of illusory, common benefits.

In the human form, based on the spontaneous division of labour, the imaginary common interest has become the only criterion for judging whether all people's concepts and behaviours, including their interests, are reasonable. All ideas and practices that conform to the imaginary common interests, because they are basically in conformity with the special interests of the bearer of the common interests, that is, the rulers, always get the advocacy and support of the rulers. Similarly, personal benefits can only be affirmed and satisfied if they are conducive to the realization of unreal common interests.

However, the contradiction between private interests and unreal common interests is confrontational, and this contradiction cannot resolve fundamental resolve through the realization of unreal common interests. As Habermas said: "When only special interests squeeze in the stakes, behavioural conflicts cannot resolve at all." Because of this, we assume that the previous solution to the contradiction between the common interests and personal interests is only superficial. In fact, in history, not only has the contradiction between private interests and common interests fundamentally overcome and resolved, but the intensification of such contradictions has occasionally triggered the struggle of personal interests against the imaginary common interests.

It is precisely this kind of fight that "necessarily made the actual interference and restraint of special interests through the illusory 'universal' benefits appearing in the state's posture. In a capitalist society, the contradiction between personal interests and common interests has reached an unprecedented level of sharpness. However, the development of the capitalist industry also created the necessary social conditions for eliminating the spontaneous division of labour and genuinely solving the conflict between personal interests and shared interests. The worldwide expansion of capitalist production methods, especially the industrial revolution of capitalism, significantly promoted the development of productive social forces, thereby creating a material basis for eliminating the division of labour with a fixed specialization.

Engels once said: "It is precisely because of this industrial revolution that human labour productivity has reached such a high level that for the first time in the history of humanity. The possibility of creating a reasonable division of labour among all people has created. Under the conditions of not only large-scale production to fully satisfy the affluent consumption and full reserves of all members of the society, but also to allow everyone to have sufficient leisure time from the culture leftover from history-science, art, and communication methods, etc. - to withstand among all real value of things. Of course, the development of the capitalist industry just for the elimination of the Spontaneous division of labour provides a possibility.

This spontaneous division of labour has not only been eliminated under the capitalist system but has continuously regenerated. Only through the socialist revolution, the elimination of the capitalist system, and the realization of communism can we finally eliminate the spontaneous division of labour and fundamentally resolve the contradictions between personal interests and shared interests. In a socialist society, especially in the current primary stage of socialism in China, although private ownership eliminates, the voluntary division of labour has not yet been fully formed and replaced the spontaneous division of labour.

It can say that the division of work in a socialist society is not only a division of energy that is utterly spontaneous in a capitalist society but also a division of power that is semi-conscious in a future communist society. Based on this division of labour, on the one hand, the contradiction between personal interests and common interests still exists. At some point, this contradiction is even sharp in some aspects.

On the other hand, the contradiction between private interests and common interests is no longer confrontational. The two are mostly the same. "We have advocated in a socialist society, the interests of the state, the collective, the individual are the same. If there is a contradiction, the individual's interests must obey the interests of the state and the collective." Although the contradiction between personal interests and common interests in a socialist society is no longer confrontational, it is essential to face up to this contradiction and coordinate and resolve this contradiction seriously to promote the stability and development of a socialist society.

At this stage in our community, to coordinate the relationship between personal interests and common interests, and to resolve the contradictions between private interests and everyday interests. we should pay attention to the following two aspects: First, we must guide people to correctly understand the relationship between their interests and common interests in a socialist society. In a socialist society, private ownership as a fundamental social system eliminates, and the masses of people have become masters of the whole community. It is no longer external to the individual's interests, it is the shared content in the personal attention of all social members, and it is the fundamental guarantee for the conscious realization of the own interests of all social members.

Although this common interest as the overall interest of all members of society may sometimes contradict and conflict with some unique and immediate benefits of individuals, it is consistent with the fundamental importance of individuals as members of the community. Therefore, in socialism, if an individual damages their common interests for their own unique and immediate benefits, it damages their fundamental interests. Only by recognizing this point, when there is a contradiction between personal interests and everyday interests, can people consciously safeguard the common interests, subordinate the individual attention to the common interests, and resolve the disagreements.

The second is to fundamentally curb all kinds of acts that pretend to be real common interests with imaginary common interests. It should say that the socialist society has provided an important institutional guarantee for eliminating the illusory form of common interests. In a socialist society, every person who assumes public office is a civil servant of the people, and truly embodying the common interests of the people should be the purpose of every public official's behaviour. However, since people are still in a semi-conscious division of labour in a socialist society, the act of pretending to be real common interests with imaginary common interests still has its parasitic reality.

Due to their unique position in the social division of labour, some people practice special interests in the name of common interests.

It is quite severe, and it has become a social issue that people generally pay him attention. At present, some corrupt elements seek the benefit of "small circles" in the name of common interests. Corporate corruption, collective bribery, and mass crime not only severely damage the reputation of the party and destroy the realization of real common interests, but also directly lead to individuals. The intensification of conflicts between interests and common interests has caused strong dissatisfaction among the broad masses of the people, which has become a significant cancer of reform and opening up.

All kinds of acts that pretend to be real common interests with imaginary common interests. In addition to the need to vigorously strengthen ideological education and increase the intensity of socialist legal construction, it is necessary to enhance socialist democratic development further and fully Recognizing that the conflict between personal interests and everyday interests, but also a political issue, so that the people have full rights to know and participate in matters related to shared interests,

How to Reform the Toxic Social Habits?

Everyone has bad habits, which for almost everyone is a problem that plays a vital role in his life. A pattern is an action, the consistent implementation of which has become a need for a person and without which he can no longer do. Bad habits are habits that harm a person's health and prevent him from fulfilling his goals and fully utilizing his abilities throughout his life. The evolution of man provided his inexhaustible body reserves strength and reliability, which are redundancy of elements of his systems. Amosov claims that the margin of safety of the "structure" of a person has a coefficient of about 10, i.e. its organs and systems can carry loads and withstand stresses about ten times greater than those that a person has to face in everyday life.

The realization of the opportunities inherent in a person depends on his lifestyle, behaviour, the habits that he acquires, the ability to intelligently manage the intrinsic capabilities of the body for the benefit of himself, his family and the state in which he lives. However, it should note that several habits that a person begins to acquire in his school years and which he cannot get rid of throughout his life seriously harm his health. They contribute to the rapid expenditure of the full potential of human capabilities, premature ageing and the acquisition of sustainable diseases. These habits primarily include the use of alcohol, drugs, and smoking. German professor Tannenberg estimates that at present, per million people, one death in a plane crash occurs once every 50 years; Bad habits have several features, among which are especially noteworthy:

1. Alcohol, drugs, and smoking are harmful to both the health of the person most exposed to them and the health of those around him.
2. Bad habits ultimately necessarily subordinate to itself all other actions of a person, all his activities.
3. A distinctive feature of bad habits is an addiction, the inability to live without them.
4. Getting rid of bad habits is extremely difficult. The most common bad habits are smoking, drinking alcohol and drugs.
5. Harmful addictions and addiction factors Addictions (habits) that hurt health are considered dangerous. Painful addictions - a select group of bad habits - the use of alcohol, drugs, toxic and psychotropic substances for entertainment. Currently, the general concern is the habit of using narcotic substances, which adversely affects not only the health of the subject and his social and economic situation but also his family (and society) as a whole. Frequent use of pharmacological drugs for entertainment causes drug dependence, which is especially dangerous for a young body. The World Health Organization (WHO) experts created the following classification of addictive substances:

substances of an alcoholic-barbiturate type (ethyl alcohol, barbiturates, sedatives - meprobamate, chloral hydrate, etc.).

- Materials such as amphetamine (amphetamine, phenmetrazine).
- Substances like cocaine (cocaine and coca leaves).
- Hallucinogenic type (lysergide - LSD, mescaline).
- Kata type substances - Catha lectures forsk.
- Materials like opiate (opiates - morphine, heroin, codeine, metal).
- Materials such as ether solvents (toluene, acetone and carbon tetrachloride).

The listed drugs are used for medicinal purposes, excluding ethereal solvents, and cause addiction - the human body is addictive to them. Recently, artificially created narcotic substances have appeared, the effect of which exceeds the action of known drugs, they are especially dangerous. A non-medical drug like tobacco is also a drug. Smoking is a substance that causes addiction and can cause physical harm to health. Nicotine is a stimulant and depressant has a relatively small effect on the central nervous system (CNS), causing minor disturbances in perception, mood, motor functions, and behaviour.

Under the influence of tobacco, even in large quantities (2-3 packs of cigarettes per day), the psychotropic effect is incomparable with pharmaceuticals. Still, the stupefying effect is observed, especially in young and childhood. Therefore, smoking is alarming not only doctors but also educators. Socio-pedagogical prerequisites for introducing bad habits. The beginning of familiarization with bad habits, as a rule, refers to adolescence. The following groups of main reasons for introducing youth to bad habits can be distinguished: Lack of internal discipline and a sense of responsibility. Because of this, young people often come into conflict with those from whom they are in absolute dependence. But at the same time, they have rather high demands.

However, they are not able to satisfy them because they do not have the necessary training for this, nor social, nor physical capabilities. In this case, bad habits become a kind of rebellion, a protest against the values professed by adults or society. Lack of motivation, a clearly defined life goal, Therefore, such people live in the present, with momentary pleasures and do not care about their future, do not think about the consequences of their unhealthy behaviour. I am feeling of dissatisfaction, unhappiness, anxiety, and boredom.

This reason is especially evident in insecure people, with low self-esteem, to whom life seems hopeless, and those around them do not understand them. Communication difficulties inherent in people who do not have healthy friendships, it is difficult to enter into close relationships with parents, teachers, and others, not easily fall under the influence of evil. Therefore, if there are harmful substances among peers, they can be more easily pressed ("try it and don't pay attention to the fact that it's bad"). Feeling under the influence of these substances, emancipation and lightness, they are trying to expand the circle of acquaintances and increase their popularity. Experimentation.

When a person hears from others about pleasant sensations from the use of harmful substances, although he knows about their adverse effects on the body, he wants to experience these feelings himself. Fortunately, most people who are experimenting with this stage of acquaintance with harmful substances are limited. But if above-provoking reasons characterize a person, then this stage becomes the first step to the formation of bad habits. The desire to get away from problems is the main reason for the use of harmful substances by adolescents.

The fact is that all hazardous materials cause inhibition in the central nervous system, as a result of which a person is "disconnected" and, as it were, avoids his problems. But this is not a way out of this situation - problems not resolve, but exacerbated, and time is running out. It is necessary to note once again the particular danger of the effects of harmful substances on adolescents.

It is due not only to the processes of growth and development that occur in them but primarily to the very high content of sex hormones in their body. Interaction of these hormones with harmful substances makes the teenager extremely sensitive to their action. For example, an adult, from a beginner to drink alcohol to an alcoholic, takes two to five years, and a teenager only three to six months! Of course, for a 14-15-year-old student who is preparing to enter adolescence, such a consequence of the use of harmful substances is especially dangerous.

All the above makes clear the crucial importance of work on the prevention of bad habits in children and adolescents. It is sufficient under the following conditions:

- It is necessary to educate and form healthy life needs, create socially significant motivations of behaviour
- Children and parents should provide objective information about bad habits, their effects on humans and the consequences of use
- Appropriate knowledge should carry out taking into account the age and individual characteristics of the child
- Children's understanding of the essence of bad habits should go hand in hand with the formation of a steadily negative personal attitude to psychoactive substances and interpersonal communication skills with peers and adults, the ability to cope with conflicts, manage emotions and feelings
- Students should gain experience in solving their problems without the help of psychoactive substances, learn how to deal with these hobbies of relatives and friends

- Instil in students the skills of a healthy lifestyle, influence the level of claims and self-esteem of children;
- In the fight against bad habits, the child, parents, and teachers must be united: you need to help the child refuse (or want to give up) bad habits himself.

Causes of drug and drug addiction Characteristics of a person, temperament, social environment and the psychological atmosphere in which a person is, can have a positive or negative effect on his habits. The experts identified and formulated the following causes that cause the development of drug and drug dependence, characteristic of young people:

- The manifestation of a hidden emotional disorder, the desire to get a fleeting pleasure regardless of consequences and responsibility;
- Criminal or asocial behaviour when, in the pursuit of happiness, a person violates social traditions and laws.
- Drug dependence as an attempt at self-medication, which occurs as a result of a mental disorder of an inorganic nature (social stress, puberty, disappointment, the collapse of vital interests, fear and anxiety, the onset of mental illness);
- With regular use of medications to alleviate physical suffering (hunger, chronic overwork, illness, the disintegration of the family, a humiliation in the family) or

to prevent some kind of disease, or enhance sexual potency;
- The abuse of pharmaceuticals to create "popularity" in a particular social group is the so-called sense of expression of social inferiority ("like all and i");
- A severe illness when the use of "saving doses of the drug" is provoked;
- Social protest, a challenge to society;
- The result of acquired reflexes due to accepted behaviour in specific sectors of society;
- Alcohol abuse, smoking at various social and cultural events (discos, presentations, gala concerts, star sickness of music idols, movies, etc.).

But any of the listed factors can cause a sensitive dependence only among those dependent on their character (cowardly, spineless, easily injured, weak physically, morally unstable, etc.). Most of these factors, which are the root cause of drug and drug dependence in young people, are due to human behaviour, their perception and the ability to imitate. Therefore, the provoking factors contributing to the formation of the future drug addict or drug addict lying in the family, kindergarten, school, student environment or another social environment. But the main educational factor still belongs to the family.

Parents should continuously strive to develop certain positive habits and skills in their children; a reasoned educational process should serve the purpose of forming a stable life position. It is a great art and patience, which is acquired in the process of life and polished for years. Alcohol and alcoholism "Alcohol" in Arabic means "intoxicating." It belongs to a group of substances that inhibit the activity of centres of the brain, reduces the supply of oxygen to the brain, which leads to weakening of the mind. Poor coordination of movements, confused speech, blurred thinking, loss of attention, the ability to think logically and make the right decisions, down to the point of insanity.

Statistics show that most of the drowned were drunk, every fifth traffic accident involved alcohol, a drunken quarrel was the most common cause of murder, and a staggering person risks robbed in the first place. Sooner or later, an always drunk person begins to have diseases of the heart, gastrointestinal tract, liver and other conditions associated with this lifestyle. But they cannot be compared to the decay of the personality and degradation of the drinker.

Speaking about the negative role of drinking alcohol in the social sphere, one should also note the economic damage associated with both the state of health of drinkers and their behaviour. So, for example, science has established that even the smallest doses of alcohol reduce efficiency by 5-10%. Those who drank alcohol on weekends and holidays have a 24-30% lower working capacity. At the same time, a decrease in the working size of mental workers or when performing thin and precise operations, especially pronounce.

The economic damage to production and society as a whole also cause by the temporary disability of people who drink alcohol, which, taking into account the frequency and duration of diseases, is two times higher than that of non-drinkers. Particular damage is caused to society by people who regularly drink alcohol and are ill with alcoholism. It is because, in addition to significant losses in the sphere of material production, the state forced to spend substantial amounts on the treatment of these persons and payment of their temporary incapacity for work. From a medical point of view, alcoholism is a disease characterized by a pathological (painful) attraction to alcohol. The direct path to addiction is drunkenness - the systematic use of alcohol for a long time or the occasional use of alcohol, accompanied in all cases by severe intoxication.

The early symptoms of alcoholism include

- Loss of gag reflex
- Loss of quantitative control over drunk alcohol
- Illegibility in alcoholic beverages, the desire to drink all purchased alcohol, etc.

One of the main signs of alcoholism is a "hangover" or "withdrawal" syndrome, which is characterized by physical and mental discomfort and manifests itself with various objective and subjective disorders.

Facial flushing, heart palpitations, high blood pressure, dizziness, headaches, trembling hands, shaky gait and Other patients with difficulty falling asleep, their superficial sleep with frequent awakenings and nightmare dreams. Their mood changes, in which depression, timidity, fear, suspicion begin to prevail. Patients misinterpret the words and actions of others. In the late stages of alcoholism, alcohol degradation appears the main signs of which include a decrease in ethics of behaviour, loss of critical functions, a sharp violation of memory and intelligence. The most specific diseases in alcoholism are liver damage, chronic gastritis, peptic ulcer, stomach cancer. Alcohol consumption contributes to the development of hypertension, the occurrence of diabetes mellitus, impaired fat metabolism, heart failure, and atherosclerosis.

Alcoholics are 2-2.5 times more likely to have mental disorders, sexually transmitted diseases and other diseases. As a result, male alcoholics develop impotence, which affects about one-third of those who drink alcohol. In women, as a rule, prolonged uterine bleeding, inflammatory diseases of the internal genital organs and infertility occur very early. The toxic effect of alcohol on germ cells increases the likelihood of having children mentally and physically disabled. So, even Hippocrates - the founder of ancient medicine, pointed out that the culprits of epilepsy, idiocy and other neuropsychic diseases of children are parents who drank alcohol on the day of conception.

The painful changes in the nervous system, various internal organs, metabolic disorders, personality degradation that occur in drunkards lead to rapid ageing and infirmity. The average lifespan of alcoholics is 15-20 years less than usual. Family habits that break your relationship. We take many practices and beliefs into adulthood from the family. Although a person develops his values over time, some things received in childhood penetrate deep into the subconscious and continue to influence us at any age. First of all, this applies to love relationships.

Parents rarely discuss such topics with their children. The idea of how to behave with the opposite sex, we have to add up independently, observing others. Nobody is perfect, and your parents, unwittingly, could teach you some wrong lessons. Here are bad habits in relationships that you could learn from them.

You always doubt your partner. It's hard to watch how your parents are going through a divorce, especially when you're still a child. Most studies show that the gap does not necessarily affect children more negatively than ongoing conflicts in the family. The termination of the relationship between mother and father can create a common fear in a person of attachment or refusal, according to the journal Psychology Today. The divorce of parents makes it too early to understand that marriage can end. Constant anxiety makes it difficult to feel safe with a partner and build a healthy long-term relationship.

You discuss problems with everyone except your partner Communication style is one of the first things that we adopt in the family. If your parents complained about issues with all their friends instead of talking to each other, you might not understand how important communication is when paired. Passive aggressiveness can kill relationships. Quarrels, misunderstanding is inevitable; you need to be able to find healthy ways to resolve conflicts.

Hide something from a partner Hiding information is as bad a sign as gossip about your boyfriend's bad habits. Many of us heard the phrase: "Don't tell mom" in childhood. Do not put up with the idea that some things are better not to say. According to Michel Kerulis, professor at American Northwestern University, even a small white lie can lead to trust problems. Agree to an unpleasant conversation with a partner understanding that the conversation intends to satisfy your needs and feelings, and not attack the personality of another person.

You Are Embarrassed to Show Feelings

If your parents never kissed each other before going to work or no one saw them hugging you, it can also be awkward to show your affection to your partner. The way you discuss family sex also affects your behaviour in the future. When parents give their child an idea of intimacy as something shameful, it can lead to severe problems in sexual life. A healthy relationship involves sexual positiveness, the ability to communicate your needs and hear what your partner needs.

You Feel Like You're Competing

If it was more important for mom and dad to prove who is right than to support each other, you could learn that relationships are competition. It's important to remember that you and the guy are partners, not opponents. In love, there are no winners or losers. You need to learn to trust your man and always remember that you are on the same side.

Toxic Relationship Low-Income Family Relationships

You get into a toxic relationship Low-income family relationship can cause you to fall into the same pattern of unhealthy relationships. It is not your fault - the surrounding physical and emotional abuse traumatizes for life. Violence in a link does not necessarily imply beatings; it applies to any form of abuse, whether it be jealousy or gaslighting. If you attract toxic men all the time, you should seriously think about your behaviour and learn to love in a healthy, non-dangerous way.

You Are Changing

Some studies show that children in whose family has been cheating have problems with emotional health. According to a report published in the Daily Mail, the main side effects of adultery for children are low self-esteem, unwillingness to work, and antisocial behaviour. In the future, this is fraught with even more significant difficulties. A person does not say what he wants in a relationship and prefers to solve problems on the side, or generally avoids dangerous attachments.

Toxic Habits in Relationship That Most People Consider Normal

Schools do not teach how not to screw up relationships with your boyfriend or girlfriend. Of course, we show the biological side of sex and gender differences, the legal aspects of marriage, and maybe in a literature lesson we will read a couple more obscure love stories from the 19th century on the subject of "what to do or not to be." But, when it comes to dealing with relational cuisine in real life, here we already have absolutely no pointers where to go and what to do. Or, even worse, we are offered advice from the pages of women's magazines. Yes, a trial and error method awaits us from the very beginning. And if you are the same as most people, then this will most likely be a method of predominantly mistakes.

But partly the problem is that many unhealthy habits in relationships are simply "sewn" into our culture. We worship romantic love - you know, that very dizzyingly stupid and irrational romantic love, which for some reason believes that throwing ceramic plates into the wall in a fit of tears is very lovely, and we deride practicality or unconventional types of sexuality. Men and women in the process of education teach to objectify each other and objectify their relationship. Accordingly, we often perceive our partners as a useful or valuable contribution to our lives, rather than as someone with whom we can share mutual emotional support.

The vast amount of literature on self-help currently existing does not help at all either (no, men and women are not from different planets, and stop spreading this nonsense). And for most of us, mom and dad were not the best role models. Fortunately, over the past few decades, a considerable amount of psychological research has been carried out in the field of healthy and happy relationships, and there are several common regularly pop-up principles that most people are unaware of or refuse to follow.

Some of these principles run counter to what is considered "romantic" or normal in a relationship. Below are the six most common relationship trends that many couples find healthy and normal, but are quite toxic and destroy everything you cherish. Stock up on handkerchiefs.

1. Report Card of Your Relationship

The phenomenon "maintaining accounts" characterized the fact that your partner continues to blame you again and again for past mistakes made in your connection. You acted like the last asshole at a party on the 28th anniversary of Cynthia back in 2010, and this fact, in the end, has methodically ruined your life ever since. Why? Yes, because a week does not pass without a reminder about this. But it's okay because the time you caught her sending flirting text messages to her colleague deprives her of the right to be jealous. So it's kind of like you are counting, huh?

Why it is toxic: The Scorecard in a relationship develops and grows more significant over time, because one or both partners use past sins to try to justify their current righteousness. And here you mess twice as big. You not only look away from the existing problem but also attract and increase even more guilt and resentment from the past, thereby making your partner feel bad in the present. It leads to the fact that, instead of solving the immediate problem, both partners spend all their energy trying to prove that he/she much less reprimand than the partner. People spend all their time trying to be less "bad" for each other, instead of being more suitable for each other.

What to do: Deal with problems in turn until you reasonably begin to see their connection with the present. If someone has already become a habit of adultery, then this, of course, is a frequently recurring problem. But the fact that you dishonoured in 2010, and was upset and ignores you all days, you have nothing to do. You must be aware that when choosing the person who is significant to you, you also want to be with all of his past. And if you do not accept his past, then you do not automatically accept the person himself. And if something bothered you so much a year ago, then you had to deal with it a year ago.

2. Accidentally Abandoned "Hints" And Other Passive Aggression

What it is: Instead of openly and openly expressing your desires or thoughts, your partner is trying to push you in the right direction so that you can guess what he/she wants. And instead of saying that it's upsetting you, you choose small and, at first glance, innocent ways to annoy your partner so that later you can justifiably complain.

Why it is toxic: Because it shows how uncomfortable it is for both of you to communicate honestly and openly with each other, a person does not feel the need for passive aggression if he can safely express his anger and fears in a relationship. We will never have the urge to drop a "hint" if we are not afraid of condemnation and criticism.

What to do: Openly express your feelings and desires. And do not forget to let your partner know that he is not responsible for them and is not obliged to run them out immediately, but you would be grateful for the support. And if you are loved, you will almost always have the opportunity to receive this necessary support.

3. Hostage Relations

What is it: When one of the partners, due to a slight discontent or complaint, begins to threaten the second partner with the destruction of relationships? For example, if someone thinks that you are cold towards him, then instead of the phrase "I feel that you are sometimes cold with me", he/she says: "I cannot meet a person who is constantly cold with me."

Why it is toxic: This is emotional blackmail, and it gives rise to kilometres of unnecessary drama. Any minimal snag in relationships perceives as a threat of severance. It is incredibly essential for both people in a relationship to know that they can express their negative thoughts and feelings to each other with a complete sense of security, and this will not threaten this relationship. Otherwise, people will suppress their real thoughts and feelings, and this, in turn, will lead to an atmosphere full of mistrust and manipulation.

What to do: It's normal to be angry with a partner may be unhappy with something in your relationship. This behaviour, called "being a normal person." But understand that devotion to obligations to those with whom you are in a relationship and unconditional sympathy is not the same thing. You can be loyal to someone and at the same time not be enthusiastic about any individual manifestations of this person. You can always be faithful and at the same time, sometimes annoyed or angry at your partner. No matter how surprising it may sound, if two are capable of expressing criticism and expressing feedback to each other without condemnation and threats, this will only strengthen their loyalty to each other in the long run.

4. Blaming A Partner for Their Own Emotions

What is it: Let's say you have a lousy day, and your partner somehow does not empathize very much or does not seek to express support? He hangs on the phone all day, discussing something at work. You come to him to hug, and he asks him not to distract. You would love to lie with him at home on the couch watching a movie, but he has plans to hang out with friends. And you are already attacking him for being so indifferent and inattentive to you. You just have a terrible day, and he does not care, and he does not try to fix it. Of course, you did not ask about this, but he is obliged to guess and certainly do something to make you feel better. He just had to quickly get off the phone and cancel all his plans because of your lousy emotional state.

Why it is toxic: Blaming partners for our own emotions is a sophisticated form of egoism and a classic example of the inability to handle our and others' boundaries. When you blame your partner for how you sometimes feel (and, conversely, he blames it on you), you develop a tendency to co-dependence. And suddenly, the partner can no longer plan anything without consulting with you. Everything that you do at home - even basic reading books or promoting TV - should be preliminarily discussed and agreed. When someone starts to get upset, all personal desires fly out the window, because now your partner's functional condition is on your shoulders. The biggest problem in developing a penchant for co-dependence is that it gives rise to resentment. Of course, if my girlfriend somehow shouted at me because she had a bad day and was upset and needed attention, this is understandable. But if she begins to believe that my life revolves around her emotional well-being constantly sincerely, then very soon, I will become quite cruel and manipulative concerning her feelings and desires.

What to do: Take responsibility for your own emotions, and expect the same from your partner. There is a very subtle but essential difference between supporting and partnering with a partner. Any sacrifice should come from everyone's personal choice and not expect for granted. As soon as the partners in the relationship begin to blame each other and shift responsibility for their feelings and decadent moods, they immediately have a desire and an occasion to hide their true feelings and manipulate each other.

5. The Manifestation of Jealousy "Out of Love"

What it is: You get enraged when your partner talks, touches, calls, write messages, hangs out or sneezes in the direction of another person, and you begin to pour anger at your partner and try to control his behaviour. It often results in absurd actions, such as hacking a partner's email, reading messages on his phone while he is in the shower, or even tracking him around the city with a sudden appearance in his eyes when he least expects it.

Why it is toxic: It surprises me when people explain such behaviour as a kind of manifestation of love. They believe that if they are not jealous, the partner will decide that they do not like him. By this behaviour, we transmit to the partner our distrust. And if you honestly, it is humiliating. If my girlfriend believes that I cannot be left alone surrounded by beautiful women, then two conclusions come up: either a) I am a liar, or b) I am not able to control my impulses. In any case, I do not want to be in a relationship with such a woman.

What to do: Trust your partner. Yes, I know this is a pretty radical idea. Jealousy is, to some extent, completely natural. But excessive jealousy and attempts to control a partner directly indicate your lack of self-esteem, and it is with him that you need to understand, and not morally rape your loved ones. Because otherwise, you will only push away the person you love.

6. Solving Relationship Problems

What is it: As soon as conflict erupts in a relationship or a problem arises, instead of resolving it, one of the partners "covers" the negative with pleasant feelings from buying some gift or organizing a joint holiday. My parents were experts at this. In their case, it went quite a long way: a vile scam with a terrible scandal and a complete ignoring of each other for 15 years - ever since they divorced. But each of them individually told me that the leading cause of the problems in their marriage was the systematic concealment of real difficulties by some superficial pleasures.

Why it is toxic: Thus, you not only stuff the real problem "under the carpet" (where it will come out anyway, only on a much larger scale) but also create an unhealthy atmosphere in the relationship. And this problem is by no means inherent in any of the sexes to a greater extent, but I will give a traditional gender example in this case. Let's imagine that every time a woman gets angry with her boyfriend or husband, the man "solves" the problem by buying something beautiful for the woman, or leads her to a good restaurant, or something like that. It not only gives rise to an unconscious desire in a woman to find more and more reasons for anger and resentment against a man but also does NOT cause a man any willingness to take on his part of the responsibility for problems in relationships.

What to do: Well, what else would you advise, except on how to solve the problem. Lost Confidence? Talk about what could bring him back. Does anyone feel ignored and devalued? Talk about how to bring back a sense of value and understanding. Talk! There is nothing wrong with fun and lovely gifts for a significant person after a quarrel to show that you are still together and once again confirm your interest in a relationship. But you can not use gifts and other amenities as a substitute for a real solution to fundamental emotional problems. Gifts and travel are called pleasures for a reason; we can truly enjoy them only when everything else is in order. If you cover up issues with them, then, in the end, you will have to deal with something much more severe and unpleasant.

The general mechanism of action of narcotic substances on the body is very reactive. All narcotic substances have a standard tool of influence on the body, as they are poisons. With systematic use (for entertainment), they cause the following phases of changes in the body.

The First Phase Is A Protective Reaction

At the first use, narcotic substances have a toxic (poisonous) effect on the body, and this causes a protective response - nausea, vomiting, dizziness, headache, etc. In this case, as a rule, there are no pleasant sensations.

The Second Phase Is the Euphoria

With repeated doses, the protective reaction weakens, and happiness arises - an exaggerated feeling of well-being. It achieves by drug stimulation of receptors (sensitive structures) of the brain, related to endorphins (natural internal stimulants that cause a feeling of pleasure). The drug at this stage acts as endorphin.

The Third Phase Is Drug Addiction

A drug that causes euphoria disrupts the synthesis (production) of endorphins in the body. It leads to a deterioration in a person's mood, and he begins to strive to enjoy taking drugs (alcohol, drugs, etc.). It further impairs the synthesis of natural "pleasure hormones" and strengthens the desire to take narcotic substances. A person's obsessive attraction to a drug gradually develops (this is already a disease), which consists in the fact that he continually thinks about taking drugs, about the effect he is causing, even when he thinks about the future use of a drug, his mood rises. The idea of medicine and its impact becomes a constant element of the consciousness and content of a person's thoughts: no matter what he thinks, whatever he does, he does not forget about the drug. He considers the situations that contribute to the extraction of drugs, and how unfavourable - the obstacles to this. However, at this stage of the disease, the surrounding people still do not notice anything unusual in his behaviour.

The Fourth Phase Is A Physical Dependence on Drugs

The systematic use of drugs leads to a complete disruption of the system that synthesizes endorphins, and the body ceases to produce them. Since endorphins have an analgesic effect, the cessation of their synthesis by the agency taking narcotic substances causes physical and emotional pain To get rid of this pain, a person is a force to make a hefty dose of a narcotic substance. It is how physical (chemical) dependence on narcotic substances develops. Having decided to refuse to accept drugs, a person accustomed to them must survive a period of adaptation that takes several days before the brain resumes the production of endorphins. This unpleasant period is called the period of withdrawal ("withdrawal"). It manifests itself in general malaise, decreased performance, trembling limbs, chills, pain in various parts of the body. Many painful symptoms are visible to others.

The most well-known and well-studied state of withdrawal symptoms, for example, after drinking alcohol is a hangover. Gradually, the patient's attraction to the drug becomes unstoppable, he has a desire immediately, as soon as possible, at all costs, despite any obstacles to get and take medicine. This desire suppresses all needs and completely subjugates human behaviour. He is ready to take off and sell clothes, take everything away from home, etc. It is in this condition that patients go for any antisocial actions, including crime. At this stage of the development of the disease, a person requires significantly higher doses of the narcotic substance than at the beginning of the illness, because, with systematic use of it, the body becomes resistant to poison (tolerance develops).

The Fifth Phase Is the Psychosocial Degradation of Personality

It occurs with systematic and prolonged use of narcotic substances and includes emotional, volitional and intellectual deterioration. Psychological degradation consists of the weakening, and then the complete disappearance of the most complex and subtle emotions, in emotional instability, manifested in sharp and unreasonable mood swings, and at the same time in the growth of dysphoria - persistent mood disorders. These include constant bitterness, depression, depression. Volitional degradation manifest in the inability to make an effort on oneself, to complete the work begun, in the quick exhaustion of intentions and motives. Everything is fleeting for these patients, and you cannot believe their promises and oaths (they will certainly fail).

They can persevere only in the desire to get a narcotic substance. This condition is obsessive in them. Intellectual degradation is manifest in a decrease in the understanding, inability to concentrate. The best tactic in dealing with bad habits is to stay away from people suffering from them. If you offer to try cigarettes, alcohol, drugs, try to dodge under any pretext. Options may be different:

- No, I do not want, and I do not advise you.
- No, this puts my workouts.
- No, I have to go - I have things to do.
- No, this is bad for me.
- No, I know that I may like it, but I do not want to become addicted.

In your situation, you can come up with your version. If the offer comes from a close friend who is just starting to try nicotine, alcohol or drugs, then you can try to explain to him the harm and danger of this activity. But if he does not want to listen, then it is better to leave him, to argue with him is useless.

You can help him only if he wants to quit these harmful activities. Remember that some benefit from having bad habits. These are people for whom tobacco, alcohol, drugs are a means of enrichment. A person who intends to try a cigarette, wine, a drug should be considered as his worst enemy, even if he was still your best friend because he offers you something that will ruin your life. Your primary life prerequisite should be the principle of a healthy lifestyle, which excludes the acquisition of bad habits.

However, if you understand that you are acquiring one of the bad habits, then try to get rid of it as soon as possible.

The following are some tips for getting rid of bad habits. First of all, tell your decision about the person whose opinion is expensive for you, ask him for advice. At the same time, consult a specialist in combating bad habits - a psychotherapist, narcology. It is essential to leave the company where bad habits are abuse, and not to return to it, maybe even change your place of residence. Look for a new circle of acquaintances who do not abuse bad habits or just as you struggle with your illness. Do not allow yourself a single minute of idle time. Take on additional responsibilities at home, at school, at college. Take more time to exercise. Choose one of the sports for yourself and continuously improve it.

Make a written program of your actions to get rid of bad habits and immediately start its implementation, each time considering what has done, and whatnot, and what prevented it. Always learn to fight your illness, strengthen your will and inspire yourself that you can get rid of a bad habit.

What to Do If A Loved One Suffers from Bad Habits?

Do not panic! Let him know about your concern without trying to yell at him or blame him for anything. Do not read morality and do not start with threats. Try to explain to him the dangers of this activity. The sooner your loved one realizes the need to stop, the more chances to achieve a positive result. Convince him to turn to specialists for help, help him make life exciting and fulfilled without bad habits, and discover the meaning and purpose in it. It is essential to interest a person in self-development so that he learns to relax and enjoy without cigarettes, wine or drugs. Well, for those who themselves suffer from bad habits, we advise once again to do everything as soon as possible to stop this dangerous activity.

Killing Assumption and Mental Leap

Another mass shooting in the United States Attack, those who Russia thinks is the most aggressive Threaten Assad. Massacres across the vast belt of the Middle East Hobbesian turmoil wholly govern, so players cannot be distinguished. Enough to make rational strategic decisions-these different events unified. The cultural premise that humans are killing other humans Represents an effective way to resolve conflicts. Someday we will see how the grotesque distortion of reality. The heart of an insane person who randomly sprays bullets among his innocent companion's Citizens is not so different from Assad dropping a barrel bomb on his allies.

Citizen or Putin Is Dropping Bombs Where His Airplane Is Targeting Today-Or Obama fired an extra-law missile from an uncrewed aerial vehicle. Killing does not solve anything. However, a general assumption that is not so hidden is killing. It explains a lot of things based on what is right. It gives in the media that the "objective" reporting of "facts" is not.

It is even necessary to set violence in the context of value, except when there was a murder. It has unavoidable tragic consequences such as a mass outflow of refugees. Journalism proudly seeks its purpose, the "genuine"—death and disappointment without any blurring of human "facts, pity, compassion, and shameful values. Whether motivated by fear, revenge, best defence attacks, or significant actionsStreamlining against the frenzy of war frenzy or "private" murder Humans live, move, and exist in vast oceans to justify murder. It covers the highest range of our technical strength. Hence, we have designed and deployed a unique death toll like the Trident The submarine, 600 feet of pure potential destruction.

A kind of Holocaust in a can be Managed by the elite and proud professionalism that we will be pleased with See it emulated somewhere in our organization or activity. Justify our need This deterrent breakwater, like the others who own these internal machines, Russians, French, British, and the Democratic People's Republic of Korea feel that protection is justified as well. With your device ready for mass murder.

It is the human paradigm on our little planet. However, the model can change. We once thought that making a hole in a person's skull was the most effective treatment method. Chronic headache or it was "real" like journalists today. "Objectivity," or the sun goes around the earth or cholera bacteria. Not in the air and over water. We, humans, have evolved from mammals that have slowly learned compassion and care. In these ecosystems, there is a constant contradiction where the creatures fit, but again—the survival and soundness of the entire system, I have a lot to learn. And as we have evolved, the ability to learn is unique within us.

It is difficult to determine how much force a positive change involves. The phrase that killing does not solve anything. I'm sure most people believe that. It's true. You can perform unrealistic thought experiments: Imagine all the news. The story of war and murder begins with the words, "murder does nothing." It is open to having a broad dialogue on whether killing will solve anything. The door to unthinkable or at least unselected possibilities-and, perhaps, Someday, to close the door to kill each other.

Nuclear weapons are a great place to start. Use in conflict will not solve anything and will inevitably make things a lot. Worse, even in our very extinct range is even worse. It's past time International conference, military and high civilian participants In the nuclear nations that are the decision-makers Completely viable abolition of these outdated weapons. Succeeded in this regard Much more comfortable than the level of cooperation needed to mitigate global climate

Insecurity can be a model for non-violent conflict resolution Includes NRA-led commitment to gun culture The U.S. with common-sense law. Killing does not solve anything. Winslow Myers, the author of Living Beyond War: A Citizen's Guide, writes globally: Raise and service issues on the Advisory Committee of the War Prevention Initiative.

1 Mental Development of Young Children

Early childhood is a particular period in the formation of organs and systems and, above all, brain functions. It proved that the features of the cerebral cortex are not only fixed hereditarily, but they also develop as a result of the interaction of the body with the environment. It is especially intense in the first three years of life. During this period, the maximum rate of formation of prerequisites observed, which determine the further development of the body. For the protection and strengthening of children's health, preventive health-improving work is of particular importance: compliance with the regime, rational nutrition, gardening, gymnastics, medical and pedagogical control over development and health. **What will they consist?**

One: -

For an early age, a fast pace of development of the body is characteristic. In no other period of childhood is there such a rapid increase in body mass and length, the development of all brain functions. A child is born a helpless creature. However, by the age of 2 months, conditioned reflexes (habits) form in him, during the first year of life, inhibition reactions form. At this time, sensors, movements are actively developing, the baby masters the speech. The rapid pace of development of a young child, in turn, has several features. First of all, the spasmodic development.

In this case, periods of slow accumulation are distinguished, when there is a slowdown in the formation of certain body functions, and so-called critical periods (jumps) alternating with them when the appearance of the child changes over a short time. It can trace to the example of the development of the function of understanding speech by a child of the second year of life. So, from the age of 1 year to 1 year three months, there is a slow accumulation of the stock of understood words.

During this period, the baby takes control of independent walking, which expands for him the possibility of direct communication with the outside world—on the one hand, walking as if temporarily delays the manifestation of reactions associated with understanding speech. The critical periods in the development of the child are one year, two years, three years, six years, 12-13 years. It was a time that drastic changes, giving a new quality in the development of children, one-year mastery of walking; 2 years - the formation of visual-effective thinking. A turning point in the event of speech; 3 years - the period when the connection between the behaviour and development of the child with the second signalling system is particularly bright, the baby recognizes himself as a person; 6-7 years - the period of school maturity; 12–13 years.

Hopping reflects the normal, regular process of development of the child's body, and, conversely, the absence of jumps is a consequence of defects in the development and upbringing of children. Therefore, it is so important during the period of accumulation of experience by the child to create optimal conditions for the timely maturation of a new quality in the development of a particular function. However, critical periods are difficult for the child. They can accompany a decrease in the baby's performance and other functional disorders. At this time, the baby especially needs proper care, in a regime that spares his nervous systemThe fast pace of development of the child is due to the rapid establishment of relations with the outside world and at the same time, the slow consolidation of reactions.

For young children characterized by instability and incompleteness of emerging skills. (Given this, repetition in training is provided, providing a link between the effects of adults surrounding the child and his independent activity.) The maturation of various functions determines the unevenness in the development of a young child at certain times. Observing this pattern, N.M. Shchelovanov and N.M. Aksarin revealed periods of a particular sensitivity of the baby to certain types of exposure and outlined the leading lines in its development.

They emphasized that when raising children, special attention should pay to the formation of those reactions that mature for the first time and which cannot develop independently, without the targeted effects of an adult. For example, the "revitalization complex" that appears in a baby at three months old, the ability to use simple sentences when communicating with an adult at two years old, the appearance of role-playing games at three years past. In the first three years of a child's life, there is a high vulnerability, lability of his condition, due to the rapid pace of development of the body. Children of this age easily fall ill, often (even from minor causes) their emotional state changes, the child is quickly tired.

Frequent morbidity, as well as increased excitability of the nervous system, are especially characteristic of stressful conditions (during the period of adaptation when children enter the nursery, etc.). However, a fast pace of development is possible only with considerable plasticity of the body, its vast compensatory capabilities. It is especially true for brain functions. In the cerebral cortex of the child, there are many so-called empty fields, therefore, through specially targeted influences, a very high level of development of the baby and the earlier formation of a particular function can be achieved. The training of young children should be based primarily on the development of such abilities as imitation, reproduction, the ability to watch and listen, compare, distinguish, compare, generalize, etc., which will be necessary for the future for the acquisition of specific skills, knowledge, life experience.

Two: -

An essential feature of early childhood is the interdependence of the state of health, physical and psychological development of children. A strong, physically full-fledged child is not only less affected by diseases but also develops better mentally. But even minor violations in the state of health of the baby affect his emotional sphere. The course of the illness and recovery to a large extent, is associated with the mood of the child, and if you manage to maintain positive emotions, his health improves, and healing comes quickly. N.M. Shchelovanov found that the development of hypotrophy is often associated with a deficit of emotions, dissatisfaction with the motor activity of the baby. It revealed that neuropsychic development, in particular, the function of speech, largely depends on biological factors: the course of pregnancy, complications during childbirth, the state of health of the baby, etc.

Three: -

Each healthy child in the first three years of life characterized by a high degree of indicative reactions to everything around. This age-related feature stimulates the so-called sensorimotor needs. It proved that if children are limited in obtaining information and processing it by age-related capabilities, the rate of their development is slower. Therefore, the lives of children must be diverse, rich in impressions. Sensory needs also cause high motor activity, and movement is the baby's natural state, contributing to his intellectual development.

Four: -

Particular importance in early childhood are emotions that are so necessary when conducting regime processes - when feeding, staying awake, shaping behaviour and skills, and ensuring full development. The early formation of positive emotions through the establishment of social ties with adults, and later with peers, is the key to the creation of a child's personality. The emotional sphere has a significant influence on the formation of the cognitive abilities of children. Interest in the environment in early childhood is involuntary and largely determined socially.

It is impossible to force a baby to watch or listen, but many can interest him. Therefore, positive emotions play a unique role in teaching young children. Often, while still not understanding the meaning of an adult's speech addressed to him, children react to her intonation, emotional mood, easily catch them and become infected with the same spirit. It is the simplicity and complexity of raising young children.

Five: -

In the development of young children, the leading role belongs to the adult. It provides all the conditions necessary for the development and optimal health of the baby. Communicating with him carries the warmth, affection and information that is necessary for the development of the mind and soul of the child. A friendly tone, a calm, even attitude to him is the key to a balanced state of the baby. One of the conditions ensuring the healthy development and well-being of young children is the unity of pedagogical influences. On the part of all those involved in their upbringing, especially in a family where often several children are included: a mother, father, grandmother and other adults - and their actions in a relationship with the baby are not always consistent and not ever constant. In these cases, the baby does not understand how he should act, how to respond.

Some children, easily excitable, cease to obey the requirements of adults, others, more powerful ones, try to adapt, each time changing their behaviour, which is an impossible task for them. So, adults themselves are often the cause of psychotic action of children. Therefore, it is essential that not only in the family but also in the preschool institution, the requirements should be equally feasible for the children, agreed between parents and carers. When accepting a child for the first time in a group, the educator must know everything about him, having received information from the doctor, in conversation with parents, in communication with the child before he came to the preschool institution.

In the first days of the baby's stay in the group, one should not violate what he is used to at home, even if these habits are not entirely correct. For example, a child is used to sleeping at home with a dummy, and at first, he should not wean. But the teacher should patiently explain to parents that, if possible, they should gradually prepare the baby for habituation: to tell what skills, abilities, should be formed in children at home, what methods to use.

Young Children Are Suggestible

The mood of others easily conveyed to them. Increased, irritable tone, sudden transitions from affection to coldness, screaming affect the baby's behaviour. It is essential to use prohibitions in raising a child. You cannot allow the baby to do everything he wants. Both many bans and permission to do whatever it pleases is harmful to the child. In one case, the child does not have the skills necessary for life; in the other, the baby sometimes forced to restrain himself, which is a lot of work for him. How to deal with young children? First of all, bans, if necessary, should be justified, requirements for their implementation should present in a calm voice. You can't allow what was forbidden before, for example, you must always demand that the child does not sit down with unwashed hands, does not go to the open window, the burning stove, does not take things from the teacher's table, etc.

However, there should be much fewer prohibitions. The requirements must be feasible for young children to fulfil. So, it is difficult for a child not to move for a long time - to sit or stand, keeping the same pose, wait until, for example, it is his turn to dress for a walk. From an early age, independence formed in children. Performing actions without the help of an adult begin to give the baby pleasure very early. Having learned to speak, he turns to an adult with the words "I". This need of the baby in the manifestation of activity, self-affirmation should, as far as possible, be supported in every possible way. In a game, often children themselves try to overcome some difficulties, and there is no need to strive to help them immediately. Let the child try to act on his own.

It is one of the conditions for the formation of skills and good mood of the baby. Often the cause of psychotic behaviour of a child is a violation of his activities. At an early age, the baby cannot quickly, arbitrarily switch from one type of business to another. Therefore, a sharp breakdown, the demand to immediately stop, for example, the game and do something else is beyond his strength, causes an intense protest. And vice versa, if an adult does this gradually - at first, he offers to finish the game, put the toys in place, then he gives an installation for a new type of activity: "Now let's go wash, the soap is fragrant—delicious pancakes for lunch. Will, you help me put the plates on the table?" - the child willingly obeys. In education, individual characteristics should consider—a child.

In children with different types of nervous activity, the limit of working capacity is not the same: some get tired faster, they often need to change cool and active games during the game and go to bed earlier than others. There are children who themselves come in contact with others, require that they are called to such communications, more often maintain their positive emotional state. Children fall asleep also not the same way: some slowly, restlessly, ask that a tutor is with them; sleep comes to others quickly, and they do not need particular influences.

During the game, some kids efficiently complete the tasks of an adult (therefore, it is essential that the job is difficult enough; the child decides independently). Others are waiting for help, support, encouragement. Knowing the individual characteristics of the child not only helps the teacher find the right approach. Often the cause of the psychotic behaviour of children is the incorrect organization of activity. When a motor activity is not satisfied, the child does not get enough impressions, suffers from a lack of communication with adults. Disruptions in behaviour can also occur as a result of the fact that organic needs met promptly. In essence, inconvenience in clothes, diaper rash, the child is hungry, has not slept.

Therefore, the regimen of the day, thorough hygienic care, the methodically correct conduct of all the regimen processes - sleep, feeding, sending sanitary needs, timely organization of the child's independent activities. The implementation of the right educational approaches is the key to the formation of the child's proper behaviour, creating a balanced mood. The features and means of raising a child correspond to the characteristics of early childhood; they include physical, mental, moral and aesthetic education. Tasks of physical education: protecting the health of children, their movements, full physical development; instilling cultural and hygienic skills.

The Primary Means of Physical Education

Providing sanitary and hygienic care hardening measures the widespread use of air, sun, water, rational feeding and nutrition, organization of massage and gymnastics. Organization of the daily routine; methodically correct conduct of all regime processes (feeding, sleep, wakefulness). Tasks of mental education: the formation of action with objects; sensory development; speech development; development of gaming and other activities; the creation of basic psychological processes (attention, memory), the development of visual and practical thinking, emotional development, the formation of initial ideas and concepts about the world, the development of mental abilities (the ability to compare, distinguish, generalize, establish a causal relationship between individual phenomena); the formation of cognitive needs (the need for information, activity in the classroom, independence in the knowledge of the world).

The primary means of mental education: emotional-business communication of an adult with a child during the child's activities; specialized training provided by the tutor in the classroom; the independent practice of the child in everyday life, games, communication. The main activities at an early age are communication with adults, as well as the development of actions with objects. For their timely development, it is necessary to create optimal conditions.

Tasks of Moral Education

The formation of a positive relationship with adults (the ability to calmly fulfil their requirements, show affection and love for parents, family members, carers, the desire to help others, show affectionate feelings, sympathy). The upbringing of positive personality traits (kindness, responsiveness, friendliness, initiative, resourcefulness, ability to overcome difficulties, bring the job started to the end). Fostering friendly relations between children (the ability to play nearby, without interfering with other children, share toys, show empathy, help with difficulties, etc.).

The upbringing of positive habits (the ability to say hello, give thanks, put away toys, etc.); training in primary forms of labour activity (all types of self-service, available assistance to younger and adult, Means of moral education. Adult behaviour patterns, approval of good deeds, teaching children positive acts; organizing special relevant situations, reading books. For the full and harmonious development of children, it is essential from an early age to cultivate their love of the beautiful in the environment, nature, life, that is, to form aesthetic feelings. Tasks of artistic education: the upbringing of the ability to notice the beauty in nature, surrounding reality, people's actions, clothing, the development of creative skills (musical ear, visual activity).

Means of Aesthetic Education

Familiarization with nature, music, teaching singing, drawing, sculpting, reading folk tricks, poems, fairy tales. All these tasks solved by the joint efforts of the preschool institution and the family. The correct organization of children's lives in a corporate environment allows the mother to work successfully, and the child to develop harmoniously under the guidance of specialists (paediatricians, educators, music workers).

Two development and maturation of physiological systems of the body of children of the second year of life. This age is called the nursery. The period is critical in the life of the baby. In essence, the growth of the body does not proceed as rapidly as in the first year, but the mental and physiological development of the child makes a new qualitative leap. In the second year of life, the weight of the child increases monthly by 200-250 g, and growth - by 1 cm.

These are average data that can guide by weighing and measuring the child. The proportions of the child's body also change; if the size of the head in a newborn baby is about ¼ of the total body length, then by the age of 2 it gradually decreases to 1/5. The central nervous system becomes noticeably more resilient. The periods of inhibition reduce the intervals of active wakefulness of the child increase. Children already know how to focus on one lesson for quite a long time - up to 10 minutes.

The Functions of The Cerebral Cortex Are Improved, Memory Is Developing

The child remembers the events that occurred several hours ago. Speech is rapidly growing; an active vocabulary is accumulating. The activity of the cardiovascular system noticeably stabilize. It functions with less voltage. The heart rate decreases to 86-90 beats per minute, which is already approaching the norm for an adult. The musculoskeletal system is improved. There is intense ossification of soft bone tissue, cartilage. And although this process will continue as long as the person grows (sometimes up to 20-25 years), the skeleton of the child in the second year of life already provides a reasonably good vertical stability of the whole body. Strengthening the muscular-ligamentous apparatus continues.

Movements become more confident, diverse. But physical fatigue still occurs quickly, and the child often changes his posture; after considerable effort, he rests for a long time. Age-related changes occur in the gastrointestinal tract. The muscular layer of the wall of the stomach develops intestinal tone increases, peristalsis increases, and the nervous regulation of the mechanism of food passage through the intestine improve. The urinary system functions much better than in infancy.

With relatively small growth of the kidneys, the volume of the bladder increases. Accordingly, the amount of once urine increase, the number of urinations per day reduced to 10 times. In toddlers, the bladder and spinal cord receptors are still underdeveloped - as a result, the urge to urinate is weak. Most children, only by the age of 3, will be able to respond on time to the overflow of the bladder.

Therefore, do not blame the baby for wet pants. Like the ability to crawl, walk and talk, the skill of neatness is formed individually for each child. Some children are ready to use the toilet before they reach the age of two, others only after the third year of life. Make sure that the child prepares for the formation of the skill of neatness, according to the following criteria.

- Stays dry for an hour or two, sometimes wakes up dry after a day's sleep.
- Draws attention to the corresponding functions of the body: finds a way to let you know that he's going to "create" something (he calms down, groans, goes into the corner, sometimes he can say, "comment" wet panties somehow).
- I am experiencing a sense of disgust at the sight of dirty hands, face, or rotation toward wet diapers.
- Begins to feel the difference between damp and dry, dusty and clean;
- Knows the specific terminology accepted in the family ("pee-pee", etc.);
- Can communicate his needs and follow simple instructions;
- Shows curiosity in the behaviour of other family members (accompanies adults to the toilet and bathroom). Bowel movement after a year usually occurs once a day.

The nature of the stool changes: it becomes more dense, dark in colour, with a characteristic unpleasant odour. It is essential to ensure that the child does not have constipation; for this, you need to observe the age-related diet strictly. If you are prone to this ailment, you should consult a doctor. A time-tested way to deal with constipation: give the child in the morning half a glass of boiled water at room temperature and offer to use the pot at the same time. SLEEP From 1 year to 1.5 years, the child should still sleep twice a day. Usually, the first day's rest happens after breakfast and a short walk.

The second - after lunch or before an afternoon snack, if after lunch, the baby is actively awake. The duration of daytime sleep is not the same for all children but averages 3 hours a day. A night's sleep lasts 10-11 hours. Sometimes weakened, premature babies, who are in the period of adaptation to kindergarten (nursery), retain their second dream for more than a year and a half. Give them that opportunity. They will go to one goal when they are ready. In general, this process is exceptionally individual.

After one year six months, the child is left with one daytime sleep only if he is healthy and is in a vigorous, active state by the time of laying. If after a while he begins to show signs of fatigue (becomes lethargic or agitated, eats poorly), then temporarily (for two to three weeks) he should again be transferred to two afternoon sleeps. An early (up to 1.5 years) transition to one dream is undesirable - babies get tired of prolonged wakefulness, are overexcited, do not fall asleep for a long time. From 1.5 to 2 years, children sleep once during the day, about 2-3 hours. The total duration of sleep should be at least 13-14 hours.

It is better to spend a nap in the fresh air. Well, there is an opportunity to put the child on the open veranda, in the loggia, in the garden. Of course, this causes specific difficulties, because he already cramps in the stroller, children cannot sleep on a cot or in a hammock to avoid curvature of the spine. You can organize a nap in the room, but there should be a constant flow of fresh air. Do not be afraid to open the window in winter, and in summer - a window or balcony door. Before bedtime, ventilate the room well, and leave a loose window or window for the night.

Sufficient oxygen content in the air is an essential condition for a sound, sound sleep. For the time of rest, tie a scarf to the child and cover with a warm blanket. At average room temperature, the child needs to be covered with a thin woollen blanket in a duvet cover, wrapping it with an envelope under the mat. In a dream, the child should not overheat, sweat. Otherwise, he will tend to free himself from the blanket and may become too cold.

Think of clothes for sleeping - spacious, not restricting movements. During the first two years of life, when the child's growth is especially noticeable (it increases by about 32 cm), the baby often needs to rest lying down. A standing child grows worse. From 1.5 years old, you can lay the child on a pillow. It should be flat, not higher than 2 cm, not downy and not feather. If there are problems on the part of the nasopharynx, before going to bed, one needs to make a toilet of the nose with Aqua-Maris water.

A well-slept baby wakes up at the same time. He is cheerful, energetic, cheerful. Do not allow the child to lie in bed for long after waking up: this habit relaxes, reduces the tone of the body already tuned to wakefulness. Woke up, stretched out - and get up! Before going to bed, we also need a certain mood - cool games, quiet reading. Then the child "switched" to sleep calmly falls asleep. SECOND YEAR OF LIFE - VERY VULNERABLE AGE At this age, the child experiences an insatiable desire for exploration and autonomy ("I", "I am alone", "I").

There is such an age-related phenomenon as tantrums of the 2nd year of life that accompany the social development of children (their manifestations: moods, unmotivated crying, negative and protesting reactions, etc.). Such behaviour reflects the child's inability to clearly express their needs and desires, as well as the relative social immaturity of only children starting to speak (lack of formation of an emotional-volitional sphere).

Bad Listening and Effective Listening

Listening is not easy. Read what skills are required and how good listening can practise.

It says that listening is quasi-innate because the ear is the first fully developed sense organ. That may be, but hearing is not yet listening, just as little as seeing is reading. Think of different situations in which you want or should look: an expert explains how a device works; You are looking to a good friend who has a serious concern; You listen to your father, who once again shows his wisdom for the best. Imagine these situations as vividly as possible and consider what you are doing and how different these situations are. What you have to do and what do you have to bring in to listen effectively in these situations? If you pay attention to different listening opportunities, you will quickly notice.

One Ear In, The Other Out

Imagine yourself sitting in the car and talking to your fellow travellers. The traffic news reports: "There are sheep on the A3 on the A3 towards Würzburg. There is, therefore, a traffic jam between the Marktheidenfeld and Wertheim exits. Please drive exceptionally carefully in this area, the end of the traffic jam lies in a curve. "You have probably not kept any of this message.

You may be able to say that it was the exact highway you are driving on; You may also remember the sheep on the road, but you probably cannot say with certainty between which junctions the danger lies and in which direction the problem lies. You heard the message, but you could not listen and process the information and consequently cannot deduce any consequence from it. You now hope that the message will be repeated in time so that you can listen carefully again. Then what do you do differently?

Why Listening Is So Difficult

Listening is a complex, multi-step process. Listening presupposes that the listener wants to experience anything at all. If a person does not want to know anything, he will not be able to make an effort to listen to something concentrated. Listening requires that you focus your attention on a topic, that you have questions about this topic, that you are curious, or that you just realize

Listening also means that you record what you communicate. The message usually arrives on several channels and with many signals: you hear what someone is saying, but you also see the facial expressions and gestures of the person, you hear the tone of voice and the voice. Messages are revealed to the listener because one learns something about the feelings, the attitudes or opinions of the speaker.

Heard Is Not Saved by Itself

Although the sound waves always reach the ear somehow, the information not automatically record. The so-called working memory, i.e. the (unfortunately minimal) storage unit of the brain in which the currently important information is kept ready, must be actively populated. What hears does not fall into it, or happens to happen by itself at most once. However, if the listener does not record what has said at this point, understanding will fall by the wayside. The listener no longer contacts the speaker.

You can easily understand every single word. But it is different if you are wondering whether you have grasped the meaning. You must have sufficient prior knowledge that you can draw on. Finally, as a listener, you also have to save what you have heard in your long-term memory. It is not enough; once you understand something, you want to know it tomorrow. As a listener, you must store the information so that you can find it again. Listening is, therefore made up of searching for information, recording information, understanding data, and storing data. Every single step must succeed

How Listening Can Be Better

In principle, the ability to listen must be learned and practised, just like reading. Sure, most people can read somehow. Still, it makes a difference in reading skills how much you read, how often you read, or what and with what intentions you understand. It also applies to listen. To train to look, you can do the following:
.

Searching for information: For looking to take place, the listener must define what. You can listen better and longer if you focus on the listening event or the speaker and hide disturbances. You will soon realize that it is tiring and takes energy and that you cannot do this for as long as you like. But the excellent listener can develop an interest in the topic and the speaker, adjust to the problem and the speaker and control distracting thoughts and motives. It is essential in this context that you, as a listener, hold back your need to say something yourself and not immediately evaluate what you hear.

Record information: The capacity of the working memory is limited, and with it the amount of what a person can keep at once. But you can expand your working memory with tricks. So it is helpful if you prepare and pre-structure the listening situation if you think about what you have in advance, what you want to know or where the difficulties in understanding might be. In a conversation that you prepare in this way, you are less likely to get caught cold. Take a lot more with you from a lecture or lecture that you attend in preparation.

Understand information: Listeners rely on being able to process what they hear very quickly. Otherwise, it can lead to premature and incorrect conclusions. A listener who pays attention to complete information, i.e. consciously with facial expressions, gestures and tone of voice, has a clear advantage here. Sometimes you think for a while that you understand everything until it becomes apparent that you were on the wrong track. The sooner you discover this, the more misunderstandings and arguments you can avoid. However, it is particularly essential to withhold evaluations and quick judgments. Because reviews colour everything you hear and you then no longer record the information that the speaker wants to communicate, but stick to what you have always thought and known anyway.

Saving information: Spoken language is volatile, which means that it is no longer accessible when the speaker has said what he wanted to say. To be able to access what you have heard, you must actively anchor it in long-term memory. You can do that by, for example, imagine an image of what you heard. It is also helpful to put what you have listened to in your own words and to think critically about it: is it all logical? Does what you just heard contradict what you previously believed? Did the speaker deny himself? What feelings mattered? The more actively you deal with the information, the better the content is anchored in your memory and the higher the likelihood that you will find the news again.

Listen with Open Ears

Listening is a demanding activity that costs a great deal of energy. That means it is exhausting and prone to failure. It is because listening is a complex, compound process in which many elements have to interlock. The listener has to focus on the pace and mental world of the speaker. If you want to do it well, you have to learn and practice listening in the individual steps.

Listening with open ears is challenging but rewarding because no one has ever thought of a new idea through an open mouth.

Some people look to the answer. Others, on the other hand, love to hear themselves speak so much that they become many talkers. Inaudible people, bags of talkers and those who interrupt are taking the floor. They are not only annoying but with their behaviour, prevent every exchange and successful communication that is important for a good relationship.

But there are still people who can hear and understand the subtle nuances of what has said. You particularly like to surround yourself with these people because they listen carefully and you feel comfortable with them. Listening helps to clarify misunderstandings and avoid unnecessary arguments. In a relationship or at work, listening is useful to treat one another with respect and resolve conflicts constructively. But the talent of listening is not so natural, and you have to practice it. You should note the following points:

1. Be A Bit of a Detective

Whether master detective Sherlock Holmes or amateur detective Miss Marple, they all have a trait that is important for listening: they have the interest and willingness to learn and discover something. Like an excellent sniffer dog, a detective sets in motion and sniffs out all the essential information to solve the case.

We also need much information as possible in a conversation so that we understand how our counterpart feels. Having compassion for one another is the basis for good listening. Listening is about discovering "truths" and learning new things; after all, we want to develop further. That means: listening presupposes that the listener wants to experience anything at all.

2. Switch to Reception

Even the best listener cannot always be attentive. It is because we cannot always be open to all outside influences, Kurt Tucholsky also knew: "If you are open on all sides, you cannot be completely tight." The "inner reception committee", as communication psychologist Friedemann Schulz Designated by Thun is not always on reception. The willingness to receive and receive is what we need to listen.

Conversely, this means that to have a good conversation, it must first clarify that all conversation partners are on reception. Because if one or both of them are still distracted, listening becomes extremely difficult. It is okay and only fair to postpone an essential conversation to a time when everyone is on reception.

3. Relaxed

People often react differently under stress and tension than in a relaxed state. For example, stress creates a feeling of inner restlessness, irritability and lack of concentration. It is because anxiety or fear prepares you for attack or flight. An essential function that still ensures our survival today. But stress is poison for good conversation and sensitive listening. An interview in which both must listen well should never be "quickly" between door and rod but should take place under conditions that are relaxed. For example, everyone involved takes the time to talk and make themselves comfortable. Also, it is helpful if no one has tight deadlines. Listening when you invite to a friend's birthday, and you're late, this is a miserable time. Here, too, you are welcome to postpone the conversation. But essential: adjournment does not mean ignoring it or "just forgetting".

4. Attunement to The Discussion, Topic and Counterpart

For most people, when you have a good conversation, it's essential to listen to each other. Why is that? Because listening has a lot to do with understanding and love - the listener gets involved with the conversation partner.

Listening means recording, processing, and storing information. It creates a sense of well-being, ideally for everyone involved, because we seek consensus in the conversation. It, in turn, satisfies a basic need, namely that of inner connection (belonging).

It will be even easier for you to get involved and attune yourself to one another if you also pay attention to facial expressions, gestures and tone of voice when listening. It is listening with all your senses. Also, we store content with emotional involvement much better in our long-term memory - which means that we can come back to it more easily later.

"To communicate with each other, you have to listen not only the speaker but to the act of listening." Jiddu Krishnamurti

6. Show Interest

Active listening also means meeting the interlocutor with interest and attention. That is why it is often easier to listen to people we appreciate and like than people we don't want a career.

But how do you show interest in listening? Think back to the last time you were in love because you instinctively showed interest.

In essence, you keep eye contact and nod in agreement, don't let each other talk you out or chat, you ask questions, criticize and don't teach, you don't judge but motivate instead and, last but not least, put a lot of effort into understanding each other. Sounds easy, what? At least for lovers who are still very patient with each other.

In a dispute or a heated situation, things look very different, because everyone wants to take their stand and fight for their personal opinion. Sometimes you get the impression that it is a question of the reason for being: Whoever wins the argument can stay. But this attitude hardens the fronts, and the bottom line is unnecessary injuries on both sides.

7. Do Not Listen Passively, But Actively

Everyone knows them, the silent ones, who make you feel disinterested in the conversation. They look quietly, if at all because it's difficult to see from the outside.

What does it all involve? Avoid distractions like watching TV, reading newspapers, or looking at cell phones. Even if you say that you are capable of multitasking, you can be sure that your counterpart will not feel that way. Every distraction always distracts something from the content of the conversation.

Active listening also includes non-verbal signals such as an approving nod or an open posture. But the speaker also sends necessary non-verbal signals (facial expressions, gestures) from which further information can derive, which may be relevant under certain circumstances. The voice position, in particular, conveys a lot of "mood" of the speaker. The sound of the voice reveals what feelings are behind the spoken words.

Last, but not least: the speaker does not say some things or expresses them unclearly. Here it makes sense to ask: "Did you mean it like this ..." or "Do I understand you correctly that ..."

Questions belong to active listening, like breathing to life. But please don't ask why, because they often seem reproachful. A classic: "Why didn't you take out the trash?"

8. Please Remain Authentic and Do Not Let Any Ear Chew

And then there are the long talks where you feel like you have gill breathing because you don't even need to take a breath when talking. As a good listener, you are welcome to interrupt ongoing speeches because nobody has to be littered. A good conversation is balanced. Some people are unable to perceive this healthy balance.

One can also interrupt many talks, on the one hand for self-protection, on the other hand, so as not to feign interest, where there might not be one. It is about keeping you authentic as a good listener. Good listeners should be on reception, but it is also their responsibility to hear what interests them. It is the only way to ensure a legitimate interest - which is essential to be able to listen well.

"Listen" and "hear" are not the same thing. Most people are born ready to attend. It is a natural physiological process that does not require conscious effort from a person.

Listening is a process in which we seek to understand and remember what we **hear**. If the presence of hearing as one of the primary sensory organs is a condition for successful adaptation of an organism to the external environment; Then the developed ability to understand is a condition for a person's social adjustment. It is a process in which a person selects from all external sounds those that meet his needs and interests. In many ways, it is similar to reading. We read some material more carefully, some quickly look through, and in some, we look only at the title or the name of the author to decide whether to read it. The selection of oral information occurs similarly: we listen to something superficially, something with intense attention.

By itself, a selective attitude to information is a fundamental feature of human perception. The problem of listening lies in the field of interpersonal communication because it is associated not much with selectivity as with distortion or even skipping messages.

Under the basic model of communication, the "life" of a message includes at least four stages:

1. The news that the sender intends to make (his thoughts);
2. The story as it expresses (it's real coding by the speaker);
3. How it interprets (decoded by the listener);
4. How it finally preserves the memory of the listener.

When a message moves from one stage to another, information loss is inevitable, as a result of which the transmitted signal may not correspond to the original at all.

It is difficult to listen carefully, due to physiological reasons: we think faster than we say. It knows that an ordinary person able to perceive up to 500 words per minute, while the average speed of oral speech is from 125 to 150 words per minute. The result is, so to speak, "free time", which the listener fills with thinking about his problems, dreams, plans, or begins to interrupt and customize the speaker.

The next group of obstacles to active listening is related to the psychological state of the listener. Let us single out three types of "concern" of the listener that impede his participation in the communication process.

Firstly, external absent-mindedness: a person does not pay attention to what consider essential since he is absorbed in something that does not contribute to establishing friendly contacts with other members of the group. He listens to what is beyond the boundaries of this group.

A particular category of causes is associated with the speaker's behaviour and the nature of the message transmitted. An understanding of the word is adversely affected by the situation when its content itself causes concern and anxiety in the speaker. As a result, his speech becomes either fussy or slows down, and he is entirely silent. Thus, the "disturbing message" acts as a double obstacle to productive listening. In essence, it leads to the speaker becoming less transparent and intelligible so that the listener himself force to fill in the "gaps". It can assume the speaker gives the listener his alarm, as well as the alarm contained in the message, as a result of which the listener's anxiety already distorts the message. Thus, both the speaker and the listener should be aware of possible communication distortions and strive to reduce them. For instance,

Let us identify some sources of systematic errors, the understanding of which can benefit both the speaker and the listener.

The middle of the message least remembers. A competent speaker, realizing this, will try to exclude the centre from the structure of his words, reducing them so that they have only the beginning and the ending.

Message completion. The listener is inclined to "round off" what you hear, dividing the content into clearly delineated fragments, reducing the logical connectives both by enlarging some elements and eliminating others. Given this, a good listener should try not to miss the nuances of what was said, even if these details contradict his own opinion. In turn, a good speaker will speak sincerely, frankly, legibly, highlighting the meaning as much as possible. If the speech becomes too complicated, and the shades of meaning begin to take up more and more space, this means that the speaker is not confident in himself or is afraid of those in front of whom he speaks. If this happens, one must have the courage to admit it to himself and analyze the speech in the light of his fears.

They hear what they expect to hear. Listeners tend to modify the message to fit their expectations. The listener has predefined categories, and no matter what he hears, it is obliged to accommodate in them or will be controlled by them. What cannot be perceived by his "computer" should delay or excluded altogether. A smart speaker, recognizing the tendency of people to patterns, will emphasize the fact that his current story is different from what he said before; that he changed his position or moved away from it (if this is true). It did destroy their listeners the natural process of stereotyping. A competent listener, realizing his tendency, continually struggles with it to hear what is said.

Black and white hearing. A person perceives a message in evaluative terms, and it is much easier to see what he heard as a whole as good or evil than to attempt the differential assessment. This underlying tendency to listen to the message in evaluative terms prevents the listener from assimilating other aspects of the word. Creative finds of the news are lost in its designation by the category "bad", and deficiencies absorb by the name "good". If the speaker realizes that his speech can impress others only as "bad" or "good," he should do something to convince the listener to refrain from a tendency to evaluate.

Recommendations aimed at increasing the effectiveness of listening attract attention to improving the skills of concentration, emotional self-control, and feedback.

Managing your attention is a skill that must be continuously improved. One of the ways to concentrate on a large volume of informational messages is the development of the ability to determine what kind of information required in a given specific situation. It establishes that the effectiveness of the listening process increases if the listener manages to formulate the goals of obtaining information, i.e. answer the question "why am I listening to this?" In the field of social communication, the purposes of the listening process can be understanding, remembering, analyzing and evaluating the content of information, as well as trusting relationships with interlocutors.

Given the wide variety of situations in which we find ourselves, we must prepare to move from one level of listening to another always. The problem of a poor listener is related to his inability to determine the level that would be appropriate for the given situation.

So, the goal of "*hearing to understand*" involves the search for keywords and phrases that summarize the main problems of the issue under discussion.

One way to help a person concentrate is to **control their emotions**. Feelings of hatred, fear, happiness or grief, in general, intense emotional experiences can cause a decrease in our ability to hear another. Emotionality in conversation reduces the accuracy of attention. An exciting feature of the irrational behaviour of people: each person has some words, phrases and topics to which he reacts especially emotionally, thereby reducing his ability to control attention. We will call such terms "red flags". For one, the "red flag" is the word "clown", for the other - "fat", for the third - "chips." To know which words, phrases, and topics cause strong emotions in your means to get means of self-control: understanding that we were so excited in the conversation,

Turning to the description of feedback techniques, we draw attention to the differences between evaluative and non-evaluative feedback.

Evaluative feedback is a message of one's opinion, one's attitude to what to discuss. Evaluations can be positive ("it's *great for you to do this*") or negative ("*what kind of nonsense are you*"). Positive evaluative feedback performs the function of supporting the "I-concept" of our partner and the interpersonal relationships that have developed with him. Negative evaluative feedback performs a corrective function aimed at eliminating unwanted behaviour, the desire to change or modify our relationship. The structure of evaluative feedback involves the use of revolutions that would indicate that we are talking about a person's own opinion, for example, "it seems to me", "I think", "in my opinion". If there are no such turns, and the assessment expresses quite definitely and openly, then the statement becomes static, often perceived as rudeness or rudeness and provokes psychological protection from the interlocutor, which makes the relationship tense or even destroys them. Compare the statements "*I think this is not so* "and" *what stupidity!* "," *in my opinion, you were too harsh* "and" *well, you are rude!* "," *I think you're too dependent on it* "and" *rag.* "

Invaluable feedback is a type of feedback that does not contain our attitude to the issue under discussion. We use it when we want to learn more about a person's feelings or help him formulate thoughts on a specific occasion, while not directly interfering in the actions of the interlocutor. These goals achieve through techniques such as refinement, rephrasing, clarification, empathy. Both types of communication find expression both in non-reflective and inactive (reflective) listening.

Non-reflective listening consists of the ability to keep silent carefully, without interfering in the interlocutor's speech with his remarks. Outwardly passive behaviour, in reality, requires a lot of stress, physical and psychological attention. The general rule is that non-reflective listening is useful when the person you want to discuss sensitive issues, shows such deep feelings as anger or grief, or simply says that it requires a minimal answer. In form, a non-reflective hearing is the use of short remarks such as "yes?", "Is it interesting," "I understand," "is it nice to hear that," "can you elaborate more?" etc. or supportive non-verbal gestures, such as an affirmative nod of the head.

Reflective (or active) listening is the feedback from the speaker to control the accuracy of the perception of what hear. Unlike non-reflective listening, here, the listener more actively uses the verbal form to confirm the understanding of the message. The main types of reflexive answers are clarification, rephrasing, summarizing.

Clarification is an invaluable technique, using which we ask people for additional information, based both on business interests and for "talking" to a person their willingness and desire to listen to him. Clarification tools are questions such as "repeat", "specify what you mean," "did you want to say something else?" etc.

Rephrasing consists in transmitting to the speaker his message but in the words of the listener. His goal is to verify the accuracy what he heard, to demonstrate to another person his idea or proposal means to you. Rephrasing can begin with the words: "as I understand you ...", "in your opinion ..." "in other words, you consider ..." In this case, it is essential to choose only the critical, main points of the message, meaning and ideas, and not the feelings of the interlocutor. Rephrasing allows the speaker to see that they are listening and understanding, and if they misunderstand, then make appropriate corrections to the message. That is why paraphrasing considers as an essential communicative skill. It increases the accuracy of communication and, therefore, the level of mutual understanding. However, the rephrasing technique is not as simple as it seems at first glance. Rephrasing is not a trick or a verbal trick. It causes a desire to understand what the other person means. T is essential to demonstrate how we know the message of our interlocutor, and in such a way that he can check whether this matches what he wanted to convey.

A summary is a **summary of the** speaker's basic ideas and feelings. Summarizing statements help to connect fragments of conversation into semantic unity. Typical phrases may be the following: "Your main ideas, as I understand (a), are ...", "If you summarize what you said, then ...", etc.

Empathic listening- A special kind of listener behaviour. By looking, one can help an individual understand his situation and problems. As a specific procedure, it involves understanding the feelings experienced by another person, and the reciprocal expression of their understanding of these feelings. Clarification, rephrasing, summarizing, in connection with which the form of an empathic statement is very close to any kind of reflective listening. At the same time, empathic listening differs from reflective listening in its goals or intentions. If the purpose of reflective listening is to realize the speaker's message. Meaning of his idea to understand the feelings experienced, then the use of empathic listening is to grasp the emotional colouring of these ideas and their significance for another person, to understand what the message means and what feelings the interlocutor experiences. Empathic listening is a more intimate form of communication than active listening; it is the opposite of critical perception (by the way, therefore, it is tough to reproduce empathic statements in writing).

Empathic listening is a response path that allows others to find solutions to their problems, even if the listener himself does not know these solutions. Listeners do not empathically judge others. They comprehend the problem, consider it, often affirm in their own words their impressions of what is happening to the speaker.

They also regularly check how closely their prints match the state of the sender. The initial condition in this type of hearing is the acceptance of the partner's feelings and the confidence that he will be able to find a solution to the problem. Therefore, one does not need to impose his ideas on him until he asks for it.

Empathic listening is by no means appropriate in all situations. Sometimes someone who turns to you for help just needs information, not work with feelings. You should not use the techniques of empathic listening, even if you have little time or no real desire to help a person.

Thus, to become a competent listener, and therefore a skilled communicator, a person must possess various types of feedback, listening styles, and skillfully use them in appropriate circumstances.

Reflective Listening Techniques

The fundamental rule of interpersonal communications states: the meaning of the message decoded by the recipient never precisely matches the sensor embedded in this message by the sender. Reflective listening consists of establishing the feedback of the listener with the speaker. The listener not only listens attentively but also tells the speaker how he understood him. Reflective listening, compared to non-reflective, helps us achieve much higher accuracy in perceiving the meaning of the message since here we continuously adjust our understanding, taking into account the corrections of the interlocutor.

Again. The fundamental rule of interpersonal communications states: the **meaning of the message decoded by the recipient never precisely matches the sensor embedded in this message by the sender**.

This rule illustrates by a study conducted by graduates of an American university. This study revealed a large discrepancy between what the doctors had in mind when speaking with patients and what the latter heard. The doctor's words, "It will almost not hurt you," were interpreted in a wide range - from nagging pain to mild inconvenience. Also, 22% of patients said that for them, these words meant "very painful." Moreover, the phrase "you will soon be discharged home" for "about half the doctors and patients" said "in two or three days", while the rest of the patients understood this phrase as "tomorrow", and the patients who put such a message into the message turned out to be three times more than doctors.

The conclusion reached by the authors of the study was as follows: for patients to better understand what doctors mean, they need to ask actively and ask again. It is this manner of listening that *is called reflective listening*.

Reflective listening consists of **establishing the feedback of the listener with the speaker**. The listener not only listens attentively but also tells the speaker how he understood him. The speaker evaluates this understanding and, if necessary, makes corrections to his story, trying to achieve a more accurate understanding by the listener.

Reasons for misunderstanding

What are the reasons why our understanding is inaccurate?

1. The first reason for the misunderstanding is the **polysemy of most words**.

In the statement: "It annoys me by whistling all the time" the word "whistling" can mean a specific high-frequency sound, but it can also use in the sense of "deceiving". Exclamation: "What an organic!" on the lips of the director means praise for the actor's play, and on the lips of the psychologist is a set of symptoms indicating the presence of an organic brain lesion. The reason lies in the fact that the particular purpose of the name appears in the speaker's head but not contain itself.

Also, the meaning of the word may vary depending on the context in which it is pronounced: "I feel uneasy," for example, it can mean indigestion and mental discomfort, depending on what discuss before.

If to clarify the meaning of the words used, we apply reflective listening techniques, for example, ask him: "*What exactly do you mean by saying this?*", Most likely, the speaker will try to express his thought in other, more understandable to us words.

2. *The second reason for inaccurate understanding* is that the **speaker intentionally introduces distortion into the original meaning of the message**. When we communicate our ideas, attitudes, feelings, assessments to each other, in order not to offend anyone or appear in the eyes of the interlocutor in a bad light, we carefully select the words. Sometimes we exaggerate or underestimate something, often we use ambiguous expressions. No fewer tricks are undertaken by people who are trying to win the sympathy and sympathy of the listener, telling him about the unacceptable behaviour of some wrong person. For example, the statement: "My neighbour is a moron", most likely, does not mean a clinical diagnosis but indicates that our interlocutor is angry with his neighbour. To identify the meaning of the message, the listener can also use feedback.

3. The difficulty **of open expression:-** This means that due to the conventions adopted and the need for approval, people often begin their presentation with a small introduction, from which their intentions are not yet visible. Wanting to talk about something important, a person can start "from afar", with some problem, which is not his primary concern—he kind of tastes the water before diving into topics with a high emotional charge. The

less self-confidence he has, the more he goes around the bush before moving on to the main thing. Only as he begins to feel secure and sees that he is understood, does he reveal his deeper feelings. Therefore, the demonstration that you know him will help him quickly move to the main thing.

4. Finally, the **fourth source of difficulty is the subjective senses of the listener**. Each person accumulates during his lifetime a massive number of unique associations associated with different words. Some words in us evoke negative memories, hurt the patient, while the speaker did not invest in them a negative meaning. For example, a person who keeps a beloved dog at home will react differently to the statement "He behaves like a dog" than a person recently bitten by a stray dog. By checking whether we correctly understood the meaning of what we heard, we can overcome the negative impact of our associations on the accuracy of perception.

All this indicates the need to be able to listen reflexively, that is, to *decipher the meaning of messages, to find out their real meaning.*

By checking the correct understanding, we simultaneously let the speaker know that what he says is essential to us. Thus, we more actively encourage him to continue his story. The reflectively listening interlocutor assures the speaker that he understood everything that speaks correctly.

Any person is pleased when they know him. We indifferently feel sympathy for those who do not condemn us, but, on the contrary, treat us with understanding. Therefore, using reflective listening, we can have a specific impact on the relationship that we have with the interlocutor.

Reflective Listening Techniques

All of the following techniques unite by the focus on the simultaneous solution of three main tasks:

1. Check the correctness of your understanding of the words and statements of the speaker.

2. Not to control the topic of conversation, but to support the speaker's spontaneous speech flow, to help him "talk," to talk not about what seems relevant and exciting to us, but about what he considers important.

3. Not only to be an interested listener but also to make the interlocutor feel this interest.

1. Misunderstanding

The first technique, aimed at improving mutual understanding, looks paradoxical at first glance: this is a **demonstration of**

disagreement. It can be useful to simply state: "I do not understand what you mean."

When, after listening to the interlocutor, we do not understand him well, we can honestly and directly say this. The principle that guides us in applying this technique is simple: *if you don't understand something, say so*. Many people are embarrassed to say that they did not understand something. Often the source of such fears are memories of school. An adult living with such a childish decision will most likely seek to hide from others that he does not understand something. He will think out, make a smart appearance, nod thoughtfully and thereby mislead the interlocutor. Although, if the interlocutor is interested in being understood, he, faced with misunderstanding, would most likely make an effort to be understood correctly.

2. Reflection (Echo)

Reflection is the repetition of words or phrases of the interlocutor. It usually takes the form of a literal repetition or repetition with minor changes.

If the speaker tries to express things that are not entirely clear to himself and gets reflected (repetition) of his words, the listener does not change the structure of the statement in any way, does not introduce additional semantic load from himself. The *speaker becomes clearer what he tried to express*.

Representation should not use too often so that the partner does not have the impression that he is mimick. This technique is most appropriate in those situations where the meaning of the interlocutor's statements was not entirely clear or where his comments carry an emotional load.

3. Rephrasing (Paraphrase)

To rephrase is to formulate the same thought differently. In conversation, a translation consists in **transmitting to the speaker his message, but in the words of the listener**. The purpose of paraphrasing is to *test the listener for the accuracy of his understanding of the message*. Paraphrasing, oddly enough, is useful precisely when the interlocutor's speech seems clear to us.

4. Summary

Summarizing is a reformulation technique by which it summarizes not a single phrase, but a significant part of the story or the entire conversation as a whole. The basic rule for formulating a resume is that it should be *effortless and straightforward*.

This technique is quite applicable in lengthy discussions, where it helps to build fragments of conversation into semantic unity. It gives the listener confidence in the accurate perception of the speaker's message and at the same time, helps the speaker understand how well he managed to convey his thoughts.

PART 2

PANIC ATTACKS

Panic Attacks

You may hear individuals discussing panic attacks and anxiety attacks like they're something very similar. They're various conditions, however. Panic attacks please out of nowhere and include extraordinary and frequently overpowering trepidation. They're joined by startling physical indications, for example, a hustling heartbeat, brevity of breath, or queasiness. The most recent release of the Indicative and Measurable Manual of Mental Issue (DSM-5) perceives panic attacks, and orders them as unforeseen or anticipated.

All-Or-Nothing Thinking

Startling panic attacks happen without a conspicuous reason. External stressors signal expected panic attacks, for example, fears. Panic attacks can transpire, yet having more than one might be an indication of the panic issue. Anxiety attacks aren't perceived in the DSM-5. The DSM-5 does, notwithstanding, characterize anxiety as a component of various regular mental issues. Indications of anxiety incorporate concern, misery, and dread. Stress is usually identified with the expectation of a distressing circumstance, experience, or occasion. It might come on step by step.

The absence of analytic acknowledgement of anxiety attacks implies that the signs and indications are not entirely clear. That is, an individual may portray having an "anxiety assault" and have side effects that another has never experienced regardless of showing that they also have had an "anxiety assault." Peruse on to discover progressively about the contrasts between panic attacks and anxiety.

Indications

Panic and anxiety attacks may feel comparative, and they share a ton of enthusiastic and physical side effects. You can encounter both an anxiety and a panic assault simultaneously. For example, you may encounter anxiety while agonizing over a conceivably distressing circumstance, for example, a significant introduction at work. At the point when the thing shows up, fear may come full circle in a panic assault. T might be hard to tell whether what you're encountering is anxiety or a panic assault. Remember the accompanying:

Anxiety is commonly identified with something that is seen as distressing or compromising. Stressors don't consistently signal panic attacks. They frequently happen all of a sudden. Anxiety can be mellow, moderate, or dangerous. For instance, stress might be going on in the rear of your brain as you approach your everyday exercises. Panic attacks, then again, for the most part, include extreme, problematic side effects. During a panic assault, the body's independent battle or-flight reaction dominates. Physical manifestations are frequently more extreme than indications of anxiety. While anxiety can fabricate bit by bit, panic attacks, as a rule, please unexpectedly. Panic attacks ordinarily trigger concerns or fears identified with having another assault. This may affect your conduct, driving you to maintain a strategic distance from spots or circumstances where you figure you may be in danger of a panic assault.

Causes

Surprising panic attacks have no unmistakable outer triggers. Similar things can activate expected panic attacks and anxiety. Some fundamental triggers include:

- A Distressing Activity
- Driving
- Social Circumstances

fears, for example, agoraphobia (dread of swarmed or open spaces), claustrophobia (dread of little spaces), and acrophobia (terror of statures)

- Updates or recollections of awful encounters
- Interminable ailments, for example, coronary illness, diabetes, fractious gut disorder, or asthma
- Interminable torment
- Withdrawal from medications or liquor
- Caffeine

- Prescription and enhancements
- Thyroid issues
- Hazard factors

Anxiety and panic attacks have comparable hazard factors. These include: encountering injury or seeing horrible mishaps, either as a kid or as a grown-up encountering a distressing life occasion, for example, the demise of a friend or family member or a separation encountering continuous pressure and stresses, for example, work obligations, struggle in your family, or budgetary troubles

- Living with an incessant wellbeing condition or perilous sickness
- Having an on-edge character
- Having another emotional wellbeing issue, for example, despondency
- Having close relatives who additionally have anxiety or panic issue
- Utilizing medications or liquor

Individuals who experience anxiety are at an expanded danger of encountering panic attacks. Be that as it may, having anxiety doesn't mean you will meet a panic assault.

- Arriving at a finding
- Specialists can't analyze anxiety attacks, yet they can explain:

- Anxiety side effects
- Anxiety issue
- Panic attacks
- Panic issue

Your PCP will get some information about your side effects and lead tests to preclude other wellbeing conditions with comparable side effects, for example, coronary illness or thyroid issues.

- To get a determination, your primary care physician may lead:
- A physical test
- Blood tests
- A heart test, for example, an electrocardiogram (ECG or EKG)
- A mental assessment or poll

Home Cures

You ought to address your primary care physician or another emotional well-being proficient at discovering what you can do to both forestall and treat anxiety-and panic-related side effects. Having a treatment plan and adhering to it when an assault strikes can assist you with feeling like you're in charge. If you feel an anxiety or panic assault going ahead, attempt the accompanying: Take moderate full breaths. At the point when you think your breath enlivening, concentrate on each breathes in and breathe out. Feel your stomach load up with air as you breathe in.

Consider down from four you breathe out. Rehash until your breathing eases back. Perceive and acknowledge what you're encountering. If you've just met an anxiety or panic assault, you realize that it very well may be unimaginably alarming. Advise yourself that the manifestations will pass, and you'll be okay.

Practice care. Care based intercessions are progressively used to treat anxiety and panic issues. Responsibility is a system that can assist you in establishing your considerations in the present. You can rehearse care by effectively watching contemplations and sensations without responding to them. Use unwinding systems. Unwinding systems incorporate guided symbolism, fragrance-based treatment, and muscle unwinding. In case you're encountering indications of anxiety or a panic assault, take a stab at doing things that you find unwinding. Close your eyes, clean up, or utilize lavender, which has to loosen up impacts.

Way of Life Changes

The accompanying way of life changes can assist you with forestalling anxiety and panic attacks, just as decrease the seriousness of indications when an assault happens:

- Diminish and oversee wellsprings of worry in your life.
- Figure out how to recognize and stop negative contemplations.

- Get ordinary, moderate exercise.
- Practice contemplation or yoga.
- Eat a decent eating regimen.
- Join a care group for individuals with anxiety or panic attacks.
- The breaking points your utilization of liquor, medications, and caffeine.

Different Medicines

Address your primary care physician about different medications for anxiety and panic attacks. Some regular medicines incorporate psychotherapy or prescription, including:

- Antidepressants
- Antianxiety drugs
- Benzodiazepines

As a rule, your primary care physician will suggest a mix of medications. You may likewise need to modify your treatment plan after some time.

The Takeaway

Panic attacks and anxiety attacks aren't equivalents. Even though these terms are regularly utilized reciprocally, just panic attacks are recognized in the DSM-5. Anxiety and panic attacks have comparable manifestations, causes, and hazard factors. Notwithstanding, panic attacks will, in general, be increasingly exceptional and are regularly joined by progressively physically severe side effects. You should contact a specialist if anxiety-or panic-related indications are influencing your regular day to day existence.

What Is A Panic Issue?

The panic issue happens when you experience repeating surprising panic attacks. The DSM-5 characterizes panic attacks as unexpected floods of severe dread or distress that top in practically no time. Individuals with the confusion live in terror of having a panic assault. You might be having a panic assault when you feel abrupt, overpowering dread that has no undeniable reason. You may encounter physical indications, for example, a hustling heart, breathing troubles, and perspiring.

The vast majority experience a panic assault a few times in their lives. The American Mental Affiliation reports that 1 out of each 75 individuals may encounter a panic issue. The panic issue is portrayed by industrious dread of having another panic assault after you have faced in any event one month (or a more considerable amount of) constant concern or stress over extra panic attacks (or their results) repeating. Even though the side effects of this issue can be very overpowering and startling, they can be overseen and improved with treatment. Looking for treatment is the most significant piece of diminishing indications and enhancing your satisfaction.

What Are the Manifestations of The Panic Issue?

Indications of panic issues regularly start to show up in youngsters and youthful grown-ups younger than 25. On the off chance that you have had at least four panic attacks, or you live in dread of having another panic assault in the wake of encountering one, you may have a panic issue. Panic attacks produce solemn dread that starts of nowhere, regularly with no notice. An assault commonly goes on for 10 to 20 minutes, yet in extreme cases, indications may keep going for over 60 minutes. The experience is diverse for everybody, and signs regularly change.

Essential manifestations related to a panic assault include:

- Hustling heartbeat or palpitations
- Brevity of breath
- Having an inclination that you are gagging
- Unsteadiness (vertigo)
- Unsteadiness
- Queasiness
- Perspiring or chills
- Shaking or trembling

changes in mental state, including a sentiment of derealization (sentiment of falsity) or depersonalization (being withdrawn from oneself)

- Deadness or shivering in your grasp or feet
- Chest agony or snugness
- Dread that you may pass on

The side effects of a panic assault regularly happen for no obvious explanation. Commonly, the side effects are not proportionate to the degree of risk that exists in nature. Since these attacks can't be anticipated, they can fundamentally influence your work. The dread of a panic assault or reviewing a panic assault can bring about another attack. What a panic assault feels like getting notification from genuine individuals who have encountered a panic assault.

What Causes the Panic Issue?

The reasons for panic issues are not comprehended. Research has indicated that the panic issue might be hereditarily connected. The panic issue is likewise connected with massive changes that happen throughout everyday life. Leaving for school, getting hitched, or having your first youngsters are, for the most part, significant life advances that may make pressure and lead to the improvement of panic issues.

Who Is In Danger Of Creating A Panic Issue?

Even though the reasons for panic issues are not comprehended, data about the malady indicates that specific gatherings are bound to build up the confusion. Specifically, ladies are twice as likely as men to build up the condition, as indicated by the National Foundation of Emotional well-being.

How Is A Panic Issue Analyzed?

If you experience the side effects of a panic assault, you may look for crisis clinical consideration. These great many people experience a panic assault just because they accept that they have respiratory failure. While at the crisis office, the crisis supplier will play out a few tests to check whether your side effects are brought about by respiratory failure. They may run blood tests to preclude different conditions that can cause comparable indications or an electrocardiogram (ECG) to check heart work. On the off chance that there is no crisis premise to your manifestations, you will allude back to your essential consideration supplier. Your essential consideration supplier may play out a psychological wellness assessment and get some information about your indications. All other clinical issues will be precluded before your critical consideration supplier makes a finding of a panic issue.

How Is the Panic Issue Treated?

Treatment for panic issue centres around decreasing or wiping out your side effects. This is accomplished through treatment with a certified proficient and, at times, drug. Treatment regularly includes psychological conduct treatment (CBT). This treatment instructs you to change your considerations and activities, so you can comprehend your attacks and deal with your dread. Drugs used to treat panic issues can incorporate specific serotonin reuptake inhibitors (SSRIs), a class of energizer. SSRIs recommended for the panic issue may include:

- Fluoxetine
- Paroxetine
- Sertraline

Different drugs now and again used to treat panic issue include serotonin-norepinephrine reuptake inhibitors (SNRIs), another class of upper antiseizure drugs benzodiazepines (ordinarily utilized as sedatives), including diazepam or clonazepam monoamine oxidase inhibitors (MAOIs), another sort of energizer that is utilized inconsistently as a result of uncommon yet genuine reactions Notwithstanding these medicines, there are various advances that you can take at home to lessen your side effects. Models include: keeping up a standard timetable practising all the time getting enough rest maintaining a strategic distance from the utilization of energizers, for example, caffeine

What Is the Drawn-Out Viewpoint?

The panic issue is regularly a constant (long haul) condition that can be hard to treat. A few people with this issue don't react well to treatment. Others may have periods when they have no side effects and periods when their side effects are severe. The vast majority with the panic issue will encounter some side effect help through treatment.

In What Manner Can Panic Issues Be Forestalled?

It may not be conceivable to forestall panic issues. Be that as it may, you can work to diminish your indications by maintaining a strategic distance from liquor and energizers, for example, caffeine just as illegal medications. It is additionally useful to see if you are encountering indications of anxiety following a troubling life occasion. On the off chance that you are annoyed by something that you met or were presented to, talk about the circumstance with your essential consideration supplier. Alarm assaults are sudden assaults where you feel dread, uneasiness. Like you're losing control in any event, when there's no risk. These assaults happen out of nowhere with no notice, and a few manifestations can feel like a coronary episode.

Fits of anxiety are commonly short, arriving at their top in under 10 minutes. An assault ordinarily keeps going anyplace from a couple of moments up to 30. However, rehashed assaults can repeat for a considerable length of time. This is what you have to think about the length of a fit of anxiety and how you can adapt or keep it from happening.

Mind Reading

What's the Longest A Fit of Anxiety Can Last?

Most fits of anxiety last just a couple of moments. However, they regularly feel like a lifetime when you're encountering one. Side effects frequently top inside 10 minutes and afterwards start to blur away. It's conceivable to have a fit of anxiety that is particularly long or short. A few assaults can top in almost no time, with the full charge enduring only minutes, while others may last more. Most research has portrayed a single fit of anxiety, enduring as long as 30 minutes. A few reports by people have described assaults enduring hours or even days. As indicated by certain specialists, if manifestations don't top inside 10 minutes, it's not viewed as a fit of anxiety (which has an abrupt beginning of frenzy). Instead, it's considered to be high tension. While this is still unimaginably awkward and upsetting, it may not be analyzed as a fit of anxiety.

It's additionally conceivable to encounter numerous fits of anxiety that happen in waves for an hour or more. Would symptoms be able to wait? While side effects of fits of anxiety can change, they regularly include: dashing heart perspiring or chills trembling brevity of breath chest agony or inconvenience dazedness the dread of losing control or of passing on sickness and other stomach inconvenience

In a fit of anxiety, side effects please unexpectedly, pinnacle, and afterwards step by step blur away. Physical side effects are frequently the first to die down, however relying upon your uneasiness levels, and you may proceed to hyperventilate and encounter chest and stomach inconvenience. After the blow of the assault, you may likewise feel worn out or pressure in your muscles. The fundamental manifestations that can wait are social or psychological indications. General nervousness may endure after the assault. Individuals frequently keep on stressing over their absence of control. On the off chance that you experience torment, a dread of death may persevere until you see a specialist.

On the off chance that you have an alarming issue, you may stress or fixate on having another fit of anxiety. This can make day uneasiness, influencing your satisfaction.

What Are Some Ways of Dealing with Stress at The Time?

First of all: Relax. You're likely hyperventilating, however balancing out your breathing can rapidly quiet your body's battle or-flight reaction. Have a go at tallying your breaths—one full breath in, one full breath out. Check up to 10 and afterwards start again until your breathing has returned to typical. Other brisk adapting methodologies include: perceiving that what you're encountering is a fit of anxiety finding an item to concentrate on rehearsing muscle unwinding rehashing a mantra Exercising you forestall a fit of anxiety? You don't need to carry on with your life in dread of fits of anxiety. There are a few apparatuses and systems you can use to help deal with your assaults and even forestall them.

A decent method to forestall alarm assaults is to make an arrangement that will assist you with feeling more in charge. If you have an agreement worked out for when an attack goes ahead, you can conceivably abbreviate the length and recurrence of assaults. Your arrangement may include: rehearsing a profound breathing activity or doing dynamic muscle unwinding centring an establishing system like the 5-4-3-2-1 method perusing a piece of paper depicting alarm assaults, to help justify the dread of kicking the bucket

having a short rundown of mantras either on a clingy note or in your telephone to open, saying something like, "I will be all right, these are only indications of frenzy." You might need to look for help and let your family, companions, or associates in on your arrangements for when you're in specific circumstances.

For Example:

At home, you can show your accomplice or flatmate an unwinding procedure that they can do with you when you're amidst an assault. Breathing together may assist you in feeling more grounded and centred. At work, you may need to give a trusted collaborator or manager a heads up that you experience alarm assaults. Sharing this data can feel startling. However, it can likewise cause your office to feel like a more secure space. Different approaches to forestall future assaults include: Information is power. With more data about fits of anxiety, you can know about your indications, feel more in charge, and abbreviate your assaults.

While numerous individuals experience a fit of anxiety only a single time or a couple of times, others experience them as a feature of a current nervousness issue. Finding out about uneasiness can assist you with bettering oversee it.

Practice Unwinding Strategies

Contemplation, breathing activities, and muscle unwinding would all be able to help at the time of a fit of anxiety. In any case, learning and rehearsing these strategies already is fundamental, so you're prepared when one occurs.

Exercise Routinely

Customary exercise has demonstrated various advantages for both mental and physical wellbeing. Working out, particularly high force or cardio exercises, can even copy manifestations of fits of anxiety. By practising routinely, you can prepare your body and brain to understand that those side effects — brave heart, perspiring, breathing hard — don't generally demonstrate alarm. You may likewise decrease your pressure, which can trigger fits of anxiety. Abstain from stress more difficult and increase your anxiety levels. That's why it's essential to maintain good sleep hygiene.

When to See A Specialist

Panic attacks can feel terrifying, particularly while encountering one just because. In any case, it doesn't mean you consequently have an anxiety issue. In essence, you can have panic attacks without a dysfunctional behaviour. Look for help if: you have a few panic attacks or experience them constantly your anxiety is influencing your everyday life you're experiencing issues adapting There are such a large number of alternatives accessible to you, and your PCP can even assist you with setting up plans, share writing, or check your crucial signs to facilitate your brain.

On the off chance that you regularly experience a dread of biting the dust or stress that something is amiss with your wellbeing, see a specialist. They can run tests to check your general welfare, or explicitly the soundness of your heart. Having a physician's approval can give you genuine feelings of serenity. You can even keep a printout of the outcomes. This piece of paper can be a piece of your arrangement to pull out during an assault to advise you that you will be okay.

Takeaway

Panic attacks may come all of a sudden and feel awkward, yet they won't keep going forever. Indeed, while they may feel longer, most panic attacks just last around 10 minutes. On the off chance that you start to encounter anxiety manifestations that influence your everyday life, your attacks increment in force or term, or you simply need additional assistance with adapting, contact psychological wellbeing proficient. For the individuals who look for treatment from psychological wellness proficient, two-third trusted Source purportedly accomplish abatement inside a half year.

On the off chance that you've at any point had a panic assault, you'll realize it very well may be both an alarming encounter and depleting experience. The panic issue is an analysis given to individuals who experience intermittent surprising panic attacks—that is, the assault seems to happen out of nowhere. Panic assault manifestations incorporate perspiring, shaking, the brevity of breath, sentiments of stifling, chest torment, and dread of kicking the bucket.

What Is an Assault?

A panic assault is an unexpected flood of exceptional dread or uneasiness that arrives at a top in no time. During which time, an assortment of mental and physical side effects happen. These side effects incorporate quick pulse, perspiring, shaking, the brevity of breath, hot flashes, and tipsiness—just as a feeling of approaching fate, chills, queasiness, stomach torment, chest agony, migraine, and deadness or shivering.

What Is Issue?

The panic issue is a conclusion given to individuals who experience intermittent startling panic attacks—that is, the assault seems to happen all of a sudden. The term intermittent alludes to the way that the individual has had more than one unforeseen panic assault. Conversely, expected panic attacks happen when there is a conspicuous signal or trigger, for example, a particular fear or summed up anxiety issue. In the U.S., generally, half of the individuals with panic issues experience both unforeseen and expected panic attacks. Panic attacks cause an assortment of upsetting side effects that can be alarming for the individual encountering the assault. A few people botch panic attacks for coronary failures, and many accept that they are passing on. Others feel a blend of self-question or looming fate. Some can likewise discover the scenes amazingly humiliating and cease from telling their companions, family, or psychological wellbeing proficient.

To get a determination of the panic issue, the panic attacks must be unforeseen. During the assault, at least four of the above indications must happen. For panic attacks that are normal, which means they probably won't be normal by the individual, however, are relied upon comparable to any fear, anxiety, or other psychological wellness issues, at least four side effects should likewise happen.

To What Extent Does A Panic Assault Last?

Although term changes between people, normally, panic attacks arrive at their top inside 10 minutes or less. Afterwards, side effects start to die down. Panic attacks infrequently keep going for over 60 minutes, with generally going on for around 20 to 30 minutes.

Are Panic Attacks Awful for Your Heart?

As indicated by an examination distributed in Brain science Medicine1, individuals who experience the ill effects of panic attacks and the panic issue might be more danger of respiratory failure and coronary illness further down the road. While the connection between the panic issue and coronary illness stays disputable, the examination found that contrasted with people without panic issues; sufferers were found to have up to a 36%

higher danger of respiratory failure and up to 47% higher danger of coronary illness. On the off chance that you experience the ill effects of panic attacks, look for consideration for any chest torment indications to preclude any issues with heart wellbeing. Would you be able to Bite the dust from a Panic Assault?

While panic attacks cause an assortment of physical issues and numerous individuals detailing feeling like they are going to bite the dust while encountering one, you can't bite the dust from a panic assault.

Panic Issue and Panic Assault Causes

On the off chance that you are inclined to encountering negative feelings and are delicate to anxiety, you might be in danger for the beginning of panic attacks and panic issues. Youth experience of physical maltreatment, smoking, and relational stressors in the months before the main panic are likewise hazarded factors.

Moreover, it is accepted that hereditary qualities assume a job in defenselessness to the panic issue. However, the specific qualities, quality items, or capacities that are ensnared are not known. People with a parent or guardians determined to have anxiety, sorrow, or bipolar issue are likewise thought to be at a greater danger of creating a panic issue.

Step by Step Instructions to Stop A Panic Assault

As for appearances top during a panic assault, it can feel like the experience will never end. While you may believe there's nothing you can do except for enduring it, there are a few methods you can practice to lessen the seriousness of your indications and divert your brain. See our inside and out article on the best way to stop a panic assault.

Has an Arrangement Set Up?

Regardless of what your arrangement is, having one set up is the most significant thing. You can think about your arrangement as your go-to set of directions for yourself when you feel a panic assault going ahead. One arrangement may be to remove yourself from your present condition, plunk down, and consider a companion or relative that can help divert you from your indications and help you to quiet down. At that point, you can fuse the accompanying strategies.

Practice Profound Relaxing

The brevity of breath is a typical side effect of panic attacks that can cause you to feel mad and wild. Recognize that your brevity of breath is a side effect of a panic assault, and this is just brief. At that point, start by taking a full breath in for a sum of four seconds, hold for a second, and discharge it for a sum of four seconds. Continue rehashing this example until your breathing gets controlled and consistent. Concentrating on the tally of four not exclusively will keep you from hyperventilating. However, it can likewise assist with leaving different side effects speechless.

Use Muscle Unwinding Systems

Amidst a panic assault, it's inescapable that you'll feel like you've lost control of your body; however, muscle unwinding strategies permit you to restore a portion of that control. Dynamic muscle unwinding (PMR) is a straightforward yet powerful strategy for panic and anxiety issues. Start by grasping your clench hand and holding this grip until the check of 10. When you get to 10, discharge the hold and let your hand unwind totally. Next, attempt a similar procedure in your feet, and afterwards, bit by bit stir your way up to your body-gripping and loosening up each muscle gathering: legs, glutes, guts, back, hands, arms, shoulders, neck, and face.

Rehash a Mantra

You may feel somewhat unbalanced doing this from the outset; however, rehashing an empowering, positive mantra to yourself during a panic assault can fill in as a way of dealing with stress. Take a stab at rehashing something as basic as "This is brief. I will be all right," or "I'm not going to kick the bucket. I simply need to relax."

Discover an Article and Spotlight on It

Pick an item that you can see someplace before you and note all that you notice about that object—from its shading and size to any examples it might have, where you may have seen others like it, or what something totally different to the article would resemble. You can do this in your mind or talk your observational so anyone might hear to yourself or a companion.

Panic Assault Treatment

Both psychotherapy and medicine have been seen as powerful in assisting with diminishing the recurrence and force of panic attacks. Your particular treatment way will rely upon individual inclination, clinical history, and the seriousness of your attacks.

A type of psychotherapy called psychological conduct treatment (CBT) has been seen by a few examinations as the best treatment for panic attacks and panic issues. During CBT, you will work with an advisor on unwinding preparing, rebuilding your contemplations and practices, care, introduction treatment, and stress decrease. Numerous individuals that experience the ill effects of panic attacks begin to see a decrease inside weeks, and manifestations regularly decline essentially or leave totally inside a while.

Your primary care physician may likewise recommend that you attempt some type of medicine as a major aspect of your treatment way. These meds can be incredibly useful in overseeing panic assault side effects, just as anxiety and wretchedness. Instances of prescriptions your primary care physician may recommend are:

Particular serotonin reuptake inhibitors (SSRIs, for example, fluoxetine (Prozac), paroxetine (Paxil, Pexeva), and sertraline (Zoloft). SSRI depressants are generally the primary decision for treating panic attacks and panic issues because of their adequacy and the okay of any genuine reactions.

Serotonin and norepinephrine reuptake inhibitors (SNRIs, for example, venlafaxine (Effexor) are FDA endorsed for the treatment of the panic issue.

Benzodiazepines, for example, alprazolam (Xanax) and clonazepam (Klonopin), may likewise be endorsed.

Anxiety Assault versus Panic Assault: What's The Distinction?

Numerous individuals utilize the terms anxiety assault and panic assault tradable, yet in actuality, they speak to two distinct encounters. The DSM-5 uses the term panic assault to portray the trademark highlights of panic issues or panic attacks that happen because of another psychological issue. To be viewed as a panic assault, at least four of the manifestations laid out in the DSM-5 must be available.

Conversely, the term anxiety assault isn't a specifier laid out in the DSM-5. Or maybe, anxiety is utilized to depict a centre component of various diverse anxiety issues. The finish of side effects that come about because of being in a condition of anxiety, for example, eagerness, the brevity of breath, expanded pulse, and trouble concentrating—may feel like an "assault," however are commonly less extraordinary than those accomplished at the tallness of a panic assault.

Given that anxiety attacks aren't explicitly sketched out as an analysis in the DSM-5, the use of the word is not entirely clear, and various people may utilize it in changing manners and conditions. For one individual, an anxiety assault may be overthinking about a particular concern to the degree that they can't focus on whatever else; for another, anxiety assault may allude to perspiring and brevity of breath when confronted with a specific circumstance.

Instructions to Help Somebody Having a Panic Assault

Seeing a companion or a friend or family member experience a panic assault can be a startling encounter. It can likewise be trying to feel frail to support that individual and to watch them endure. While you're probably not going to have the option to leave your adored one's panic assault speechless, there are things you can do and say to help them through the experience.

Basically, it is imperative to remain quiet, patient, and comprehension. Help your companion hold up out the panic assault by urging them to take full breaths in for four seconds and out for four seconds. Remain with them and guarantee them that this assault is just transitory, and they will traverse it. You can likewise advise them that they can leave the earth they are in on the off chance that they would feel increasingly great somewhere else and attempt to connect with them in the happy discussion.

When the panic assault is finished, and the individual has come back to a quiet state, urging them to look for help from emotional wellbeing proficient at their soonest comfort, in the event that they haven't as of now. You can assist them with facilitating by helping with the quest for an authorized proficient, inquiring about adapting methods on the web, and searching for self-improvement guides that may be valuable.

Panic Assault Help and Backing

In the event that you've been encountering panic attacks or figure you may have a panic issue, we urge you to look for analysis and treatment from your primary care physician and psychological wellness proficient. In spite of the fact that panic attacks can feel like a weakening and humiliating condition, recollect that you aren't the only one and your emotional wellbeing is not something to be humiliated about. There is an assortment of assets accessible to you for guidance and backing, both on the web and as care groups.

When May I Have Panic Attacks?

Panic attacks can occur during the day or night. A few people have one panic assault at that point never experience another, or you may find that you have them consistently, or a few out of a short space of time. You may see that specific spots, circumstances, or exercises appear to trigger panic attacks. For instance, they may occur before an upsetting arrangement.

Most panic attacks last between 5–20 minutes. They can come on rapidly. Your side effects will typically top (be even under the least favourable conditions) inside 10 minutes. You may likewise encounter indications of a panic assault over a more drawn out timeframe. This could be on the grounds that you have a subsequent panic assault, or you're encountering different manifestations of anxiety.

"My panic attacks appear to come all of a sudden at this point. In any case, truth be told, they appear to be activated primarily around evening time when I need to rest yet can't stop my psyche dashing, encountering stress and panic over whatever might be at the forefront of my thoughts."

What Assists with Overseeing Panic Attacks?

Panic attacks can be alarming, yet there are things you can do to enable yourself to adapt. It could assist with keeping print these tips out and keep them someplace simple to discover.

During A Panic Assault

Concentrate on your relaxing. It can assist with focusing on breathing gradually in and out while checking to five.

Stamp on the spot. A few people discover this helps control their relaxing.

Concentrate on your faculties. For instance, taste mint-enhanced desserts or gum, or contact or snuggle something delicate.

Take a stab at establishing methods. Establishing systems can assist you with feeling more in charge. They're particularly helpful in the event that you experience separation during panic attacks. (See our page on self-care for dissociative disarranges for more data on establishing methods.)

After A Panic Assault

Consider self-care. It's critical to focus on what your body needs after you've had a panic assault. For instance, you may need to rest someplace discreetly or eat or drink something.

Tell somebody you trust. In the event that you feel ready to, it could assist with telling somebody you've had a panic assault. It could be especially useful to make reference to how they may see in case you're having another, and how you'd like them to support you.

What Is the Panic Issue?

In case you're having loads of panic attacks at capricious occasions, and there doesn't appear to be a specific trigger or cause, you may be given a determination of the panic issue. It's entirely expected to encounter panic issues and agoraphobia (a kind of fear) together. Individuals who experience panic issue may have a few periods with few or no panic attacks, yet have parcels on different occasions.

My first day of secondary school was likewise the first occasion when I understood I was on edge. Maybe a switch had flipped in my psyche from quiet to off-the-outlines froze. I had been apprehensive previously. However, this was another variety of stress. Strolling into the structure, I felt a feeling of fear I was unable to comprehend and was powerless to battle off. Maybe it was a dread of progress—would I be able to truly deal with being in Secondary SCHOOL? Maybe, it was that old, natural dread of talking. I've been a person with speech issues for as long as I can remember and having a stammer instructed me to fear circumstances that necessary me to acquaint myself with a room or even just to one new individual.

Whatever the explanation was, I spent the entire school day mentally and really tense just as setting myself up for an attack that never came at this point was determinedly drawing closer. I conquered that first day by the skin of teeth. I potentially talked when around kids, I unquestionably knew from focus school and when a kindhearted teacher mentioned that we dodge the room and familiarize ourselves with the class as an icebreaker. Besides those conditions, I barely talked that day, and the dread never wavered. Right, when school completed, I came clearly home and went choice to rest at 4 PM, exhausted as if I had as of late run a significant distance race.

Like all sentiments, that anxiety passed moderately rapidly, and in a couple of days, I was going to class without totally debilitating myself with dread. Regardless of this experience and innumerable different minutes throughout my life despite what might be expected, I never thought of myself as somebody with "anxiety."

At that point, I had my first panic assault at age 20. I was lesser in school, and about a month already, I had been having serious stomach issues, which looking back was, in all likelihood, my anxiety showing in physical torment. I could scarcely eat without my body rebelling against me. Multiplied over in torment after every supper, I started to remain alive as a rule on apples and toast. I shed 30 pounds in a month. The specialists were flummoxed. Nobody recognized what wasn't right with me.

"Definitely, you're biting the dust," my anxiety let me know in its smooth, evil voice.

What's more, one night, the possibility that I was biting the dust overpowered me. I was persuaded whatever was going on within me couldn't be fixed. On the off chance that the specialists couldn't make sense of it, that implied it was hopeless. Thus, started the panic assault.

A Nonsensical Reaction

For me, a panic assault feels like this: You need to flee, the extent that away as could be expected under the circumstances, yet there's no sheltered harbour hanging tight for you in light of the fact that the risk is in your own head. You are persuaded you are going to bite the dust, and there is no hope to stop it. You have lost control of everything. Life is lurching off into a void, and there is no returning. This is the manner in which it closes. You will either bite the dust at the present time or be at this time of degraded panic for eternity. There are no different choices. No end as far as anyone can tell.

On this specific occasion, I particularly recollect walking about the washroom in my nearby lodging. Irregularly, I sat on the floor with my legs pulled up to my chest, shaking and shaking, murmuring incomprehensibly trying to self-mitigate. I lost all feeling of time. I could have been in there for a considerable length of time or hours. It's impossible to say. I simply realize I truly figured somebody would definitely discover me dead in that washroom. That night, my closest companion arrived in a rescue vehicle with me to the emergency clinic where I quieted down, was revealed to I had a panic assault, was inquired as to whether I needed Xanax (which I can't and now understand THAT reaction was presumably a slip-up.

In any case, that second started an acknowledgement in me: I wasn't simply restless. I had anxiety. Furthermore, it had turned crazy.

My attack into the universe of subjective conduct treatment (CBT) has instructed me that my anxiety's specific image is "disastrous reasoning," which basically implies I ruminate on most pessimistic scenario situations and intensify the force of issues to world-completion extents. Did I wreck at work? I will get terminated, and I'm moving to be destitute. At the point when I get up toward the beginning of the day, my standard inclination is generally anxiety or on an especially awful day, veritable fear, and a sinking feeling that whatever the day has coming up for me, I won't have the option to deal with it.

At whatever point I am encountering something new or a change occurs in my life, the primary feeling is consistently dread, which I've understood is the reason I loathed that first day of secondary school to such an extent. I overthink pretty much each and every choice I make, a collaboration I have, step I take. I lie alert around evening time going over things I said and did during the day, suffocating in shame over things I've persuaded myself others made a decision about me for or are frantic at me about in spite of having no evidential confirmation.

I invest hours at energy agonizing over the future, imagining a day when I'm old and wake up to acknowledge I squandered as long as I can remember accomplishing something I detest, never beginning to look all starry eyed at, simply existing and failing to experience all the things I need to. In some cases, for reasons unknown by any stretch of the imagination, my mind will advise me to panic. I could be strolling down the road or sitting in a cinema, and the light goes off in my cerebrum, blazing the words YOU Ought to B.E. Stressing RIGHT NOW over my vision in large, intense, red letters, and my pulse gets, which thusly, makes me believe I'm having a cardiovascular failure, which just adds to the anxiety. Fundamentally, my mind is certifiably not a great spot to be now and again. On the entirety of this, when I am in an anxiety winding (a genuine article I swear I didn't simply imagine!), there is constantly a degree of blame and feebleness that frequently is far and away more terrible than the anxiety itself. For instance, my anxiety spirals regularly resemble this:

The previous quite a long while, there have been stunning steps in taking out the shame around psychological wellness. Realize that somebody battling with anxiety or some other mental sickness can't merely kill their sentiments anything else than somebody with a messed-up arm can will their unresolved issues. Questions like "Why not simply consider something different?" or "Why not simply unwind?" while good-natured, are unfathomably unhelpful and regularly cause an on-edge individual to feel much more dreadful. As though they ought to have the option to wake up, and when they can't, they feel just as they've fizzled.

The Agonizingly Moderate Procedure of Giving Up

Be that as it may, shockingly, it has set aside me an extremely long effort to get out from under the propensity for considering my emotional wellness. All the time, I feel feeble. I feel like a weight to my loved ones since I know here. There I need additional help and care in my darker minutes; minutes, I can't even indeed clarify because of I, despite everything, don't wholly comprehend where my anxiety originates from and what it's about. I feel just as I ought to have the option to control it, since it's an imperceptible disease occurring inside my cerebrum, and on the off chance that I can't control my musings, doesn't that make me frail and feeble? The appropriate response is no. In any case, my brain frequently can't be persuaded.

The treatment makes a difference. Medication and contemplation (the Uncommon occasions I'm ready to ruminate effectively, I mean), as well. Be that as it may, even with every one of these devices, I will most likely consistently have anxiety. As a rule, we can coincide calmly now. I can take a gander at those falsehoods and realize I don't need to tail them down the anxiety winding bunny opening. Once in a while, however, it shows signs of improvement of me. There are days when I have a feeling that I may implode from fear when my brain turns into jail with no chance to get out when I accept the untruths; my anxiety lets me know.

I'm despite everything figuring out how to be benevolent to myself around these times. Instructions to isolate myself from my anxiety and realize that it is a piece of me. However, it doesn't need to characterize me. I'm despite everything figuring out how to acknowledge that, in any event, when it hasn't appeared in some time, it will consistently return and that I will always come out of it on the opposite side when it does. In any case, above all, I'm despite everything discovering that my day by day battle with my psyche doesn't make me frail or feeble or unlovable. It makes me a boss.

Win Big or Bust Reasoning

At the point when you take part in win big or bust reasoning, you assess your life in outrageous terms: It's either great or a calamity. You're either a complete achievement or a total disappointment.

This is contorted reasoning since life is a diverse assortment for us all. Going to one of these two boundaries while assessing your life is fertile ground for self-fault. Even self-loathing since what you're truly doing is requesting flawlessness from yourself, since the main elective you're willing to consider is a disappointment, and nobody is content with that. Win big, or bust reasoning can take two structures.

1. You don't give yourself the breathing space to do anything such that you assess as not precisely "An"— or even an "A+." I used to be like this about my exhibition in the homeroom. Although I adored educating, I verged on stopping since I didn't think I was doing A+ work. This out of line (and uncompassionate) request that you be anything short of impeccable can come up in both your workplace and in things you accomplish for joy, for example, drawing or weaving or playing an instrument.

This kind of win big or bust reasoning can likewise crush any endeavour to support yourself. For instance, in case you're slimming down or attempting to practice ordinarily if you go off the eating regimen once or skip exercising for only one day, you give yourself an "F" and, in appalling, abandon the endeavour inside and out. (Self-fault is practically certain to follow.) You treat yourself like a disappointment in case you're not feeling all around ok, genuinely or intellectually, to play out an undertaking you'd intended to do.

This specific type of win significant or bust reasoning is a progressing challenge for me as an individual who lives with incessant torment and ailment. I, in some cases, need to advise myself that I'm not a disappointment because, on a specific day, I couldn't play out an errand I'd intended to do—in any event, something as necessary as the clothing. Far more atrocious, when you take part in this sort of win or bust reasoning, you can persuade yourself that, since some minor assignment didn't complete one day, the entire family is self-destructing.

What follows are two recommendations for beating this agonizing and ridiculous standard that a significant number of us hold ourselves to. In examining these recommendations, I'll allude to the two kinds talked about above: #1—win or bust reasoning for how you played out an errand and #2—win or bust reasoning in regards to what you're ready to do. To start with, bring out empathy for yourself. Self-sympathy is my go-to rehearse at whatever point I begin deciding for myself brutally. I trust you'll make it you're go-to repeat as well. All it requires is that you do whatever you can to facilitate your psychological torment. In less complicated terms, it implies being pleasant to yourself.

How you treat yourself is one of only a handful, not many things you control throughout everyday life. In my view, there will never be a valid justification not to be benevolent to yourself. Treating yourself with sympathy encourages you to bring an end to the propensity for win or bust reasoning since, when you're caring to yourself, it's simpler to see the manners by which you're not kind to yourself. This empowers you to get mindful of the enthusiastic mischief brought about by over and again outlining for yourself (about whatever the issue is): "It's win big or bust... that is the thing that I expect of myself."

We should come back to the two different ways this psychological twisting appears in our reasoning. 1. You don't give yourself the breathing space to do anything such that you assess as not precisely "An"— or even an "A+." The mild reaction to a not precisely flawless presentation delicately states to yourself something like: "Nobody makes an occupation on everything. It's not reasonable for request from myself what I don't request from others. I did as well as could be expected, and that is everything I can decently ask of myself."

Self-sympathy is additionally called for in model 2. You treat yourself like a disappointment in case you're not feeling all right, truly or intellectually, to play out an assignment you'd intended to do. Nothing positive originates from treating yourself along these lines. The empathetic reaction would be something like: "I'd planned to do the clothing today, yet I'm over agony. That is not my deficiency. I'll improve."

Second, centre around what you did well and on what you accomplished. At the point when you participate in win or bust reasoning, you markdown as irrelevant or shameful all that you did well and all that you accomplished. Consider that for a couple of seconds: limiting the positive along these lines is both uncalled for to you and foolish because it leaves you feeling like a disappointment.

Once more, staying with our two sorts of win or bust reasoning, in regards to #1, when you consider how you played out an assignment, centre around what you're satisfied with: "When class was finished, I worked admirably addressing understudies' inquiries," or "I adhered to my eating routine four out of five days." Concerning, state to yourself something like: "I might not have done the clothing, yet unfortunately, given how much torment I'm in, I made the bed and showered." In the two models, in case you're prone to go directly to self-analysis, you may need to consider every option from the start to think of the positives. In any case, they're there, and they're worth the push to discover. Why exacerbate yourself feel when you can cause yourself to feel better.

Magnification

To outline, with the win big or bust intuition, when you fall underneath 100 per cent in your estimation, that 100 per cent goes to zero. Thus, when I was instructing, if I thought my class execution was in the "B+" run, I gave myself an "F." Or, in case you're attempting to get in shape when you think as far as to win or bust, you'll give yourself an "F" if you go off your eating regimen for one day. Not exclusively is that not a legitimate method to assess your life (100 per cent and 0 are not by any means the only rates accessible to you!). However, you're by and large unjustifiably unforgiving and harsh to yourself. I trust you'll take steps to search for that centre ground by getting mindful of when you're thinking in total win big or bust terms. You'll spare yourself a ton of grief.

Many years of mental research have distinguished useless examples in believing that they are related to an expanded danger of misery, anxiety, and sadness. One of those sorts of reasoning is something I work much of the time with my customers on destroying: win or bust reasoning. Likewise called dark or-white reasoning or dichotomous reasoning, the essential thought is that as opposed to being capable precisely to evaluate a circumstance (particularly a somewhat antagonistic one), an individual sees the thing.

A little misrepresentation from time to time is likely not going to be mentally harming, and a large portion of us have accessible routes in our discourse that overgeneralize for the good of simplicity. Yet, the genuine mischief comes when win or bust reasoning gets interminable and begins to offer shape to how we process our condition: We start to see the world in distorted and regularly negative terms. This can, thus, cause us to feel vulnerable and skeptical about ourselves, our friends and family, and our general surroundings. Need to check whether you are taking part in this sort of reasoning? Start with seeing how you utilize the accompanying words.

Continuously

One of the most widely recognized expressions of win or bust reasoning, "consistently" is regularly utilized in a pessimistic way, to take one or a couple of explicit occurrences and sum up to censure the character of an individual or the idea of our encounters. It is frequently joined with speculation about another person's conduct or character, similar to "No doubt about it," "You generally do that," or "I generally get exploited." Positively, there might be commonly when "consistently" feels exact. In any case, different occasions, it keeps you in a pattern of accepting that things can't beat that, or it keeps you from stretching out some tolerance and comprehension to somebody who has fouled up.

"Never"

The underside of "consistently," "never," can-do rise to harm when it is utilized to dispose of expectation, adaptability, or the opportunity to be vindicated. There aren't that multiple occasions where "never" is valid in relational relations, and it's once in a while accommodating to see things in these terms. Additionally, "never" can regularly be turned internal in negative manners, similar to "I never get a break," "I never comprehend what to state at gatherings," or "I never well in introductions." Besides, it very well may be utilized as a method for staying stuck in a negative vision of things to come, similar to "I'll never add up to anything," or "Things will never show signs of improvement."

"Everything"

"Everything" is frequently unhelpful when it is utilized to make a mountain out of a molehill, to go from something explicit that happened to make worldwide speculation. It very well may be so enticing to state that "everything" is turning out badly during a progression of get-away incidents, for example, and on the off chance that it's ready to be shaken off soon with a giggle, at that point that is not all that broken. In any case, when it feels like "everything" is turning out badly, and that itself turns into a mentality that restricts you from seeing what is going right, it can turn into an unavoidable outcome, as you'll consider things to be turning out badly that indeed weren't so awful — keeping you from trying to investigate them.

"Completely"

A word that has been exceptionally famous from the Valley-Young lady slang days of the 1980s and is regularly utilized in constructive manners ("Absolutely rad, dude!"), it similarly as now and again is by all accounts some portion of win significant or bust speculation a pessimistic way: "This activity thoroughly smells"; "Something's thoroughly amiss with her"; "My home is an all-out pigsty." When you go from part to entire so rapidly and mistakenly, you daze yourself from seeing the potential positives of a circumstance or an individual, putting on sift that keep through the positive qualities to line up with your effectively settled point of view that perceives the awful — which keeps you stuck.

"Destroyed"

Yes, a few things in life get totally demolished: your telephone when it experiences the clothes washer, a place of cards when it's thumped over. Be that as it may, "demolished" is additionally regularly used to catastrophize during times of fault or struggle. Have you at any point blamed your accomplice or youngsters for "destroying" an exceptional occasion, or thought when you had a misfortune on an individual venture you were progressing in the direction of that it was currently all "demolished?" It might be useful in those circumstances to reframe the experience. Is the battle some portion of development that will take care of later? Are there parts of the time that can be rescued positively? Has another way been lit up that will assist you with getting the hang of something, or resolve for the last time contention that was continually covering up under the surface? Provided that this is true, at that point, nothing's demolished.

"Can't."

Much the same as with "demolished," there are undoubtedly times when "can't" bodes well. Yet, there are bunches of different occasions when it is utilized in an overgeneralizing way that lone mixes sentiments of educated weakness and sadness, and serves to sustain an example of self-damage: "This can't be fixed"; "I can't do anything right"; "I can't deal with this." Focus on how you utilize this word in your day by day life. As much as it has become something of a self-improvement banality to oust "can't" from your jargon, is it conceivable that you genuinely are utilizing this word in manners that get you into a trench of contrary reasoning? Is it barging in on a practical evaluation of your capacities?

"Everybody" Or "Nobody"

It appears that in this exceptionally charged world of politics, a "us versus them" attitude has grabbed hold. Outrage has risen, and generalizing of different gatherings is very reasonable — which, when those two consolidate powers, can prompt despise. One of the components of partiality is to make clearing speculations about collections of individuals that are not precise. Be that as it may, individuals in the throes of negative deduction will, in general, do it about considerably bigger gatherings, particularly on the off chance that they utilize the words "everybody" or "nobody" excessively much. Do you sum up, particularly contrarily, to accept that "everybody" doesn't use their blinker any longer, or "nobody" else thinks about something essential to you? Shouldn't something be said about the broad decisions you may make when it feels like you against the world since you have been harmed or deceived? Discounting the remainder of humankind regularly aggravates you think — and deadens you from pushing ahead.

"Any longer."

Similarly, as with different words, there are times when this word can be utilized in positive manners: Choosing to stop negative behaviour patterns and relinquishing laments ring a bell. In any case, different occasions, it's used to moan about things that have changed and speak to an intellectual twisting that can cut you down. Regular in this classification are musings like "Individuals simply aren't as decent any longer," or "I'm bad at X any longer." To expect that something positive can't occur any longer, or that things have changed for the more terrible, denies you the chance to have trust later on.

It is safe to say that you are a win or bust mastermind? Maybe you consider yourself to be a triumph or a disappointment, appealing or appalling, savvy, or inept. Also, you find others to be with you or against you, right or off-base, mindful, or childish.

Considering things to be absolutes, dark or white without any shades of dim in the middle of, can leave you feeling stuck – unmotivated, incapable of beginning new activities, seek after your objectives, or even perceive your advancement.

What Is Win or Bust Reasoning?

Win big, or bust reasoning is a typical sort of psychological contortion. This fair implies your thinking has gotten turned up and depends on wrong data or suspicions. Win significant, or bust reasoning is regularly founded on things we were told as youngsters, which we've acknowledged as realities, fortified, and disguised. These bogus or overgeneralized messages become our convictions about ourselves and the world – and they will, in general, be excessively negative and essential.

Here's A Case of How This May Function

As a kid, Paul battled in school. English class was especially troublesome, and he preferred not to peruse. His folks were consistently on his case about his less than stellar scores. They contrasted him with his sister, who got straight An's and his mom as often as possible, lost her temper, and called him "moronic" and "lethargic." In his 20's, Paul was determined to have dyslexia. In any case, regardless of now realizing that a learning inability, not ineptitude or lethargy, were the reason for his horrible showing in school, Paul, despite everything, calls himself dumb when he commits any sort of error. Pauls' involvement in an undiscovered learning distinction and the negative and mistaken things his folks said to him, persuaded that he's not as keen as every other person. Paul has partitioned individuals into just two classifications – brilliant and dumb. He considers things to be absolutes, as opposed to seeing all the stuff in the middle of these two limits. Furthermore, thus, he's unjustifiably marked himself as moronic.

At the point when you utilize win or bust reasoning, you're deciding for yourself as well as other people unjustifiably. On the off chance that you just observe two outrageous classes, a great many people and encounters will be arranged into the lesser classification – because they're blemished. Win big or bust deduction centres around errors and imperfections and limits qualities, achievements, and exertion. It discloses to us that on the off chance that we can't accomplish something splendidly, it's not worth doing.

6 Different Ways to Change Your Win or Bust Reasoning

As should be obvious, win or bust reasoning makes unreasonable desires for ourselves as well as other people. What's more, this can make us brutal and disparaging of ourselves as well as other people. Win or bust reasoning generally torment fussbudgets and is a sign of anxiety and sadness. All in all, how would we change win significant or bust reasoning? Here are six different ways to begin.

1) Search for The Positives

We have a proclivity to see and recollect negatives in our lives – botches, terrible news, frustrations, times things didn't go as arranged. This cynicism predisposition is the explanation you're probably going to recall the one time you were late to a significant gathering, however not the many occasions you were on schedule. This prompts win considerable or bust speculation, for example, "I'm in every case late" and most likely a string of self-basic articulations chiding yourself for something that isn't correct. It requires exertion, yet you can prepare yourself to see the encouraging points throughout your life – the effort you make, new things you learn, things you like about yourself as well as other people, and straightforward delights and satisfactions that improve your life.

2) Be Interested

We can extend our past intuition divisions, for example, fortunate or unfortunate, set in stone, by being interested and testing our win significant or bust reasoning. These mutilated idea designs will, in general, be very much drilled and typically not even in our mindfulness, so we have to begin by seeing them. At that point, when you notice that your win or bust reasoning, you can pose yourself a few inquiries to challenge it and check whether there are some different ways you can take a gander at things. You may ask yourself:

3) Extend Your Reasoning and Search for the "Shades of The Dark."

Since win or bust reasoning depends on absolutes and unreasonable desires, attempt to abstain from utilizing words, for example, consistently, never, all, every, should, should, and should. Furthermore, think amazing like an achievement, disappointment, high, and terrible and check whether you can concoct increasingly exact descriptors that don't reflect such limits.

4) Take into Account Catch 22s

Another supportive procedure is to acknowledge that two contrary energies can both be valid; you don't need to pick one outrageous or the other. For instance, your better half can be both irritating and cherishing. Your activity can be exhausting and testing. You can be innovative and organized.

5) Search for Fractional Victories

Rather than arranging your undertakings into victories or disappointments, take a stab at utilizing the procedure of fractional triumphs. This portion from The CBT Exercise manual for Compulsiveness shows what to look like for fractional joys and the advantages of doing as such.

"It's enticing not to begin things when we figure we can't do them consummately. This sort of win or bust reasoning makes it difficult to see that frequently there is as yet an advantage in doing some portion of an assignment or venture or that a few things don't should be done to incredibly exclusive expectations. Suppose I chose to go to the exercise centre each morning before work. However, I hesitated too long over my morning espresso, and now I don't have the opportunity to go to the turn class that I like. On the off chance that I let my stickler figuring direct, I'd state, 'It's past the point of no return now. I surmise I can't practice today.' Then again, I could state, 'Well, I missed my turn class, yet I could at present go strolling for twenty minutes before work.' My fussbudget self would be slanted to consider this to be a disappointment since I didn't meet my pledge to go to the turn class, and the walk wasn't as accepting of an exercise. An increasingly humane and tolerating approach to consider this— one that will shield me from falling into disillusionment and tarrying later on—is as an incomplete achievement.

"It's tough to rouse ourselves when we outline things just as 'achievement' or 'disappointment.' Such a significant amount of life is genuinely shading of the dark. At the point when we set unreasonable desires and accept, we are disappointments (or sluggish or idiotic) when we don't perform immaculately, it's simpler not to get things done by any means. Taking a short walk wasn't my optimal exercise, however, even though everything gave me medical advantages. The equivalent is valid for journaling, following a financial limit, pondering, proper dieting, and any positive movement we're attempting to do. We don't need to do things superbly for them to have esteem." (Martin, 2019, page 95-96)

6) Don't Let Botches Characterize You

Win big, or bust reasoning persuades that slip-ups are disappointments and that disappointment is deadly. In all actuality, we as a whole commit errors; nobody consistently says or does the right things. Probably the best individuals on the planet will disclose to you that disappointment is an essential piece of achievement. As it were, you can be a triumph and a disappointment – and everything in the middle. Rather than attempting to stay away from botches, acknowledge them, and gain from them, consider them to be open doors for development. At the point when you notice your win significant or bust reasoning, an attempt at least one of these systems to challenge these unbending, perfectionistic considerations. Doing so will welcome more sympathy – for yourself as well as other people – into your life. It will prompt more outstanding inspiration, confidence, and satisfaction.

Sadly, such reasoning regularly makes us, at that point, feel serious about a circumstance or ourselves. It turns into a terrible cycle. Typical psychological mutilation is Win or bust Reasoning, where we take a gander at things as carefully dark or white. Such understandings are regularly twisted from the real world and can bring about extraordinary negative emotions. In the examination, if our translation wasn't so carefully dark or white, our subsequent emotions can be increasingly moderate and likely simpler to manage and have a less enduring impact. For instance, a colleague says something to you that you decipher in a win big or bust way. The before you know it, you're disturbed and acting in an outrageous way and causing contention with your associate that wasn't even there to begin with.

A primary initial phase in halting intellectual contortions is to perceive when they're going on and recognize them. For instance, to state to yourself something like, "Gracious, I'm thinking about this in a win big or bust way. Such reasoning may not be precise and can bring about superfluous negative sentiments. The truth may be someplace in the centre." At that point, conceivably enjoy a reprieve from pondering the theme until your feelings have facilitated, at that point, return to it. Regularly doing so permits you to see it in a less win big or bust light. Agony is a piece of the human experience. Yet, it's the unhelpful contemplations we have about our torment, and our reaction to these musings, that fuel mental misery. In the realm of brain science, these contemplations are regularly alluded to as subjective mutilations.

Subjective mutilation is an idea that speaks to a distorted perspective on self, others, and conditions. Regularly, personal twists bring about ineffectual examples of conduct and heightened awkward passionate states, for example, discouragement and anxiety. Now and again, a psychological contortion starts things out, prompting an inept physical, social, or emotional response. Different occasions, intellectual mutilations outline our view of an opportunity, intensifying an effectively excruciating encounter or feeling. There are, in any event, ten regular intellectual contortions perceived in the field of Subjective Conduct Treatment (CBT).

CBT is a type of treatment that recognizes and challenges intellectual twists and the fundamental convictions driving them to reshape subsequent sentiments and practices. Contingent upon singular contrasts, a few people are increasingly inclined to take part in particular sorts of psychological mutilations over different kinds, and with shifting force. A great many people experience subjective contortions in some way or another in their everyday lives.

How about we investigate how one brand of intellectual bends, win or bust speculation, associates with our sentiments, practices, situations, and connections. Additionally, known high contrast thinking, win significant or bust reasoning is related in with extraordinary emotional episodes and social clash. Be that as it may, it can show up quietly in our regular daily existences, consequently arranging our encounters into classifications. In case you're feeling stuck in an exhausting story, win significant or bust reasoning could be the offender.

Win or bust reasoning is the "enraptured focal point" of intellectual bends. At the point when we take part in taking all things together or-nothing thinking, we decipher ourselves, others, and conditions in a dualistic, resolute way. We consider something to be all acceptable or all terrible, all glad or all dismal. Win big, or bust reasoning communicates in the language of absolutes. It seems like: Continuously, Never, Ever, Eternity, All, None, Pass, Fall flat, Right, Wrong, Love, Detest.

We could add many more words to this rundown. Along these lines of reasoning is a typical piece of the human experience because the mind cherishes classes. Classifications are proficient and help foresee designs. The cerebrum's definitive activity is to keep you alive, so it utilizes classes to enable you to recognize what's sheltered and perilous to protect you from torment and damage—both physical and mental. At the point when you're in a circumstance that feels undermining or safe, the mind recollects both, and gives that experience a name to reference for future conditions:

- "She never tunes in to me."
- "He's the main individual who gets me."
- "I'm constantly ready to dodge results."
- "All dangers lead to disappointment."

In adolescence, win or bust reasoning is our default mode; it's a fundamental piece of our turn of events, building up our feeling of right, off-base, protected, and dangerous. There's no hazy area with regards to never under any circumstance heading off to the storm cellar to look at a peculiar sound, particularly in case you're in a thriller. We learn not to contact the oven and not to converse with outsiders. As we move into youthfulness, the cerebrum picks up the capacity to think dynamically and move between absolutes. We discover that the oven is just hot when a burner is lit and that in numerous specific situations, being neighbourly with outsiders is an approach to construct our ability for association and compassion.

It's Simpler for Us to Consider the Hazy Area Between Different Sides

Notwithstanding, when we are in circumstances that vibe undermining or dubious—like a significant life change, political change, or contention with a colleague—the defensive alerts go off in the cerebrum. We look to win significant or bust intuition to restore a feeling of security and consistency. We reference past encounters that we've arranged into classes as a guide for our conduct and dynamic. Indeed, even master basic masterminds can slip into programmed reactions when character and dependability are in question. The Results of Win significant or bust Intuition in Various Areas of Your Life

While win or bust reasoning can be useful, it can limit our encounters and breaking point open doors for development. High contrast musings are regularly the guilty party when we are stuck in an example of inadequate conduct. Possibly you end up having a similar battle with an accomplice again or sitting home alone on another Friday night. Likely you can't shake the bothering instability that is settled over your profession like a dim cloud.

Might It Be Able to Be Win or Bust Reasoning?

Here are how high contrast contemplations could be characterizing various areas of your life, and how you can include more "shades of dim" to your story: Your Relationship with Yourself Marks reinforce a feeling of self, yet what names have you been taking care of yourself of late? Possibly you consider yourself to be a complete disappointment or just not a brave individual. Perhaps you battle to think yourself to be esteemed and loveable because you don't match a subjective standard of achievement.

"In case I'm not (great, rich, Chief, truly fit), I'm a disappointment." These classifications overlook the numerous emphasizes of yourself that exist in the middle of boundaries. They could empower examples of conduct that strengthen these convictions about yourself. Shades of Dim: Outrageous marks are once in a while noticeable. At the point when you find yourself believing you're an all-out disappointment, excessively bashful, or exhausting, characterize your terms all the more explicitly.

"I'm bashful," means, "I am peaceful in enormous gatherings and chatty with individuals who realize me well." "I am a disappointment," means, "I did exclude an area about objectives in my introduction, and I've realized what to do any other way for the following instructions.

Your State of Mind

How we name our conditions can propagate how we feel about them. At the point when we're in a terrible spot, we may figure, "I will feel this way perpetually" or "Nobody might see how awful I feel." This can close the entryway on trust, dynamic adaptation, and connecting for social help. On the other side, we might be in a peak period of life and attempting to do everything we can to continue. Rather than getting a charge out existing apart from everything else, we become unhinged, attempting to look after it. "I will possibly feel certain and glad if I continue having accomplishment at work." Living in all great or every terrible set us up for an enthusiastic crazy ride. Shades of Dark: In case you're feeling stuck in an enthusiastic encounter, inquire as to whether the mark you've given your feeling is suitable. Maybe you're not feeling cheerful, yet you likewise aren't tragic.

Keep an eye on a sentiments outline like the one underneath to work on depicting shades of feeling. "I am confronting difficult conditions at this moment. Here and there, I feel disheartened about it, and I have assets to help me." On the off chance that it doesn't feel nullifying, you can take a stab at rehearsing "inverse activity," which includes acting inverse to the feeling you're feeling (for example, In case you're feeling uncertain, change your body stance to a progressively specific position). You most likely won't propel yourself totally to the opposite side. However, it could assist you in moving into the hazy area.

Your Public Activity

Online life and FOMO have come to characterize our social encounters. We have steady roads for contrasting our public activities with those of our companion and A-rundown superstars. It's harder to be content and live at the time. "I don't have the most likes, so I am unlikeable." Shades of Dark: I work a great deal with high schoolers, and we, as of late, endured the homecoming move season. As is valid throughout everyday life and adolescent romantic comedies, not every person gets asked to the move. Not being asked to the move is an impartial point between being asked or being dismissed. Be that as it may, numerous youngsters I work with see this as a negative. Notice when you may be thumping impartial data about your social collaborations into positive or negative classifications, and check it back in the dim where it has a place.

Your Work and Objectives

What amount of additional time do you put into your work, worrying about every detail? Or then again pummeling yourself when something doesn't turn out entirely? "On the off chance that it's not great, it's trash." Dynamic is trying, feeling like you need to pick the absolute best choice. With these contemplations driving you, you may wind up wore out, or surrendering before you arrive at your objectives. Shades of Dark: Win big, or bust reasoning can take care of a fussbudget disposition. In the middle of flawlessness and disappointment, there's "adequate." Psych Bytes supporter Laura Hamilton offers intelligence about relinquishing hairsplitting and making harmony with "sufficient." You can look at that article by tapping on the connection beneath!

Your Connections

Without being aware of the thought processes of others, we rush to decipher slip-ups of others through the perspective of mal-expectation. "She hurt me so that she couldn't care less about me." We meld the conduct of others with their personality. This kind of reasoning is regularly liable for the depleting "hot and cold" dynamic in individual connections, or the development of disdain that can make a few links appear to be unsalvageable. Shades of Dim: It tends to be as hard to acknowledge the conjunction of other's very own qualities and shortcomings as it is our own. When deciphering the conduct of those you associate with, change from However to AND. Be that as it may, "He's typically there for me, Yet he overlooked me today. He should not think about me." This closes out other options. What's more, "He's as a rule there for me, AND he disregarded me today." The two can coincide, and we can acknowledge defects in our connections.

Your Legislative Issues

An important mentality in our political atmosphere is "you're either with me or against me." On the off chance that somebody isn't our ally, it tends to be anything but difficult to outline them as the foe. At the point when we clutch the thought of absolutes, it's challenging to tune in to the opposite side. Shades of Dark: I tuned in to a superb meeting with Frances Kissling from On-Being, tied in with discovering high in the situation of the other. She calls us to pose a few inquiries:

- What esteems exist in the situation of the other?
- What am I pulled in to in the situation of the other?
- What do I question about my position?

It takes boldness to overcome any issues, realizing we should concede vuln eat the point when life doesn't fit flawlessly into classes, as it once in a while does, the mind fights. Considering outside classes requires additional work, however, brings the prize of breaking out of highly contrasting, win or bust. The exploration shows that extending our ability for different reasoning is a lengthy-lasting procedure, and requires effectively testing the programmed understandings of our conditions. Approach names and decisions carefully, asking yourself what truth exists in apparently restricting powers.

Fortune Telling

Fortune telling is the act of anticipating data about an individual's life. The extent of fortune-telling is on a fundamental level, indistinguishable with the action of divination. vI MET KIM Looked when he gave an introduction at Ohlone School in October 2009, only half a month before his passing. During the discussion, look dumbfounded my understudies by displaying his surprising ability for schedule counts. Just from realizing my understudies' introduction to the world dates, Look had the option to decide the day of the week they were conceived and could review the headline news that day. Known as a uber academic or a "Komputer," Look had one of the most exceptional recollections individuals have ever observed. Doctors who inspected Look found that he had harm to the cerebellum. This cerebrum locale directs consideration and language, just as passionate.

Responses, for example, joy and fear. Perhaps most strikingly, doctors found that Look had no corpus callosum. This basket case interfaces the mind's both ways halves of the globe. They conjectured that the nonappearance of this basic structure permitted Look's neurons to make new and abnormal associations between his privilege and left halves of the world. These significant associations in all probability clarify his strange memory limit. As indicated by Look's dad, Look could remember each word in the books they read before he was two years of age. Look advanced to perusing two pages all the while. Albeit how he did so stay a puzzle, some have estimated he examined the left page of a book with his left eye and the correct page with his proper eye.

The look could absorb the material in any subject and turn into a specialist ever, sports incidental data, topography and music. He remembered postal districts, zone codes and telephone directories. He could tell if an artist was "off" by a couple of notes in an ensemble setting—and would even call them on it. Look's one of a kind capacity motivated the character Raymond Babbitt, played by Dustin Hoffman, in the 1988 film Downpour Man. To precisely depict Look, Hoffman met him and different academics; be that as it may, in contrast, to Look, Babbitt was described as having mental imbalance.

On the off chance that you are somewhat of a worrier, however, a few days simply appear to be especially overpowering, your breathing gets shallow. You can't centre, at that point what you are in all likelihood having is an anxiety assault. Be that as it may, on the off chance that you're feeling fine and, at that point, for no obvious explanation, your heart begins to race, you can't regain some composure. You have to plunk down because you are feeling sick, at that point you probably have a panic assault. Even though they share comparable indications, anxiety attacks and panic attacks are two distinct encounters, clarifies Amanda M. Splash, PhD, chief of NYU Langone's Steven A. Cohen Military Family Place and clinical aide educator in the Division of Psychiatry. "The contrast between the two is about the suddenness of the sentiments—for the most part (however not generally) individuals who get panic attacks will feel all right before it occurs," she says.

Subjective conduct treatment (CBT) is the best treatment for anxiety issue, including panic issue and summed up the anxiety issue, which frequently leads to panic attacks and what individuals allude to as anxiety attacks. The drug, the executives, is additionally a choice. At the time, breathing activities can be compelling to de-raise anxiety manifestations. "It's useful to have you breathe out to be longer than your breath in to reestablish the equalization of CO_2 and oxygen in your body," Dr Splash says.

- Run of the mill side effects of panic attacks
- Panic attacks can generally incorporate at least four of the accompanying:
- Beating heart
- Perspiring

- Shaking
- The brevity of breath which can include:
- Sentiment of stifling
- Chest torment
- Sickness/belly cramps
- Feeling mixed up or precarious
- An out of body or stunning inclination
- Shudders or hot flushes
- A tingling sensation

Panics can be all out, or milder "close" panics and they ordinarily work to a crescendo quickly. Regularly the individual naturally makes a cataclysmic understanding of what's going on. Panic Issue might be analyzed when there are repetitive panics that disturb an individual's life. When somebody has one, they justifiably dread another will happen which can regularly create new scenes.

A Case of An Ordinary Agoraphobic Panic:

Jump on the train – careful about getting caught, adhered – begin to feel tense, sweat-soaked – attempt to quiet self-down – remain close to exit – clutch something too consistent self – strengthens the possibility that something awful is in transit – train stops between stations – I am caught – attempt to get breath – quick breathing – causes bleary-eyed – the dread of swooning – to feel stunning – extreme fear – dread I am kicking the bucket – leave at next station.

Do Panic Assault Side Effects Fluctuate?

The physical side effects will, in general, be a lot of the equivalent. Yet, the focal point of dread will, in general, change for various individuals. Some dread is falling, others a cardiovascular failure or others a sentiment of losing control Trigger circumstances that incite the panics can change too. The dread of being a long way from home - agoraphobia evening panics kept spaces stress incited panic or then again panic activated by injury recollections How would you realize it is a panic assault and doesn't have a real reason? By taking a gander at the indications and the way that the principle sensation is dread.

A couple of clinical issues can impersonate panic. However, the signs are typically genuinely clear of the clinical problem. Basic models are:

- Overactive thyroid or adrenal organ
- Specific sorts of seizures
- Heart palpitations
- Lung issues like asthma

A great many people speculate a clinical reason with their first panic and go to An/E or their GP Some are misdiagnosed having a clinical or heart issue; however, there is more consciousness of panic now than there used to be. Could panic attacks be a side effect of another emotional well-being issue? Indeed, definitely. Not precisely half have separated alleged panic issue. Panics regularly go with gloom, and if mind-set and vitality are low, this ought to be considered as a potential hidden reason. At the point when we are down, we will, in general, be increasingly on edge and progressively defenceless against panic sentiments.

- Half create agoraphobia – a dread of being endlessly from security typically home
- Panic may likewise be an indication of another anxiety issue, for example,
- Social anxiety
- Fanatical habitual issue
- Fear or even
- Post-horrendous pressure issue

In 33% of individuals, the panic is blended in with liquor or medication abuse. How regular are panic attacks? Panic attacks are regular, 7-9% of the populace experience the ill effects of them and twice this sum if milder panics are incorporated. Who is bound to experience the ill effects of panic attacks? Panic attacks are increasingly regular in ladies with a proportion of 3:2. Most panic issues start late teenagers mid-20s, yet they can happen at any age. Regularly connected with upsetting occasions, life changes or injuries either past or present, for example, Loss of work or being bereaved or isolated

Early Life Difficulty or Misuse

What is the ideal approach to manage a panic assault? Breathing and unwinding preparing is not, at this point, though about the best methodology. They will, in general, quietly keep up the possibility that panic is risky or dangerous.

We presently suggest for a run of the mill panic: To "go with it". This is like the meditational thought of "disengaged acknowledgement". Test out whether the panic will genuinely hurt you by braving it. Remain in the circumstance on the off chance that you can until fear dies down. Discover that albeit upsetting panic isn't perilous and won't cause enduring mischief

In any case, every individual is extraordinary. On the off chance that panic is connected with another issue, as past injury or deserting sentiments or wretchedness, then it may not be ideal to endure it. A progressively caring restorative methodology might be required at first. This features the significance of a cautious evaluation. When do you have to begin searching for master help? If panics are making massive disturbance your life, they ought to be tended to right on time, the prior the better. A short-engaged treatment utilizing Subjective Conduct Treatment means to break the support cycle and is viable for familiar panic. It, for the most part, takes 4 to 10 meetings.

In any case, as referenced prior, note that panic can show a progressively mind-boggling fundamental issue, so a careful psychological wellness appraisal is expected to begin with. Where would I be able to get a psychological wellness appraisal? Master evaluations should be possible by psychological wellness groups or CBT specialists and can be set up through GPs. Expanding quantities of GPs have great skill in anxiety; however, not all GPs know about the most recent improvements here, so it's useful to do your exploration on what demonstrated treatments are accessible.

What Kinds of Medications Are Available?

Here and there serotonin-boosting antidepressants are utilized mainly if despondency is available yet acceptable psychotherapy is the favoured treatment for most. Valium like tranquillizers is best kept away from. A few people require longer-term treatments to address underlying issues with certainty, connections or past injuries. This drawn-out treatment will, in general, be taken on by specialists with the other preparing to the standard CBT treatment referenced previously. It is imperative to note additionally that a few people have addictions to liquor or narcotic medications and panics are a side effect of drugs or liquor withdrawal. These people need their habit tended to first.

This program, given Intellectual Social Treatment and Sympathy Care Based methodologies, centres around tending to the physical, mental and conduct parts of the anxiety issue utilizing bunch psychotherapy. The Anxiety Issue Program was extraordinarily established to accommodate the necessities of individuals with an Essential Anxiety Issue. This is a central element of the Anxiety Issue Administration and is an exceptional demonstrative treatment program for this customer gathering. The program caters for the requirements of a full scope of disarranges - Panic Issue, Agoraphobia and Explicit Phobic Issue, Social Anxiety Issue, Over the top Urgent Issue, (OCD) Summed up Anxiety Issue. The points of the program incorporate expanding information and comprehension through psycho-instruction, gathering and individualized psychotherapy.

Moreover, it gives people the chance to learn healing abilities and methodologies to help conquer their challenges. It centres around tending to the physical, mental and social parts of the anxiety issue utilizing bunch psychotherapy. The helpful structure of the program depends on Subjective Conduct Treatment and Sympathetic Care Based Methodologies. The Anxiety Issue Administration is a thorough, multi-disciplinary, evaluation, treatment and aftercare administration for sufferers from essential Anxiety Issue. It means to convey the best accessible medicines for anxiety in a convenient and adaptable manner just as giving follow up care and backing for those that need it.

Characterizing a Panic Assault

Panic attacks can flag the nearness of a Summed-up Anxiety Issue or, in all likelihood, can happen to miss of a related passionate issue. They show as the quick beginning and extraordinary occasions in which an individual encounters extreme anxiety, expanded pulse, and even brevity of breath and trembling. At the point when Panic Attacks Occur A panic assault regularly goes on for around 10 minutes. To the patient, these 10 minutes can appear to go for any longer. In the approach to an attack, patients may encounter sentiments of stress. In the result, the individual can feel spent in any event 24 hours. Patients may likewise confront anxiety and fear that the assault may reoccur.

Once in a while, a panic assault is a once in a blue moon occasion. For other people, panic attacks can come back over and over. In these circumstances, patients may be evaluated for a panic issue. Physical Responses with no Outside Boosts The one of a kind figure included panic attacks is that they happen with no outside reason or upgrades. While somebody in an auto collision, for instance, may feel anxiety or stun in the result, somebody with a panic assault has no apparent, physical reason for their experience.

This reality can cause those with panic attacks to feel senseless or even as though they are losing their brains. It is significant for them to understand that it is a diagnosable and treatable condition.

Panic Assault Insights

- Panic attacks influence 1 of every 75 individuals sooner or later.
- 1 million individuals in the US experience panic attacks each month
- 1 of every three individuals with panic issue additionally have agoraphobia
- 40 per cent of individuals with panic issue likewise experience discouragement
- The Indications of a Panic Assault
- Indications of a panic assault include:
- Tipsiness
- Chest torment
- I am feeling that one is losing control.
- Sentiments of shortcoming
- Expanded pulse
- A feeling of approaching fate
- Trouble relaxing
- Shivering in the limbs

- Chills or potentially perspiring

Now and then, panic attacks can feel like respiratory failures. If you are uncertain on the off chance that you are encountering a coronary episode, consider 911 and tell the administrator the manifestations.

Halting Panic Attacks

The individuals who experience the ill effects of panic attacks should search out assistance from emotional wellness proficient. At the point when patients are not in meetings, in any case, they can at present experience panic attacks. Coming up next are manners by which one can improve or stop a panic assault.

Concentrating on The Breath

Close your eyes and attempt to concentrate on your breath. Follow the air with your inner being as it goes in and out. The reason for this activity is to centre and accordingly quiet the psyche during times of panic.

Distinguish the Assault

Distinguish the panic assault as a panic assault as it occurs. This encourages you to adapt to and acknowledge the truth of the occasion and serves to kill the intensity of the panic assault.

Ground Yourself with Your Environment

One strategy for easing back dashing considerations includes establishing oneself in your environment. Concentrate on you detects and distinguish three things around you, be they aromas, sensations or sounds.

Muscle Unwinding

Start at the toes and hold and loosen up every little muscle bunch along the body.

Recounting a Mantra

Online life and FOMO have come to characterize our social encounters. We have steady roads for contrasting our public activities with those of our companion and A-rundown superstars. It's harder to be content and live at the time. "I don't have the most likes, so I am unlikeable." Shades of Dark: I work a great deal with high schoolers, and we, as of late, endured the homecoming move season. As is valid throughout everyday life and adolescent romantic comedies, not every person gets asked to the move. Not being asked to the move is an impartial point between being asked or being dismissed. Be that as it may, numerous youngsters I work with see this as a negative. Notice when you may be thumping impartial data about your social collaborations into positive or negative classifications, and check it back in the dim where it has a place.

Your Work and Objectives

What amount of additional time do you put into your work, worrying about every detail? Or then again pummeling yourself when something doesn't turn out entirely? "On the off chance that it's not great, it's trash." Dynamic is trying, feeling like you need to pick the absolute best choice. With these contemplations driving you, you may wind up wore out, or surrendering before you arrive at your objectives. Shades of Dark: Win big, or bust reasoning can take care of a fussbudget disposition. In the middle of flawlessness and disappointment, there's "adequate." Psych Bytes supporter Laura Hamilton offers intelligence about relinquishing hairsplitting and making harmony with "sufficient." You can look at that article by tapping on the connection beneath!

Your Connections

Without being aware of the thought processes of others, we rush to decipher slip-ups of others through the perspective of mal-expectation. "She hurt me so that she couldn't care less about me." We meld the conduct of others with their personality. This kind of reasoning is regularly liable for the depleting "hot and cold" dynamic in individual connections, or the development of disdain that can make a few links appear to be unsalvageable. Shades of Dim: It tends to be as hard to acknowledge the conjunction of other's very own qualities and shortcomings as it is our own. When deciphering the conduct of those you associate with, change from However to AND. Be that as it may, "He's typically there for me, Yet he overlooked me today. He should not think about me." This closes out other options.

What's more, "He's as a rule there for me, AND he disregarded me today." The two can coincide, and we can acknowledge defects in our connections.

Your Legislative Issues

An important mentality in our political atmosphere is "you're either with me or against me." On the off chance that somebody isn't our ally, it tends to be anything but difficult to outline them as the foe. At the point when we clutch the thought of absolutes, it's challenging to tune in to the opposite side. Shades of Dark: I tuned in to a superb meeting with Frances Kissling from On-Being, tied in with discovering high in the situation of the other. She calls us to pose a few inquiries: At the point when life doesn't fit flawlessly into classes, as it once in a while does, the mind fights. Considering outside classes requires additional work, however, brings the prize of breaking out of highly contrasting, win or bust.

The exploration shows that extending our ability for different reasoning is a lengthy-lasting procedure, and requires effectively testing the programmed understandings of our conditions. Approach names and decisions carefully, asking yourself what truth exists in apparently restricting powers. Fortune Telling

It a month of before his passing. During their discussion, Look dumbfounded my understudies by displaying his surprising ability of schedule counts. Just from realizing my understudies' introduction to the world dates, Look had the option to decide the day of the week they were conceived and could review the headline news that day.

Known as a uber academic or a "Komputer," Look had one of the most exceptional recollections individuals have ever observed. Doctors who inspected Look found that he had harm to the cerebellum. This cerebrum locale directs consideration and language, just as passionate.

Responses, for example, joy and fear. Perhaps most strikingly, doctors found that Look had no corpus callosum. This basket case interfaces the mind's both ways halves of the globe. They conjectured that the nonappearance of this basic structure permitted Look's neurons to make new and abnormal associations between his privilege and left halves of the world. These significant associations, in all probability, clarify his strange memory limit.

As indicated by Look's dad, Look could remember each word in the books they read before he was two years of age. Look advanced to perusing two pages all the while. Albeit how he did so stay a puzzle, some have estimated he examined the left page of a book with his left eye and the correct page with his proper eye.

The look could absorb the material in any subject and turn into a specialist ever, sports incidental data, topography, and music. He remembered postal districts, zone codes, and telephone directories. He could tell if an artist was "off" by a couple of notes in an ensemble setting—and would even call them on it.

Look's one of a kind capacity motivated the character Raymond Babbitt, played by Dustin Hoffman, in the 1988 film Downpour Man. To precisely depict Look, Hoffman met him and different academics; be that as it may, in contrast, to Look, Babbitt was described as having mental imbalance.

On the off chance that you are somewhat of a worrier, however, a few days simply appear to be especially overpowering, your breathing gets shallow. You can't centre, at that point, what you are in all likelihood having is an anxiety assault. Be that as it may, on the off chance that you're feeling fine and, at that point, for no obvious explanation, your heart begins to race, you can't regain some composure. You have to plunk down because you are feeling sick, at that point you probably have a panic assault.

Even though they share comparable indications, anxiety attacks and panic attacks are two distinct encounters, clarifies Amanda M. Splash, Ph.D., chief of NYU Langone's Steven A. Cohen Military Family Place and clinical aide educator in the Division of Psychiatry. "The contrast between the two is about the suddenness of the sentiments—for the most part (however not generally) individuals who get panic attacks will feel all right before it occurs," she says.

Subjective conduct treatment (CBT) is the best treatment for anxiety issues, including panic issues, and summed up the anxiety issue, which frequently leads to panic attacks and what individuals allude to as anxiety attacks. The drug, the executives, is additionally a choice. At the time, breathing activities can be compelling to de-raise anxiety manifestations. "It's useful to have you breathe out to be longer than your breath in to reestablish the equalization of CO_2 and oxygen in your body," Dr Splash says. Panics can be all out, or milder "close" fears, and they ordinarily work to a crescendo quickly. Regularly the individual naturally makes a cataclysmic understanding of what's going on.

What Is the Panic Issue Now?

Panic Issues might be analyzed when there are repetitive panics that disturb an individual's life. When somebody has one, they justifiably dread another will happen, which can regularly create new scenes.

What May A Panic Assault Feel Like?

A Case of An Ordinary Agoraphobic Panic

Jump on the train – careful about getting caught, adhered – begin to feel tense, sweat-soaked – attempt to quiet self-down – remain close to exit – clutch something too consistent self – strengthens the possibility that something awful is in transit – train stops between stations – I am caught – attempt to get breath – quick breathing – causes bleary-eyed – the dread of swooning – to feel stunning – extreme fear – dread I am kicking the bucket – leave at next station.

Do Panic Assault Side Effects Fluctuate?

The physical side effects will, in general, be a lot of the equivalent. Yet, the focal point of dread will, in general, change for various individuals. Some dread falling, others a cardiovascular failure or others a sentiment of losing control

How Would You Realize It Is A Panic Assault and Doesn't Have A Real Reason?

By taking a gander at the indications and the way that the principle sensation is dread. A couple of clinical issues can impersonate panic. However, the signs are typically genuinely clear of the clinical problem. A great many people speculate a clinical reason with their first panic and go to AN/E or their GP Some are misdiagnosed having a clinical or heart issue; however, there is more consciousness of panic now than there used to be. Could panic attacks be a side effect of another emotional well-being issue? Indeed, definitely. Not precisely half have separated the alleged panic issue.

Panics regularly go with gloom, and if mind-set and vitality are low, this ought to be considered as a potential hidden reason. At the point when we are down, we will, in general, be increasingly on edge and progressively defenceless against panic sentiments, Panic attacks are regular, 7-9% of the populace experience the ill effects of them, and twice this sum if milder panics are incorporated. Who is bound to experience the ill effects of panic attacks? Panic attacks are increasingly regular in ladies with a proportion of 3:2. Most panic issues start late teenager's mid-20s, yet they can happen at any age. Regularly connected with upsetting occasions, life changes or injuries either past or present.

Emotional Reasoning

What is the ideal approach to manage a panic assault? Breathing and unwinding preparing is not, at this point, though about the best methodology. They will, in general, quietly keep up the possibility that panic is risky or dangerous.

We Presently Suggest for A Run of The Mill Panic

To "go with it." This is like the meditational thought of "disengaged acknowledgement." Test out whether the panic will genuinely hurt you by braving it. Remain in the circumstance on the off chance that you can until fear dies down. Discover that albeit upsetting panic isn't perilous and won't cause enduring mischief In any case, every individual is extraordinary. On the off chance that panic is connected with another issue, as past injury or deserting sentiments or wretchedness, then it may not be ideal to endure it. A progressively caring restorative methodology might be required at first. This features the significance of a cautious evaluation.

When Do You Have to Begin Searching for Master Help?

If panics are making massive disturbance your life, they ought to be tended to right on time, the prior the better. A short-engaged treatment utilizing Subjective Conduct Treatment means to break the support cycle and is viable for familiar panic. It, for the most part, takes 4 to 10 meetings.

In any case, as referenced prior, note that panic can show a progressively mind-boggling fundamental issue, so a careful psychological wellness appraisal is expected to begin with. Where would I be able to get a psychological wellness appraisal? Master evaluations should be possible by psychological wellness groups or CBT specialists and can be set up through GPs. Expanding quantities of GPs have great skill in anxiety; however, not all GPs know about the most recent improvements here, so it's useful to do your exploration of what demonstrated treatments are accessible.

What kinds of medications are available? Here and there, serotonin-boosting antidepressants are utilized mainly if despondency is available. Yet, acceptable psychotherapy is the favoured treatment for most. Valium, like tranquillizers, is best kept away from.

A few people require longer-term treatments to address underlying issues with certainty, connections, or past injuries. This drawn-out treatment will, in general, be taken on by specialists with the other preparing to the standard CBT treatment referenced previously. It is imperative to note additionally that a few people have addictions to liquor or narcotic medications, and panics are a side effect of drugs or liquor withdrawal. These people need their habit tended to first. This program, given Intellectual Social Treatment and Sympathy Care Based methodologies, centres around tending to the physical, mental, and conduct parts of the anxiety issue utilizing bunch psychotherapy.

The Anxiety Issue Program was extraordinarily established to accommodate the necessities of individuals with an Essential Anxiety Issue. This is a central element of the Anxiety Issue Administration and is an exceptional demonstrative treatment program for this customer gathering. The program caters to the requirements of a full scope of disarranges - Panic Issue, Agoraphobia and Explicit Phobic Issue, Social Anxiety Issue, Over the top Urgent Issue, (OCD) Summed up Anxiety Issue. The points of the program incorporate expanding information and comprehension through psycho-instruction, gathering, and individualized psychotherapy. Moreover, it gives people the chance to learn healing abilities and methodologies to help conquer their challenges. It centres around tending to the physical, mental, and social parts of the anxiety issue utilizing bunch psychotherapy. The helpful structure of the program depends on Subjective Conduct Treatment and Sympathetic Care Based Methodologies.

The Anxiety Issue Administration is a thorough, multi-disciplinary evaluation, treatment, and aftercare administration for sufferers from an essential Anxiety Issue. It means to convey the best accessible medicines for anxiety in a convenient and adaptable manner just as giving follow up care and backing for those that need it. This program is accessible for inpatients and day patients. Characterizing a Panic Assault Panic attacks can flag the nearness of a Summed-up Anxiety Issue or, in all likelihood, can happen to miss of a related passionate issue. They show as the quick beginning and extraordinary occasions in which an individual encounters extreme anxiety, expanded pulse, and even brevity of breath and trembling.

At the point when Panic Attacks Occur A panic assault regularly goes on for around 10 minutes. To the patient, these 10 minutes can appear to go for any longer. In the approach to an attack, patients may encounter sentiments of stress. As a result, the individual can feel spent in any event 24 hours. Patients may likewise confront anxiety and fear that the assault may reoccur.

Once in a while, a panic assault is a once in a blue moon occasion. For other people, panic attacks can come back over and over. In these circumstances, patients may be evaluated for a panic issue. Physical Responses with no Outside Boosts

The one of a kind figures included panic attacks is that they happen with no outside reason or upgrades. While somebody in an auto collision, for instance, may feel anxiety or stun. As a result, somebody with a panic assault has no apparent physical reason for their experience. This reality can cause those with panic attacks to feel senseless or even as though they are losing their brains. It is significant for them to understand that it is a diagnosable and treatable condition.

Now and then, panic attacks can feel like respiratory failures. If you are uncertain on the off chance that you are encountering a coronary episode, consider 911 and tell the administrator the manifestations.

Halting Panic Attacks

The individuals who experience the ill effects of panic attacks should search out assistance from emotional wellness proficient. At the point when patients are not in meetings, in any case, they can at present experience panic attacks. Coming up next are manners by which one can improve or stop a panic assault.

Concentrating on The Breath

Close your eyes and attempt to concentrate on your breath. Follow the air with your inner being as it goes in and out. The reason for this activity is to centre and accordingly quiet the psyche during times of panic.

Distinguish the Assault

Distinguish the panic assault as a panic assault as it occurs. This encourages you to adapt to and acknowledge the truth of the occasion and serves to kill the intensity of the panic assault.

Ground Yourself with Your Environment

One strategy for easing back dashing considerations includes establishing oneself in your environment. Concentrate on you detects and distinguish three things around you, be they aromas, sensations or sounds.

Muscle Unwinding

Start at the toes and hold and loosen up every little muscle bunch along the body.

Recounting a Mantra

The point of treatment is to help ease anxiety manifestations and diminish the recurrence of panic attacks. The most widely recognized methodology is talking therapy and drugs. Contingent upon your conditions, you may profit by possibly only one or a mix of the two. In the primary example, you'll likely be prescribed to attempt intellectual conduct treatment (CBT). Your primary care physician might allude you, or you can allude yourself straightforwardly. You may likewise need to investigate private specialists if this is available to you. CBT can assist you with seeing how you respond and think when you have a panic assault and how you can change these. Your specialist can train your breathing systems and other social changes that can help with anxiety. Your primary care physician may likewise suggest a stimulant drug. It might require some investment to locate the correct kind of prescription and portion that suits you, so guarantee you keep your primary care physician refreshed on how you're feeling. On the off chance that CBT and prescription aren't helping, you might have alluded to an authority who can investigate other treatment draws near.

Discovering Support

Close by your treatment, and you may likewise profit by conversing with other people who have anxiety. Care groups and the noble cause can be unbelievably steady as individuals can share encounters and what works/doesn't work for them.

Overseeing Anxiety

Just as following your treatment plan, there are a few ways of life transforms, and you can attempt to ease anxiety and forestall further attacks. Organizing self-care is significant. Attempt to guarantee you're getting enough rest and eating an even eating regimen (what we eat can influence the state of mind and anxiety levels). Maintain a strategic distance from a lot of sugar caffeine and nicotine as these would all be able to fuel anxiety side effects. Discover approaches to decrease pressure and empower more unwinding in your life. This could be through physical exercise, breathing activities, or in any event, investigating complementary treatments like a back rub and fragrant healing. Building up a care practice can help as well, regardless of whether this is through reflection or exercises like yoga. In case you're battling to bring down your feelings of anxiety, care-based pressure decrease (MBSR) might merit investigating.

Step by Step Instructions to Stop A Panic Assault

On the off chance that you can feel a panic assault going ahead, attempt the accompanying: Concentrate on your breathing, expect to inhale gradually, breathing out somewhat longer than you breathe in. Do whatever it takes not to battle the assault and, if conceivable, stay where you are. Reveal to yourself that this inclination will pass and help yourself to remember past attacks that you've survived. Stamp your feet on the ground. This can assist you with returning to your body and control your relaxing. Concentrate on your faculties. Take a stab at eating a mint, smelling an essential oil or contact something delicate and consider how it feels/tastes/smell.

Take in solace and straightforwardness and breath out pressure and dread. Rehash multiple times. Dr. David Kraft imparts his tips for managing to a panic assault At the point when the panic assault passes, relax, and ask yourself what your body and brain needs. You might need to sit someplace calm or drink some water. On the off chance that you can, mention to somebody what's occurred and share with them ways they can support you on the off chance that you have a panic assault later on. What would it be a good idea for me to be searching for an advocate or psychotherapist?

There are, at present, no laws set up specifying what preparing and capabilities an instructor must have to treat the panic issue.

In any case, the National Foundation for Wellbeing and Care Greatness (Pleasant) has built up many rules that give guidance about the suggested medications. In the first occurrence, those experiencing panic issues ought to be offered access to a care group and self-improvement data suggestions by their PCP. On the off chance that this doesn't help, or the panic issue is increasingly extreme, mental medications, for example, psychological, humane treatment, as well as applied unwinding, are suggested. Further treatment may require a prescription.

Peruse the Full Pleasant Rules
.

There are a few accredited courses, capabilities, and workshops accessible that can improve an advocate's information on a specific territory, so for significant serenity, you may wish to verify whether they have had further preparation in treating the panic issue.

Anxiety is portrayed as a state of stress, defenselessness, and fear coming about due to the desire for reasonable or imagined trading off event or condition. It is in like manner a tendency of stress, anxiety, or fear about an event or situation. It is a normal reaction to push. It makes you stay alert for a troublesome When all is said in done, it encourages you to adapt. In any case, anxiety can be handicapped if it meddles with everyday life, for example, making you fear nonthreatening everyday exercises like riding the transport or conversing with a colleague. Anxiety can likewise be an unexpected assault of dread when there is no danger. Anxiety issue happens when unreasonable concern meddles with your regular exercises, for example, going to work or school or investing energy with companions or family. Anxiety issue is not kidding psychological maladjustments. They are the most widely recognized mental issue in the United States. Anxiety issue is more than twice as regular in ladies as in men.

The significant sorts of anxiety issues are: Summed up the anxiety issues (GAD). People with GAD stress exorbitantly over common, everyday items, for example, wellbeing, cash, work, and family. With GAD, the psyche regularly hops to the direst outcome imaginable, in any event, when there is next to zero motivation to stress. Ladies with GAD might be on edge about simply traversing the day. They may have muscle pressure and different pressure-related physical side effects, for example, inconvenience resting or irritated stomach.

Now and again, stressing shields people with GAD from doing ordinary assignments. Ladies with GAD have more danger of sorrow and another anxiety issue than men with GAD. They likewise are bound to have a family ancestry of depression.3 Frenzy issue. Frenzy issue is twice as essential in ladies as in men.4 People with alarm issues have abrupt assaults of dread when there is no real threat. Fits of anxiety may cause a feeling of falsity, a terror of approaching fate, or a fear of losing control. One's very own dread unexplained physical side effects is likewise an indication of a frenzy issue. People having alarm assaults here and there accept they are having coronary failures, losing their brains, or passing on—social fear. Social fear, additionally called social anxiety issues, is analyzed when people become on the edge and unsure in ordinary social circumstances. People with social phobia have a solid dread of being watched and made a decision by others. They may get humiliated effectively and regularly have a fit of anxiety indications—understandable fear. A particular concern is an extraordinary dread of something that presents practically no real peril. Specific phobias could be fears of shut-in spaces, statures, water, articles, creatures, or particular circumstances. People with understandable concerns regularly find that confronting, or in any event, pondering confronting, the dreaded article or situation expedites a fit of anxiety or extreme anxiety.

Some different conditions that are not viewed as anxiety issues, however, are comparative include: Over the top habitual issue (OCD). People with OCD have undesirable considerations (fixations) or practices (impulses) that cause anxiety. They may check the broiler or iron over and over or play out a similar daily schedule again and again to control the anxiety these musings cause. Frequently, the customs wind up controlling the individual—post-awful pressure issue (PTSD). PTSD begins after a startling occasion that included physical mischief or the danger of physical damage. The individual who gets PTSD may have been the person who was hurt, or the accident may have happened to a friend or family member or even an outsider. Anxiety issues influence around 40 million American grown-ups each year.

Anxiety issues likewise influence kids and teenagers. About 8% of teenagers ages 13 to 18 have an anxiety issue, with side effects beginning around age 6.5 Ladies are more than twice as likely as men to get an anxiety issue in their lifetime.2 Also, a few sorts of anxiety issue influence a few ladies more than others Women with anxiety issue experience a mix of on edge contemplations or convictions, physical manifestations, and changes in conduct, including evading ordinary exercises they used to do. Every anxiety issue has various expressions. They all include a dread and fear about things that may happen now or later on. Your primary care physician or attendant will ask you inquiries about your side effects and your therapeutic history. Your primary care physician may likewise do a physical test or different tests to preclude other medical issues that could be causing your side effects. Anxiety issue is analyzed when dread and fear of non-threatening circumstances, occasions, places, or articles become over the top and are wild. Anxiety issue is likewise examined if the anxiety has gone on for in any event a half year, and it meddles with social, work, family, or different parts of everyday life.

Treatment for anxiety issues relies upon the sort of anxiety issue you have and your history of medical problems, savagery, or misuse. Your primary care physician may allude you for a kind of directing for anxiety issues called subjective social treatment (CBT). You can converse with prepared emotional wellness proficient about what caused your anxiety issue and how to manage the symptoms. For instance, you can speak with a therapist, clinician, social specialist, or instructor. CBT can assist you in changing the intuition designs around your feelings of dread. It might help you in changing how you respond to circumstances that may make anxiety. You may likewise learn approaches to decrease feelings of anxiety and improve explicit practices brought about by incessant anxiety. These systems may incorporate unwinding treatment and critical thinking. Some of the time, you may need to work with your primary care physician to attempt a few distinct medicines or mixes of medications before you discover one that works for you. If you are experiencing difficulty with symptoms from medications, converse with your PCP or attendant. Try not to quit taking your drug without talking with a specialist or attendant. Your primary care physician may alter how much medication you make, and when you take it. At times side effects of an anxiety issue return after you have completed treatment. This may occur during or after a distressing occasion. It might likewise happen with no notice. Numerous people with anxiety issues improve treatment. Yet, if your side effects return, your primary care physician will work with you to change or modify your drug or treatment plan. You can likewise converse with your primary care physician about approaches to distinguish and keep anxiety from returning.

This may incorporate recording your feelings or meeting with your guide if you think your anxiety is wild. On the off chance that your treatment is guiding, it won't influence your pregnancy. On the off chance that you are on medication to treat your anxiety issue, converse with your primary care physician. A few medications used to treat anxiety can influence your unborn infant. It depends. A few prescriptions used to treat anxiety can go through breastmilk. Certain antidepressants, for example, a few SSRIs, are sheltered to take during breastfeeding. Try not to quit taking your prescription too rapidly. Converse with your primary care physician to discover what drug is best for you and your child. Get familiar with drugs and breastfeeding in our Breastfeeding area. You can likewise enter your medication into the LactMed® database to see whether your prescription goes through your breastmilk and any conceivable reactions for your nursing child. Specialists are contemplating why ladies are more than twice as likely as men to create anxiety issues and wretchedness. Changes in levels of the hormone estrogen all through a lady's menstrual cycle and regenerative life (during the years a lady can have a child) presumably assume a job.

Specialists Additionally, as of late, concentrated the male hormone testosterone, which is found in ladies and men yet usually at more elevated levels in men. They found that treatment with testosterone had comparative impacts as antianxiety and energizer prescription for the ladies in the study.15 Other research centers around anxiety issues and melancholy during and after pregnancy and among overweight and stout ladies. For progressively clinical preliminaries identified with anxiety issues and ladies, Anxiety can cause meddling or fanatical considerations. An individual with anxiety may feel befuddled or think that it is difficult to focus. Feeling anxious or baffled can, likewise, be an indication of stress. Others with anxiety may feel discouraged. Side effects of stress can also be physical. Anxiety can cause excessively, tense muscles, or hypertension. Trembling, perspiring, a hustling heartbeat, unsteadiness, and sleep deprivation can likewise originate from fear. Stress may even reason migraines, stomach related issues, trouble breathing, and sickness. On the off chance that physical indications of anxiety are severe and abrupt, it might be a fit of anxiety. People can give evidence of stress from multiple points of view. Some may turn out to be progressively chatty, while others pull back or self-disconnect. Indeed, even people who appear to be cordial, neighborly, or daring can have anxiety.

Since anxiety has numerous manifestations, what it looks like for one individual isn't how it shows up for another. People who have concerns might be pulled back, yet this isn't the situation for everybody with anxiety. Now and again, stress may trigger a "battle" instead of a "flight" reaction, in which case an individual may seem fierce. Bumbling over words, trembling, and anxious tics are regularly connected with anxiety. While they can show up in people with anxiety, they are not always present, and a few people who don't have concern likewise give these indications. If you are uncertain on the off chance that somebody you know might be encountering distress, it may not be useful to bring it up except if they do. Be that as it may, there are a few moves you can consider making on the off chance that you need to make an individual who may be on edge progressively agreeable. Summed up, anxiety is otherwise called free-skimming fear. It is recognized by ceaseless feelings of fate and stress that have no immediate reason. Numerous people feel on edge about specific things, similar to cash, prospective employee meetings, or dating. Be that as it may, people with free-skimming anxiety can think on the side for no obvious explanation. Summed up, fear can likewise mean inclination an excessive amount of stress over a specific occasion.

Developing Your Anxiety

You can find it when you experience extreme anxiety or stress and think that it is hard to control. You can find it when stress or anxiety cause you to feel exhausted or fractious. You can find it stress or anxiety meddle with your rest or capacity to focus. You can nd it when you experience redundant and diligent considerations that are upsetting and undesirable. You can find it when you experience solid dread that causes alarm, the brevity of breath, chest torments, a beating heart, perspiring, shaking, sickness, tipsiness, or potentially dread of kicking the bucket. You can find it when you ever dodge spots or social circumstances because of a paranoid fear of this frenzy. You can find it when you ever participate in dull practices to deal with your stress? (for example, checking the stove is off, locking entryways washing hands, tallying, rehashing words)

How To Find Your Anxiety

They all issue are analyzed when dread and fear of non-compromising circumstances, occasions, places, or articles become over the top and are wild. Anxiety issue is likewise examined if the anxiety has gone on for in any event a half year, and it meddles with social, work, family, or different parts of the day by day life. With regards to the measure of time they go through with one another, guardians and teenagers wander in their evaluations, with guardians undeniably bound to state it's insufficient. Among guardians who live with their youngsters, 45% state they invest too little energy with their adolescent kids; a fourth of teenagers say the equivalent regarding the time they go through with their parents.2 Most adolescents (65%) state they invest the perfect measure of time with their folks, while 9% state they spend much time. Teenagers from lower-salary families are the well on the way to state they invest too little energy with their folks: Four-in-ten adolescents in families with yearly wages below $30,000 state this, contrasted and approximately one-in-five in families with higher salaries. These equivalent salary contrasts are not apparent among guardians, in any case. Equal portions of guardians across pay levels state they invest too little energy with their young kids.

Among guardians who live with their adolescents, fathers are more likely than moms to state they invest too little energy with their high school youngsters (53% versus 39%). When getting some information about cooperation's with their folks, around six-in-ten youngsters (59%) state they get an embrace or kiss from their people consistently or consistently. Around three-in-ten (31%) state they find support or counsel from their folks with schoolwork or school extends on day by day or practically consistent schedule, and 19% state they routinely get into contentions with their parents. Young ladies and young men are about similarly liable to state they get an embrace or kiss from their folks consistently or consistently, as are youngsters from various financial foundations. The portion of adolescents who say their parents help them with schoolwork or school extends each day or pretty much consistently is significantly lower than it was two decades back. An Open Plan review led in 1996 found that, around then, about the portion of adolescents (48%) detailed day by day or practically everyday contribution from guardians in their schoolwork. Successful social critical thinking requires both a versatile direction toward the issue and the fundamental aptitudes to produce significant and compelling arrangements. Shockingly hardly any examinations have inspected critical social thinking with regards to social anxiety. We examined critical social thinking in 38 members with social anxiety issues (Tragic) in contrast with 30 healthy control (HC) members with no history of anxiety issues. Members appraised their critical thinking mentalities and capacities (i.e., issue direction) and afterward produced answers for speculative problems relational from both their point of view and that of a goal other.

These arrangements were coded for adequacy and significance, just as how much the mechanism was dynamic versus inactive. Members with Dismal displayed a more negative issue direction than HC members. Moreover, albeit Miserable and HC members showed no general contrasts in creating meaningful and successful answers for relational issues, using an individual viewpoint encouraged the age of progressively dynamic solutions for HC members, however less potent responses for those with Dismal. Discoveries enlighten new research headings in regards to critical social thinking in social anxiety, with potential ramifications for applied intervention. Your mind begins dashing when your head hits the pillow. You're considering your plan for the day, that thing you should (or shouldn't) have said to your chief, or how costly your youngster's supports will be. Sooner or later, it's difficult to tell whether you're experiencing difficulty dozing because you're on edge, or you're restless because you can't rest. The appropriate response might be both. It's a two-way road: Stress and anxiety can mess, resting up, or intensify existing ones. In any case, the absence of rest can likewise cause an anxiety issue. On the off chance that anxiety or upset rest manifests just every so often, these basic techniques may assist you with loosening up your body and brain so you can get the rest that you need.

Attempt contemplation. Figuring out how to calm your brain can be useful expertise, both for exploring upsetting daytime periods and for nodding off around evening time. If you've never attempted it, start with as meager as a few minutes of sitting unobtrusively and concentrating on you breathe in and breathe out. You can likewise investigate applications that will help direct you. Add exercise to your day. Regular exercisers nod off quicker and rest all the more adequately. Even a solitary moderate-power exercise, similar to an energetic walk, can improve rest among individuals with constant sleep deprivation. Set aside some effort to slow down. A healthy sleep time routine allows your body and psyche time to slow down before lights out. Take at any rate 30 minutes to play calm music, scrub down, or read a book. Avoid upsetting exercises before bed. Leave the bill paying for prior in the day, avoid warmed internet-based life trades, and skirt the nightly news. Put your to-dos in writing. Rather than letting your mind whirl with all the things that you would prefer not to neglect to deal with, record them so your cerebrum can unwind and give up. Tense and unwind. Attempt this unwinding exercise in bed: Crush your toes for a few seconds, and afterward loosen up them.

At that point do something very similar with your lower legs and on up your body, feeling each piece of yourself ask pressure to take a hike. Try not to lie in bed conscious. If you can't nod off for over 20 minutes, give yourself a do-over. Find a workable pace, lights low, and accomplish something unwinding (and preferably rest instigating). Have some homegrown tea and read a book. In any case, stay away from screens: The light that they produce can move toward your mind that it's a great opportunity to wake up. Still not resting? If you feel that you may have progressively genuine rest issues, clinical anxiety, or clinical sadness, converse with your PCP.

A pro can assist you with finding a treatment plan, so you can deal with your side effects and get the rest you need. The long early stretches of the 21st century have seen an overall plague of poor psychological wellbeing and related ailments. In any case, while misery is the condition most will connect with mental wellness issues, and the primary source of handicap around the world, it isn't the main emotional wellbeing concern individuals face. That undesirable award goes to anxiety. An expected 275 million individuals experience the ill effects of anxiety issues. That is around 4% of the worldwide populace, with a spread of somewhere in the range of 2.5% and 6.5% of populace per nation. Approximately 62% of those experiencing anxiety are female (170 million), contrasted, and 105 million male sufferers. The Duke of Cambridge, Sovereign William will go to Davos 2019, where he will discuss Psychological wellness Grinding away, his drive to improve enthusiastic and mental prosperity in the working environment. The full degree of emotional wellbeing issue is probably going to be significantly higher than the most recent information demonstrates, as it will, in general, be under-recorded across both the created and creating universes. Indeed, even the individuals who are analyzed don't generally get the correct treatment.

As the World Wellbeing Association notes, having your heart race as you watch a thriller is a normal physiological reaction. So is experiencing difficulty dozing the previous night conveying a significant introduction. Not all that ordinary is encountering those similar sentiments on a steady close premise, paying little mind to the conditions. For the 18 percent of the U.S. populace with an anxiety issue, it is as a rule hard for sufferers to carry on with a typical life. In a meeting with The Gatekeeper, one young lady who had to drop out of school because of her frenzy issue disclosed what her every day the truth resembled: "I hate sitting at home throughout the day," she stated, yet I indeed can't do whatever else right now. It's as if an interruption button has been pushed on my life. I'm simply... pausing. As indicated by the National Organization of Psychological wellness (NIMH), alarm assaults are only one manifestation of anxiety issues. Others can incorporate a sentiment of approaching fate, fretfulness, sickness, and trouble falling and staying unconscious. Those rest related indications of anxiety can make an endless loop, with the absence of rest, making it increasingly hard for an individual to adapt to their fear, which at that point makes it much harder for them to rest—it's a ceaseless cycle. It is imperative to take note of that interminable anxiety isn't an issue with one single arrangement. It's a constant nearness that must regularly be assaulted on various fronts.

Ending Perfectionist Thinking

Prescriptions help, however right now, they can't fix anxiety issues. Just treat their manifestations. For specific individuals, the way toward finding a medication that works with their body's one of a kind science can be a wellspring of stress all its own. As per the NAMI, a few drugs can take a long time to start working and cause undesirable symptoms. In the wake of breaking down the logical writing that has been delivered in peer audit articles through the span of the last 50 years, Whitaker saw that some mental prescriptions show up as compelling over the present moment, yet that these medications eventually increment the likelihood that an individual will turn out to be constantly sick over the long haul.

This doesn't imply that drug doesn't work (it accomplishes work, and for many individuals). Or maybe, what it means is that our present medications have various issues and don't work (or don't function admirably) for all individuals. Right now, we are gaining ground; however, we have a great deal of work that, despite everything, should be finished. Wellbeing frameworks have not yet satisfactorily reacted to the weight of the mental issues.

How to Stop Inhibiting Yourself?

You can stop inhibiting yourself by inherently constraining yourself to supersede your indiscreet inclination to permit your restraints to govern. They will slowly scatter. The more occasions you prevail with regards to doing this... and wind up accomplishing something which in any case your restraints wouldn't have permitted you to do, the simpler it will become to do it once more. Inevitably of doing this, they will leave totally, and you'll be allowed to do whatever you like! On the off chance that that sounds more difficult than one might expect... you understand it appropriately. In any case, despite being troublesome, there is no more straightforward, nor increasingly powerful, the method for doing it. Coarseness your teeth, summon your dauntlessness, and stroll with certainty... Open the entryway which drives outside of your customary range of familiarity, and make only one little stride out. Utilize your psyche to get to that courage and truly power your foot to make that initial step... If anxiety gets through and you retreat, that is all right. Try not to thrash yourself about it. Simply attempt again later on, yet make two strides when you do it. Continue doing this, trying to continue expanding the means.

Overcoming Self Anxiety

There's no surge, do what needs to be done in your stead. Eventually, at some point or another. After one of those shaky advances, something unforeseen and energizing will happen. An invigorating new sensation will devour you. It will feel astonishing... You will likewise see that your restraint has been decimated. Right off the bat, be content with your finding that you might be restrained. It is a significant finding. Besides, realize that you are not the only one to have this. Thirdly unwind, because of the progression of time, all the encounters accumulated have you ascend above it in the long run. A large portion of what our identity is and become discover their root in adolescence, both the great and the terrible. Yet, in adulthood, we at long last get into the driver's seat of our lives. It's a two-way road: Stress and anxiety can mess, resting up, or intensify existing ones. In any case, the absence of rest can likewise cause an anxiety issue. On the off chance that anxiety or upset rest manifests just every so often, these basic techniques may assist you with loosening up your body and brain so you can get the rest that you need—attempt contemplation.

Figuring out how to calm your brain can be useful expertise, both for exploring upsetting daytime periods and for nodding off around evening time. In the event that you've never attempted it, start with as meager as a few minutes of sitting unobtrusively and concentrating on you breathe in and breathe out. You can likewise investigate applications that will help direct you. Add exercise to your day. Regular exercisers nod off quicker and rest all the more adequately. Truth be told, even a solitary moderate-power exercise, similar to an energetic walk, can improve rest among individuals with constant sleep deprivation. One book that helped me is ' I am OK, you are OK sections proceed in my memory and sometimes ring a bell. This production by creator Harris is World popular and clarifies such a significant amount about who we are that it lifts our comprehension. Somebody with advanced anxiety might be the image of achievement. You may land to work sooner than every other person, perfectly dressed, with your hair conveniently styled. Collaborators may realize you as driven in your work you've never missed a cutoff time or missed the mark in a given errand. Not just that, you're continually ready to help other people when inquired. Also, your social timetable additionally appears to be occupied and full. What others probably won't know, and what you could never share, is that underneath the outside of a bright exterior, you're battling a steady agitate of anxiety.

It might have been apprehensive vitality, the dread of disappointment, and the terror of disillusioning others that drove you to progress. Even though you urgently need a three-day weekend work to get yourself together, you're regularly too reluctant to also consider calling in wiped out. Do you relate to the qualities of an individual with advanced anxiety? How about we investigate what you may be understanding of what others may see of you right now. The constructive parts of advanced anxiety are commonly the results and victories that you and others observe. On the surface, you may have all the earmarks of being extremely fruitful in work and life and truth be told. This might be unbiasedly valid on the off chance that you assess yourself basically on what you accomplish. On account of advanced anxiety, underneath that cover of accomplishment lies a struggle. Success doesn't come without an expense, and now and again, the stress that you feel discovers out. A portion of these attributes may be seen by others as charming or only part of your character; however, they may, in actuality, be driven by underlying anxiety. A portion of these attributes are inward and are never at any point seen by others; however, they are super in any case. Since people don't have the foggiest idea that these activities are brought about by anxiety, they may see them as merely part of your character. The run of the advanced mill individual with concern seems, by all accounts, to be an overachiever. This observation is shallow, however, because it neglects to consider the battle engaged with arriving. On the off chance that you asked a great many people, they would most likely not understand that you battle every day with anxiety.

Nonetheless, you realize that your life is constrained by your anxiety in some significant manners. Maybe you accomplish first assignments, however, limit your life in different ways, for example, not veering off outside your customary range of familiarity. Your activities are likely directed by your anxiety, to such an extent that you decide to fill your existence with exercises as an approach to quiet your dashing contemplations, as opposed to depending on what you may appreciate or what could assist you with growing your points of view. You've additionally gotten proficient at introducing a bogus persona to the world since you never demonstrate your actual feelings to anybody. Instead, you keep everything contained inside, and compartmentalize your senses with an arrangement to manage them later, obviously later never comes. Some portion of the issue is that a significant number of us have a picture of having an anxiety diagnosis. We may imagine an individual who is housebound, can't work, or battles to keep up connections of any sort. We don't think about an inward action as being reason enough to look for help, regardless of how much internal disturbance we experience. It is mainly the existence of disavowal. You may even persuade yourself that there is nothing incorrectly. You're only an obsessive worker, germaphobe, list-producer, etc. What does this mean? We truly need to call advanced anxiety, just anxiety. It's extraordinary, sure, in that you are clearing your path through life generally well. Be that as it may, the concern is the equivalent, and it's simply covered up. With an ascent in people recognizing themselves as having "advanced" anxiety, it might get simpler to look for help. If you feel less disengaged and alone in what you are encountering, it's almost certain you will feel great showing signs of improvement.

Furthermore, considering anxiety in the two, its positive and negative terms may assist with diminishing stigma. We all need some stress to complete things throughout everyday life. As opposed to seeing anxiety as a shortcoming, one thing that this "development" has done is to feature that people with anxiety can, in any case, live full and gainful lives. It's useful some of the time to recognize well-known people who are adapting to similar battles that we face. On account of advanced anxiety, we can consider stars, for example, Barbra Streisand and Donny Osmond, and competitors like Zack Greinke and Ricky Williams. Scott Stossel, manager of The Atlantic, expounded broadly on his encounters with anxiety and how he, despite everything, figured out how to appear and accomplish. These people have discovered their way through their fear to succeed. Unfortunately, there truly is next to no exploration on this point. We realize that there is an ideal degree of anxiety that helps fuel execution (as indicated by the Yerkes-Dodson Law) — and it's someplace trying to be excessively low or excessively high. In this way, it bodes well that on the off chance that you endure with mild or moderate anxiety when contrasted with severe anxiety, the chances of you working at a more significant level would be better. Level of intelligence may likewise assume a job, as a recent report found that budgetary directors who were high in anxiety made the best cash administrators if they additionally had a high IQ. If you've never been analyzed as having anxiety and perceive yourself in the manifestations over, it's ideal for making a meeting with your family specialist for an appraisal or a referral. On the off chance that you are determined to have an anxiety issue, for example, summed up anxiety issue (GAD) or social anxiety issue (SAD), numerous successful treatment alternatives exist, for instance, subjective conduct treatment (CBT), prescription, (for example, particular serotonin reuptake inhibitors; SSRIs), and care to prepare. Regardless of whether your anxiety manifestations don't meet the full criteria for anxiety issues, treatment with psychotherapy or medicine may even now be useful.

Are there any reasons why you clutch your anxiety? Are you dreadful that in case you're never again determined by your stress, that you will quit being an overachiever? These are genuine worries that you should address as you move in the direction of diminishing the effect of anxiety on your life. Be that as it may, don't surrender to the idea that you can't achieve things without your concern. Long stretches of being a specialist list-creator won't be lost on a less-restless you. It might take some modification, yet you will locate another furrow that adjusts your psychological prosperity with getting things done. High working anxiety is, in fact, a twofold edged sword. While you may fear to relinquish what may feel like a piece of your character, realize that you don't should be covertly on edge to accomplish and succeed.

Clutch your positive characteristics through the propensities that you've grown, yet let go of the strain and inward battle. You may be charmingly shocked to discover that not exclusively do achievement should be simply the aftereffect of action, yet that opening yourself up to your feelings and imparting them to others will assist you with having an increasingly credible encounter of your general surroundings.

Preventing Anxiety from Coming Back

Numerous treatment alternatives are accessible to assist people with dealing with their anxiety and to forestall it controlling their lives. The individuals who have had an anxiety issue for a long time may likewise require help to make a way of life changes once the limitations forced by ceremonies or shirking are no longer needed. Checking for early indications of backsliding is significant, and early mediation may forestall all outside effects returning. A healthy correction of the board systems may likewise be useful. Directing and mental treatments Different methodologies might be utilized in mix. These can incorporate subjective conduct treatment (CBT), desensitization, and critical thinking methodologies. The method will be custom fitted to the individual and sort of anxiety, including Psycho-instruction about stress, including data about signs and manifestations of concern, the consolation that the feelings don't imply that the individual is 'going insane' or out of control and reaffirmation that fear is a normal physiological reaction (the 'battle or flight' response) in a strange circumstance. Your Behavioral systems to enable the individual to control the physical impacts of anxiety (for the model, breathing and unwinding).

A fundamental method to control hyperventilation is an essential breathing and unwinding exercise. Taking in profoundly (utilizing the muscular strength) to a tally of five, holding the breath for five, and afterward breathing out to a poll of five saying the word 'unwind.' This lessens hyperventilation and eases a portion of the physical manifestations. This system should be rehearsed in a calm state to guarantee that it very well may be utilized at the point when required. Unwinding can be repeated in various manners, including Tai Chi, reflection, or on the other hand, yoga. Thus, a necessary dynamic muscle unwinding procedure shows the individual to know about muscle strain and how to discharge the pressure following an efficient and dynamic process. Medical attendants and maternity specialists can help an individual to distinguish unhelpful systems (for example, the utilization of liquor or shirking) and advance unwinding exercises (for instance, scrubbing down, tuning in to music, taking a walk, playing sport or a game.

Empaths and vagus nerve

A guide to complete healing for highly sensitive people. Stop absorbing negative energy and anxiety, depression and other chronic diseases. Use your gift and overcome your fears and narcissists' abuses with emotional intelligence.

By

George brown

Table of Contents

Who Is an Empath, And How Do You Know If You're One? 251

Empaths and Social Anxiety. 259

How to Protect Yourself From "Energy Vampires" 268

Reserve the Option to Regard Your Energy 271

Energy Is Infectious 274

Tips For Supporting Young Empaths... 276

Reasons Why You Clutch Your Anxiety.. 279

Overpowered by Improvements.. 283

They Invest A Great Deal of Energy Thinking. 286

Empathy Toward Lifeless Things 287

Love of Nature 289

Youngsters Who Invest A Ton of Energy Outside......................... 290

Energetic Peruses or Data Wipes 291

Striking Visionaries 292

Masterful or Musically Slanted 294

Wired That Way.. 299

How Would We Acquaint Empaths with The World? 300

Show Children Contemplation.. 300

Practical Exercises for Empaths. 306

Exercises for The Troubled and Creating Empath 310

Essential Oil Recipes for Anxiety 315

Extracurricular Exercises 324

Various Evaluations 327

Instructing yourself about your condition 333

How to Identify Negative Thoughts Patterns When They Present Themselves? 336

Replace Your Poor Coping Strategies with Good Ones 338

Short & Long-Term Rewards 340

Stop Absorbing Negative Energies 342

Get Grounded 345

Accomplish the Work 347

Ending Perfectionist Thinking 362

PART 2 365

Vagus Nerve 367

   Vagus Nerve Stimulation Dramatically Reduces Inflammation .. 374

   Vagus Nerve and Anxiety 380

   Vagus Nerve Stimulation and Depression 393

   The Importance of Vagus Nerve to Health 396

   Vagus Nerve Stimulation and its Many Benefits 401

   Anatomy and Function of the Vagus Nerve 410

How to Stimulate Your Vagus Nerve for the Better Mental Health 414

How to Overcome Fear and Anxiety 426

Secrets About Stress and Health 433

Vagus Nerve Stimulation 444

Anti-Inflammatory Diet.. 452

Most Anti-Inflammatory Foods You Can Eat 459

Can Diet Help with Inflammation? 468

Ways, the Vagus Nerve, can Relax You 473

Vagus Exercises 478

Vagus Nerve Could Be Affecting Your Mood 483

How to Strengthen Your Vagus Nerve to Upgrade Your Whole Body 487

Massage for Vagus Nerve Stimulation 494

PART 1
EMPATHS

Who Is an Empath, And How Do You Know If You're One?

What are Empaths? Empaths are profoundly touchy people, who have a sharp capacity to detect what individuals around them are thinking and feeling. Therapists may utilize the term empath to portray an individual that encounters a lot of sympathies regularly to the point of assuming the agony of others at their own cost. In any case, the term empath can likewise be utilized as a profound term, depicting a person with unique, mystic capacities to detect the feelings and energies of others. This specific article will concentrate on the mental parts of being an empath. There are numerous advantages to being an empath. On the splendid side, empaths will, in general, be great companions. They are eminent audience members. They reliably appear for companions in the midst of hardship. They are enormous hearted and liberal. Empaths additionally will, in general, be exceptionally intuitive and genuinely canny.

Nonetheless, a portion of the very characteristics that make empaths such fabulous companions can be no picnic for the empaths themselves. Since empaths feel what their companions are experiencing, they can get overpowered by painful feelings, for example, uneasiness or outrage. Empaths tend to assume the issues of others as their own. It is regularly hard for them to define limits for themselves and state no, in any event, when an excessive amount of is being asked of them. Furthermore, it is essential for empaths to feel depleted after investing energy around individuals. Empaths are typically contemplative people, and they require a specific measure of alone time to revive. An examination from 2011 proposes there might be a connection between profoundly empathic people and social uneasiness. Groups can feel especially overpowering to empaths, who are frequently profoundly touchy to specific clamors and constant chatter. They often feel their best when they are encompassed commonly. Am I An Empath? Ask yourself: Have I been named as "excessively passionate" or excessively delicate? If a companion is troubled, do I begin feeling it as well? Are my emotions effectively stung? Am I genuinely depleted by swarms, require time alone to restore? Do my nerves get frayed by clamor, smells, or over the top talk? Do I incline toward taking my vehicle puts with the goal that I can leave when I please? Do I indulge in adapting to passionate pressure? Am I scared of turning out to be overwhelmed by personal connections? As per Dr.

You have great instincts. Ever felt like you have a robust gut response to things that vibe somewhat off? Possibly you get on deceitfulness effectively or realize when something appears to be a decent (or impractical notion. This might be your empath quality at work. Empaths will, in general, have the option to get on unobtrusive prompts that give knowledge on the contemplations of others, proposes Barrie Susskind, an advisor in Los Angeles who represents considerable authority seeing someone. "An empath's instinct regularly discloses to them whether somebody is honest or not," she says. You breathe easy in light of nature Anybody can profit by investing energy in natural settings. In any case, empaths may feel significantly progressively attracted to nature and remote territories, since typical habitats give a quieting space to rest from overpowering sensations, sounds, and feelings. You may feel settled when climbing alone in a sunlit woodland or watching waves run into the shore. Indeed, even a tranquil stroll through a nursery or an hour sitting under trees may lift your spirits, mitigate overstimulation, and help you relax. You don't do well in packed spots. As per Susskind, empaths can retain positive and negative vitality just by being in somebody's quality. In swarmed or occupied spots, this affectability may appear to be amplified to the point of being practically agonizing.

Numerous treatment alternatives are accessible to assist people with dealing with their anxiety and to forestall it controlling their lives. The individuals who have had an anxiety issue for a long time may likewise require help to make a way of life changes once the limitations forced by ceremonies or shirking are no longer needed. Checking for early indications of backsliding is significant, and early mediation may forestall all outside effects returning. A healthy correction of the board systems may likewise be useful. Directing and mental treatments Different methodologies might be utilized in mix. These can incorporate subjective conduct treatment (CBT), desensitization, and critical thinking methodologies. The method will be custom fitted to the individual and sort of anxiety, including Psycho-instruction about stress, including data about signs and manifestations of concern, the consolation that the feelings don't imply that the individual is 'going insane' or out of control and reaffirmation that anxiety is a normal physiological reaction (the 'battle or flight' response) in a strange circumstance. Your Behavioral systems to enable the individual to control the physical impacts of anxiety (for the model, breathing and unwinding).

A fundamental method to control hyperventilation is an essential breathing and unwinding exercise. Taking in profoundly (utilizing the muscular strength) to a tally of five, holding the breath for five, and afterwards breathing out to a score of five saying the word 'unwind.' This lessens hyperventilation and eases a portion of the physical manifestations. This system should be rehearsed in a peaceful state to guarantee that it very well may be utilized at the point when required. Unwinding can be repeated in various manners, including Tai Chi, reflection, or on the other hand, yoga. Thus, a necessary dynamic muscle unwinding procedure shows the individual to know about muscle strain and how to discharge the pressure following an efficient and dynamic process. Medical attendants and maternity specialists can help an individual to distinguish unhelpful systems (for example, the utilization of liquor or shirking) and advance unwinding exercises (for instance, scrubbing down, tuning in to music, taking a walk, playing sport or a game.

Empaths and Social Anxiety.

Anxiety is characterized as a condition of worry, vulnerability, and dread coming about because of the expectation of a practical or envisioned compromising occasion or circumstance. It is likewise an inclination of stress, anxiety, or dread about an opportunity or time. It is a typical response to push. It causes you to remain alert for a problematic circumstance, busy working, study more earnestly for a test, or stay concentrated on a meaningful discourse. When all is said in done, it encourages you to adapt. In any case, Anxiety can be handicapped if it meddles with everyday life, for example, making you fear nonthreatening everyday exercises like riding the transport or conversing with a colleague. Anxiety can likewise be an unexpected assault of dread when there is no danger. Anxiety issue happens when unreasonable Anxiety meddles with your regular exercises, for example, going to work or school or investing energy with companions or family. Anxiety issue is not kidding psychological maladjustments. They are the most widely recognized mental issue in the United States. Anxiety issue is more than twice as regular in ladies as in men. The significant sorts of anxiety issues are: Summed up the anxiety issues (GAD). People with GAD stress exorbitantly over common, everyday items, for example, wellbeing, cash, work, and family. With GAD, the psyche regularly hops to the direst outcome imaginable, in any event, when there is next to zero motivation to stress. Ladies with GAD might be on edge about simply traversing the day. They may have muscle pressure and different pressure-related physical side effects, for example, inconvenience resting or irritated stomach.

Now and again, stressing shields people with GAD from doing ordinary assignments. Ladies with GAD have a greater danger of sorrow and another anxiety issue than men with GAD. They likewise are bound to have a family ancestry of depression.3 Frenzy issue. Frenzy issue is twice as underlying in ladies as in men.4 People with alarm issues have abrupt assaults of dread when there is no real threat. Fits of Anxiety may cause a feeling of falsity, a fear of approaching fate, or a dread of losing control. One's very own dread unexplained physical side effects is likewise an indication of a frenzy issue. People having alarm assaults here and there accept they are having coronary failures, losing their brains, or passing on—social fear. Social fear, additionally called social anxiety issues, is analyzed when people become on the edge and unsure in ordinary social circumstances. People with social phobia have a solid dread of being watched and made a decision by others. They may get humiliated effectively and regularly have a fit of anxiety indications—understandable fear. A particular concern is an extraordinary dread of something that presents practically no real peril. Specific phobias could be fears of shut-in spaces, statures, water, articles, creatures, or precise circumstances. People with understandable concerns regularly find that confronting, or in any event, pondering confronting, the dreaded article or situation expedites a fit of Anxiety or extreme Anxiety.

Some different conditions that are not viewed as anxiety issues, however, are comparative include: Over the top habitual issue (OCD). People with OCD have undesirable considerations (fixations) or practices (impulses) that cause Anxiety. They may check the broiler or iron over and over or play out a similar daily schedule again and again to control the Anxiety these musings cause. Frequently, the customs wind up controlling the individual—post-awful pressure issue (PTSD). PTSD begins after a startling occasion that included physical mischief or the danger of physical damage. The individual who gets PTSD may have been the person who was hurt, or the accident may have happened to a friend or family member or even an outsider. Anxiety issues influence around 40 million American grown-ups each year.

Anxiety Issues Likewise Influence Kids and Teenagers

About 8% of teenagers ages 13 to 18 have an anxiety issue, with side effects beginning around age 6.5 Ladies are more than twice as likely as men to get an anxiety issue in their lifetime.2 Also, a few sorts of anxiety issue influence a few ladies more than others Women with anxiety issue experience a mix of on edge contemplations or convictions, physical manifestations, and changes in conduct, including evading ordinary exercises they used to do. Every anxiety issue has various events. They all include a dread and fear about things that may happen now or later on. Your primary care physician or attendant will ask you inquiries about your side effects and your therapeutic history. Your primary care physician may likewise do a physical test or different tests to preclude other medical issues that could be causing your side effects. Anxiety issue is analyzed when dread and fear of non-threatening circumstances, occasions, places, or articles become over the top and are wild. Anxiety issue is likewise examined if the Anxiety has gone on for in any event a half year, and it meddles with social, work, family, or different parts of everyday life. Treatment for anxiety issues relies upon the sort of anxiety issue you have and your history of medical problems, savagery, or misuse. Your primary care physician may allude you for a kind of directing for anxiety issues called subjective social treatment (CBT). You can converse with prepared emotional wellness proficient about what caused your anxiety issue and how to manage the symptoms. For instance, you can speak with a therapist, clinician, social specialist, or instructor. CBT can assist you in changing the intuition designs around your feelings of dread. It might help you in changing how you respond to circumstances that may make Anxiety. You may likewise learn approaches to decrease feelings of Anxiety and improve explicit practices brought about by constant Anxiety. These systems may incorporate unwinding treatment and critical thinking. Some of the time, you may need to work with your primary care physician to attempt a few distinct medicines or mixes of medications before you discover one that works for you. If you are experiencing difficulty with symptoms from medications, converse with your PCP or attendant. Try not to quit taking your drug without talking with a specialist or attendant. Your primary care physician may alter how a lot of medication you choose, and when you take it. At times side effects of an anxiety issue return after you have completed treatment. This may occur during or after a distressing occasion. It might likewise happen with no notice. Numerous people with anxiety issues improve treatment. Yet, if your side effects return, your primary care physician will work with you to change or modify your drug or treatment plan. You can likewise converse with your primary care physician about approaches to distinguish and keep Anxiety from returning.

This may incorporate recording your feelings or meeting with your guide if you think your Anxiety is wild. On the off chance that your treatment is guiding, it won't influence your pregnancy. On the off chance that you are on medication to treat your anxiety issue, converse with your primary care physician. A few medications used to treat Anxiety can influence your unborn infant. It depends. A few prescriptions used to treat Anxiety can go through breastmilk. Certain antidepressants, for example, a few SSRIs, are sheltered to take during breastfeeding. Try not to quit taking your prescription too rapidly. Converse with your primary care physician to discover what drug is best for you and your child. Get familiar with drugs and breastfeeding in our Breastfeeding area. You can likewise enter your medication into the Lasted® database to see whether your prescription goes through your breastmilk and any conceivable reactions for your nursing child. Specialists are contemplating why ladies are more than twice as likely as men to create anxiety issues and wretchedness. Changes in levels of the hormone estrogen all through a lady's menstrual cycle and regenerative life (during the years a lady can have a child) presumably assume a job. Specialists Additionally, as of late, concentrated the male hormone testosterone, which is found in ladies and men yet usually at more elevated levels in men. They found that treatment with testosterone had comparative impacts as antianxiety and energizer prescription for the ladies in the study.15 Other research centres around anxiety issues and melancholy during and after pregnancy and among overweight and stout ladies.

For Progressively Clinical Preliminaries

Identified with anxiety issues and ladies, Anxiety can cause meddling or fanatical considerations. An individual with Anxiety may feel bewildered or think that it is difficult to focus. Feeling anxious or baffled can, likewise, be an indication of Anxiety. Others with Anxiety may feel discouraged. Side effects of Anxiety can also be physical. Anxiety can cause excessively, tense muscles, or hypertension. Trembling, sweating, a hustling heartbeat, unsteadiness, and sleep deprivation can likewise originate from Anxiety. Anxiety may even reason migraines, stomach related issues, trouble breathing, and sickness. On the off chance that physical indications of Anxiety are severe and abrupt, it might be a fit of Anxiety. People can give signs of Anxiety from multiple points of view. Some may turn out to be progressively chatty, while others pull back or self-disconnect. Indeed, even people who appear to be cordial, neighbourly, or daring can have Anxiety.

There's no surge, do what needs to be done in your stead. Eventually, at some point or another after one of those shaky advances, something unforeseen and energizing will happen. A refreshing new sensation will devour you. It will feel astonishing. You will likewise see that your restraint has been decimated. Right off the bat, be content with your finding that you might be restrained. It is a significant finding. Besides, realize that you are not the only one to have this. Thirdly unwind, because of the progression of time, all the encounters accumulated have you ascend above it in the long run. A large portion of what our identity is and become discover their root in adolescence, both the great and the terrible. Yet, in adulthood, we at long last get into the driver's seat of our lives. It's a two-way road: Stress and Anxiety can mess, resting up, or intensify existing ones. In any case, the absence of rest can likewise cause an anxiety issue. On the off chance that anxiety or upset rest manifests just every so often, these basic techniques may assist you with loosening up your body and brain so you can get the rest that you need—attempt contemplation.

Figuring out how to calm your brain can be useful expertise, both for exploring upsetting daytime periods and for nodding off around evening time. If you've never attempted it, start with as meager as a few minutes of sitting unobtrusively and concentrating on you breathe in and breathe out. You can likewise investigate applications that will help direct you. Add exercise to your day. Regular exercisers nod off quicker and rest all the more adequately. Even a solitary moderate-power exercise, similar to an energetic walk, can improve rest among individuals with constant sleep deprivation. One book that helped me is ' I am OK; you are OK sections proceed in my memory and sometimes ring a bell. This production by creator Harris is World popular and clarifies such an enormous amount about who we are that it lifts our comprehension. Somebody with advanced Anxiety might be the image of achievement. You may land to work sooner than every other person, perfectly dressed, with your hair conveniently styled. Collaborators may realize you as driven in your work you've never missed a cutoff time or missed the mark in a given errand. Not just that, you're continually ready to help other people when inquired. Also, your social timetable additionally appears to be occupied and full. What others probably won't know, and what you could never share, is that underneath the outside of a bright exterior, you're battling a steady agitate of Anxiety.

It might have been apprehensive vitality, the dread of disappointment, and the fear of disillusioning others that drove you to progress. Even though you urgently need a three-day weekend work to get yourself together, you're regularly too reluctant also to consider calling in wiped out. Do you relate to the qualities of an individual with advanced Anxiety? How about we investigate what you may be understanding of what others may see of you right now. The constructive parts of advanced Anxiety are commonly the results and victories that you and others observe. On the surface, you may have all the earmarks of being extremely fruitful in work and life and truth be told; this might be unbiasedly valid on the off chance that you assess yourself basically on what you accomplish. On account of advanced Anxiety, underneath that cover of accomplishment lies a struggle. Success doesn't come without an expense, and now and again, the Anxiety that you feel discovers out. Others may see a portion of these attributes as charming or only part of your character. However, they may, in actuality, be driven by primary Anxiety. A piece of these attributes is inward and is never at any point seen by others; however, they are super in any case. Since people don't have the foggiest idea that these activities are brought about by Anxiety, they may see them as merely part of your character. The run of the advanced mill individual with Anxiety seems, by all accounts, to be an overachiever. This observation is shallow, however, because it neglects to consider the battle engaged with arriving. On the off chance that you asked a great many people, they would most likely not understand that you battle every day with Anxiety.

How to Protect Yourself From "Energy Vampires"

What Is An Energy Vampire?

It's not unexpected to have connections throughout your life that challenge you. Regardless of whether it's a collaborator, a companion, or even somebody in your family, a few people simply take somewhat more energy to associate with than others. Be that as it may, there's a contrast between a relationship that has a little pull and-pull to it and one that depletes your energy to where you fear ever observing or conversing with the individual. That is the thing that an energy vampire is, old buddy: somebody who ridiculously depletes you of your life power, which leaves you feeling intellectual and truly exhausted in the wake of conversing with them. "An energy vampire is extremely ground-breaking," Natalie Miles, a clairvoyant profound guide and tutor, lets me know via telephone.

Some energy vampires do this on a conscious level, and many do it on an oblivious one." Significantly, Miles brings up this doesn't mean energy vampires are innately awful individuals. The clairvoyant reveals to World-class Every day that this kind of conduct usually originates from low self-esteem or low confidence — something we as a whole battle with now and again. In any case, Miles clarifies, this additionally doesn't mean you ought ever to want to keep an energy vampire around in your life if they are reliably taking from you more than they are giving. "[Energy vampires] look for energy from you since they would prefer not to accomplish the work themselves at discovering what their identity is," Miles reveals to World-class Day by day. As it were, a few people experience difficulty making sense of what their identity is — hell, everybody experiences pain making sense of ~who they are~, isn't that so? Yet, the distinction here is that an energy vampire, as indicated by Miles, has such trouble with their personality that they regularly incline toward others for approval or support, and never appear to place in their work toward personal development. Definitely, at that point, the task falls onto the individuals around them, and no doubt, that sounds lovely cracking depleting, isn't that right? Also, Miles discloses to Tiptop Every day that energy vampires will, in general, be individuals who need to feel like they have more force in their associations with others. "They need to feel all the more monetarily plenteous, or some way or another need to feel 'good' or increasingly fruitful," the mystic clarifies. Strikingly, she includes, energy vampires, will, in general, seem to be individuals who genuinely have their she*t together, regardless of whether it's profession savvy, impractically, whatever. Be that as it may, if you strip back a couple of layers, Miles says it frequently turns out to be evident that an energy vampire's obvious enthusiastic knowledge or strong character is to a higher degree an obtained quality from the individual whose energy they're depleting — regardless of whether that is a dear companion, a relative, or even a sentimental accomplice — and not their very own genuine attribute.

"It can appear in a variety of ways." Furthermore, concerning how an energy vampire can influence you when you're companions with one? "Indeed, it can feel like fatigue, disarray, and not having the option to explain yourself," Miles discloses to the First-class Day by day. It can likewise cause you to feel like you have a piece of you missing, or you aren't yourself." Perhaps the ideal approach to perceive that a friend or family member is having this impact on you, Miles says, is to invest some energy alone, away from this individual, and truly check in with yourself. Generally, the mystic clarifies, you're better ready to see precisely how depleted and depleted you feel whenever you have the chance — regardless of whether it's brief — to genuinely withdraw yourself from the individual who is taking the entirety of your energy. As per Miles, this may appear as a reflection.

Reserve the Option to Regard Your Energy

At last, Miles clarifies, it's tied in with realizing that you reserve the option to regard your energy first, and subsequently the opportunity to expel yourself from this dangerous circumstance. Venturing into your capacity, and expelling yourself from an energy vampire's critical handle, can be amazingly hard. What it eventually comes down to, says Dr Nancy Irwin, Psy.D., a clinical analyst and essential advisor at the California recovery focus Seasons In Malibu, is figuring out how to set up sound limits inside these sorts of connections Primary concern: Energy vampires are individuals; any of us can fall into this example of conduct. Be that as it may, you reserve each privilege to shout out when you feel that somebody is exploiting you. Always remember that. The human body creates an electromagnetic field. At the point when that field is handily upset, it can show from various perspectives, including being "delicate" to individuals and situations. You may perceive the sentiments of being an exceptionally delicate individual. Being around somebody of note sets you feeling awful. Hosting to go into a packed get-together overpowers you. At the point when somebody isn't content with you, you feel as though you're as a rule genuinely assaulted. Being vivaciously delicate implies that you're getting on and absorbing negative energy from people around you.

Ensure your energy framework is robust and adjusted. There are numerous approaches to do this, yet one of my top picks is the "thymus pound." Pounding an organ in the focal point of your chest, called the thymus organ, gives you resistant framework support and is additionally powerful for quieting trepidation and adjusting your whole framework rapidly. Primarily utilize your clench hand and "pound" like Tarzan for around 30 seconds and some large full breaths. Ground your energy. The more grounded, or associated with the world's powers you are, the less shaken you'll be by your condition. An incredible method to "ground" is by actually getting your energy down through your feet. Spot your hands on the sides of your midriff. With your thumb in the front and fingers toward the back, slide your hands gradually and solidly down your legs. At the point when you get to your feet, crush along the edges of your feet. Doing this on grass, earth, or sand makes it significantly progressively amazing. By following your focal meridian, an energy pathway running up the front of your body, likewise exceptionally receptive to musings and feelings, you can reinforce it.

Spot your hands at the base finish of the focal meridian, which is at your pubic bone. Breathe in profoundly as you at the same time, pull your hands straight up the focal point of your body, to your lower lip. Rehash multiple times. With the electromagnetic power of your hands, you are moving the energy in the meridian toward its quality, and thus, the apex is fortifying you. While doing this activity, you can likewise include an insistence; for example, Breathing permits energy development in your body. On the off chance that you hold your breath in swarms or around troublesome individuals, you are keeping any negative energy from moving directly through you. Cross your arms/legs when feeling enthusiastically helpless. This protects your emanation and makes an enthusiastic shield. Negative energy being aimed at you will result in general skip off of you and come back to the sender.

Pick your area carefully. Remain by a window or entryway in swarms and abstain from sitting at the front of a class or room where individuals direct their energy toward you. Dark tourmaline, a gem that can be bought for only two or three dollars, is a fantastic negative energy safeguard. Put it in your pocket, handbag, or simply keep it near to when feeling helpless. Presently you have bunches of moment or-less apparatuses to keep you adjusted, grounded, and protected. Simply remember, they possibly work if you use them.

Energy Is Infectious

At the point when you encircle yourself with constructive individuals, you get on to the inclination and are lighter and more joyful. Energy vampires, notwithstanding, will drain the light out of you before you know it, leaving you depleted and depleted of your vivacious stores. The initial step to managing energy vampires is to recognize them, which isn't generally as straightforward as it sounds. Not all energy vampires seem to be indistinguishable. They may work in manners that are exceptional to them. However, the draining impacts on people around them are the equivalent. Regardless of whether it's the ceaseless "poor me" from a specific relative, the ceaseless showmanship originating from your neighbour the twit, or the through and through perniciousness of a partner at work, the energy vampire will unavoidably take your great vibes. After an experience with an energy vampire, you feel genuinely and intellectually depleted, and conceivably restless, pitiful, or angry. The breaking point the measure of time you burn through with effort vampires. It makes sense that the less time you are in their essence, the less energy you'll lose. Begin to execute procedures that will keep discussions short and non-obtrusive (i.e., "I just have a second to talk.")

Breaking point eye to eye connection. At the point when you need to associate with somebody, eye to eye connection is something worth being thankful for. On account of an energy vampire, in any case, you will need to evade association. Stay confined indeed, intellectually, and sincerely by avoiding eye to eye connection, however much as could reasonably be expected. Characterize your own space plainly and sincerely. This incorporates passionate space just as physical space. Abstain from being caught with an energy vampire in a little or shut area, or being separated from everyone else with them. Keep in mind; energy is infectious! Ensure you articulate your needs obviously to the vampire (i.e., "I'd preferably not talk about that specific individual/place/thing."). Do whatever it takes not to respond inwardly; instead, stay unbiased and rational. Try not to endeavor to fix their issues. Energy vampires are regularly ridden with problems that are not yours to fix, although the vampire will attempt to persuade you that they are. Stay disengaged from their dramatization and spotlight instead of leaving. The more you do it, the simpler it gets the chance to expel yourself from the circumstance. Attempt perception rehearses. In some cases, leaving isn't a choice. You can imagine a protective white light around you, a virtual energy shield. You will, at present, since the interruption of the vampire into your space, yet it will be held at a careful distance away from you. Your psyche will be distracted with the representation of light; thus, the vampire's voice and nearness will be extraordinarily diffused by your distraction with something additionally delighting. Most importantly, regard yourself. Try not to stress over being rude. Your essentialness is a valuable asset and merits protection. You are the watchman of your own fiery space. To lead an upbeat and reliable life, you totally should encircle yourself with individuals who develop constructive energies and wipe out those individuals who don't. It isn't impolite to monitor your prosperity; it's confirming of your self-esteem.

Tips For Supporting Young Empaths

Most grown-ups are pretty receptive to their feelings, yet youngsters aren't. They're encountering numerous things just because, and their little universes are whirlwinds of feelings that they can't generally comprehend. This is amplified a thousand-fold for young empaths. Since they can have such trouble understanding their sentiments, it tends to be extraordinarily difficult for empathic youngsters to appreciate that the feelings they're feeling aren't forever their own. In case you're an empath, you can likely intuit if your youngster is as well. Individuals who aren't might experience issues perceiving empathic capacities in their children, not to mention making sense of how to help them. Ideally, this article can give somewhat of a rule, and offer some supportive tips that can facilitate the route for every one of you.

How Might You Disclose to If Your Youngster Is an Empath?

Most youngsters display some level of otherworldly mystic attunement with their companions. However, some are unquestionably more empathic than others. The characteristics recorded beneath are only a couple of approaches to figure out where your children's capacities lie.

Exceptionally Touchy Or "On the Range"

As a matter of first importance, they may have been analyzed as being profoundly delicate, regardless of whether by instructors or kid clinicians. It might have even been proposed that they have real preparing issues or chemical imbalance range issues. Not exclusively are empathic youngsters unbelievably touchy to the energies around them, they're typically delicate to a wide range of tangible improvements. Many have a full scope of nourishment sensitivities. Others may break out in hives when their skin interacts with specific textures or cleansers. Rather than constraining them to wear a scratchy sweater that makes them go nuts, regardless of whether it's to satisfy the grandparent who sewed it, comprehends that it causes them to feel horrendous. Let them pick their dress.

On the off chance that they have issues with specific nourishments, figure out what these issues are and make settles. Do they like to crunch, however, loathe anything vile? You can work with that. And so on.

Furthermore, considering Anxiety in the two, its positive and negative terms may assist with diminishing stigma. We all need some anxiety to complete things throughout everyday life. As opposed to seeing Anxiety as a shortcoming, one thing that this "development" has done is to feature that people with Anxiety can, in any case, live full and gainful lives. It's useful some of the time to recognize well-known people who are adapting to similar battles that we face. On account of advanced Anxiety, we can consider stars, for example, Barbra Streisand and Donny Osmond, and competitors like Zack Reinke and Ricky Williams. Scott Stossel, manager of The Atlantic, expounded broadly on his encounters with Anxiety and how he, despite everything, figured out how to appear and accomplish. These people have discovered their way through their Anxiety to succeed. Unfortunately, there truly is next to no exploration on this point. We realize that there is an ideal degree of Anxiety that helps fuel execution (as indicated by the Yerkes-Dodson Law) — and it's someplace trying to be excessively low or excessively high. In this way, it bodes well that on the off chance that you endure with gentle or moderate

Anxiety when contrasted with acute Anxiety, the chances of you working at a more significant level would be better. Level of intelligence may likewise assume a job, as a recent report found that budgetary directors who were high in Anxiety made the best cash administrators if they additionally had a high IQ. If you've never been analyzed as having Anxiety and perceive yourself in the manifestations over, it's ideal for making a meeting with your family specialist for an appraisal or a referral. On the off chance that you are determined to have an anxiety issue, for example, summed up anxiety issue (GAD) or social anxiety issue (SAD), numerous successful treatment alternatives exist, for instance, subjective conduct treatment (CBT), prescription, (for example, particular serotonin reuptake inhibitors; SSRIs), and care to prepare. Regardless of whether your anxiety manifestations don't meet the full criteria for anxiety issues, treatment with psychotherapy or medicine may even now be useful.

Reasons Why You Clutch Your Anxiety

Are there any reasons why you clutch your Anxiety? Are you dreadful that in case you're never again determined by your Anxiety, that you will quit being an overachiever? These are genuine worries that you should address as you move in the direction of diminishing the effect of Anxiety on your life. Be that as it may, don't surrender to the idea that you can't achieve things without your Anxiety. Long stretches of being a specialist list-creator won't be lost on a less-restless you. It might take some modification, yet you will locate another furrow that adjusts your psychological prosperity with getting things done. High working anxiety is, in fact, a twofold edged sword. While you may fear to relinquish what may feel like a piece of your character, realize that you don't should be covertly on edge to accomplish and succeed. Clutch your positive characteristics through the propensities that you've grown, yet let go of the strain and inward battle. You may be charmingly shocked to discover that not exclusively do achievement should be simply the aftereffect of action, yet that opening yourself up to your feelings and imparting them to others will assist you with having an increasingly credible encounter of your general surroundings.

Orloff says. When you start to comprehend your empathic nature, you can figure out how to care more for yourself inwardly. The most effective method to Deal with Your Compassion Without Getting Depleted Set Sound Limits Being typically thinking about others, empaths make some hard memories saying "no." This can prompt issues as you overcommit and channel yourself inwardly. Dr Orloff proposes, "Control how much time you burn through tuning in to upsetting individuals, and figure out how to state 'no.' Set clear cutoff points and limits with individuals, pleasantly cutting them off at the pass on the off chance that they get basic or mean. Keep in mind, 'no' is a finished sentence." Practice Care Since empaths will, in general, become involved with what is happening around them, it is especially significant for them to put aside time to tune in. Rehearsing Care can help you reconnect to yourself. Concentrating on your breath, for request, calms the brain and focuses you on your body. It very well may be useful in contemplation to rehearse "non-recognizable proof" with others, attempt to consider yourself to be your feelings as isolated from anybody else's. Disregard Your Internal Pundit the Basic Internal Voice resembles a dreadful mentor that lives inside our heads, sitting tight for any chance to censure us. Empaths, being delicate, are defenceless against these self-basic considerations.

What's up with you?" or "You're simply excessively touchy." Notwithstanding, it is significant not to accept these self-assaults or follow up on your internal pundit's flawed guidance. You can find out about how to defeat your inward pundit here. Practice Self-Sympathy While it is simple for empaths to feel sympathy for other people, it is frequently hard for them to feel empathy for themselves. Self-empathy is only essential (yet testing) practice of treating yourself like a companion. It is known as training since it is something that you show signs of improvement after some time. As per Dr Kristen Neff, there are three segments to rehearsing self-empathy:) Recognize and notice your torment. Be thoughtful and minding in light of affliction. Recollect that defect is a piece of the human experience and something we as a whole offer. You can get self-sympathy practices on Dr Kristen Neff's site. Invest Energy in Nature, and nature has high recuperating impacts for all people; however, especially for empaths. Writer John Burroughs stated, "I go to nature to be mitigated and recuperated, and to have my faculties taken care of." Because empaths are profoundly touchy to the individuals (just as commotions and conditions) around them, time in nature is the ideal path for them to unwind and energize. Regardless of whether you live someplace that permits you to stroll on the seashore, climb through the forested areas or sit in a recreation centre, it is essential to make time to revive in a lovely, common setting, particularly when you are feeling overpowered or genuinely drained.

Nonetheless, you realize that your Anxiety constrains your life in some significant manner. Maybe you accomplish first assignments, however, limit your life in different methods, for example, not veering off outside your customary range of familiarity. Your activities are likely directed by your Anxiety, to such an extent that you decide to fill your existence with exercises as an approach to quiet your dashing contemplations, as opposed to depending on what you may appreciate or what could assist you with growing your points of view. You've additionally gotten proficient at introducing a bogus persona to the world since you never demonstrate your actual feelings to anybody. Instead, you keep everything contained inside, and compartmentalize your senses with an arrangement to manage them later, obviously later never comes. Some portion of the issue is that a significant number of us have a picture of having an anxiety diagnosis. We may imagine an individual who is housebound, can't work, or battles to keep up connections of any sort. We don't think about an inward struggle as being reason enough to look for help, regardless of how much internal disturbance we experience. It is mainly the existence of disavowal. You may even persuade yourself that there is nothing incorrectly. You're only an obsessive worker, germaphobe, list-producer, etc. What does this mean? We truly need to call advanced Anxiety, just Anxiety. It's extraordinary, confident, in that you are clearing your path through life generally well. Be that as it may, the Anxiety is the equivalent. It's simply covered up. With an ascent in people recognizing themselves as having "advanced" Anxiety, it might get simpler to look for help. If you feel less disengaged and alone in what you are encountering, it's almost certain you will feel great showing signs of improvement.

Overpowered by Improvements

Envision the entirety of your faculties being ambushed in one go, consistently. In a horde of individuals, you wouldn't merely be "mindful" that there is a lot of people processing around you...

You'd hear each expression of each discussion, smell each fragrance, and sense all the feelings that those others are feeling.

At the Same Time. At Full Volume.

Empathic kids individually can get overpowered effectively, particularly in swarmed, open spaces or when an excessive amount of is going on around them on the double. This causes a tactile over-burden that will either cause them to have a screaming emergency or numb out/disassociate to get past it. Tips: Become more acquainted with their triggers, and help to decrease them however much as could reasonably be expected. Besides, show them care reflection, so they realize how to ground and focus themselves when they begin spiraling from all the mind-boggling everything. Leave room in their bustling timetables for decompression time, and ensure they have a committed calm space to withdraw to.

Setting up a little tent in their room can be an incredibly small "home" for them. Let them fill it with delicate surfaces and relieving toys, and kindly don't upset them when they're in there. They'll come out when they're ready to. They Cry When Others Are Harmed or Vexed. This is a characteristic that most empaths can identify with, and will, in general, appear in early stages. Does your youngster cry when they see others – human or creature colleagues – get injured or upset? Do they hurry to comfort the individuals who are crying?

Most infants instinctually attempt to comfort and relieve other people who are disturbed, and this attribute can either decrease or escalate as they get more established. A few little children will turn out to be exceptionally self-included, while others keep up their compassionate extreme touchiness. Tips: Show your children the 5 detects contemplation when they're reflecting others' damages and being influenced by them. Inquire as to whether they're feeling agony or harmed feelings. On the off chance that they don't have the foggiest idea, centre around what they can smell, contact, hear, taste, and see. This takes them back to the current second. When they've quieted, acclaim them for being thoughtful and worried for other people, and perhaps cooperate to make something encouraging yet-separated.

Composing a card or a letter or preparing treats shows care and worry, without taking on the other individual's agony. Emotions Run Profound Empathic youngsters regularly feel things substantially more profoundly than others do. Though one youngster may disregard a reprimanding and return to playing in no time, an empathic child might be crushed. Not exclusively will they hurt profoundly on account of the objection; however, they'll likewise feel horrible about having frustrated a parent. And shame at being berated before their companions. Also, blame/disgrace about not having the option to control their feelings. Also, you get the thought. These children need to manage enthusiastic multi-layer cakes consistently.

They're savagely mindful of what every other person is feeling, which amplifies their enthusiastic reactions. Whatever it is they're feeling at the time, they think it a few times more seriously than most different children ever will. This is similarly as legitimate for rapture for what it's worth for despair. Tips: Kindly don't negate what they're feeling, and don't ridicule them for their passionate reactions. A kid who's derided or prodded when they skip or move in enjoyment may learn rapidly that their profoundly felt delight can't be communicated. The same goes for their distress. Robust Associations with Creature Companions It's frequently more uncomplicated for empaths to interface with non-human companions.

Their practices bode well and aren't loaded with frequently clashing non-verbal communication and verbal articulation. Also, creature companions acknowledge their people genuinely and aren't critical or brutal how human youngsters can be. (Particularly to the extraordinary individuals.) Tips: Energize this conduct, and ensure your child has a creature partner that they get the chance to invest a ton of energy with. Please guarantee that any vital hypersensitivity testing is done on all relatives before embracing a creature companion.

They Invest A Great Deal of Energy Thinking.

There are not many things as crushing to an empathic kid than holding with a creature, just to have it detracted from them given sensitivities – their own, or somebody else's. Empathic children are regularly the ones who are informed that they invest a lot of energy "in their heads." They can once in a while be blamed for staring off into space, and will in general, likewise be advised to help up, be less genuine, and so forth. These youngsters are dissecting each part of presence, attempting to comprehend their general surroundings while likewise delighting in its marvels. They attempt to get guile, mockery, and endless other opposing practices. Tips: Get some information about, and if they decide to let you know, listen effectively. Show genuine enthusiasm for their considerations, approve their point of view, and ask them to try (and empowering, and aware) age-suitable inquiries concerning them. Empowering this sort of profound thought may assist them with pushing toward impressive professions in which they can tackle their astuteness and exceptionally logical nature.

Empathy Toward Lifeless Things

On the off chance that your youngster cries when you toss out an old, broken trash can because the person is frightened that said can feel hurt and deserted, the odds are high that they're an empath. Children who understand with others can experience issues with humanoid attribution. They don't comprehend that their stuffed bear doesn't have nerve endings and, in this way, doesn't feel torment when it gets a blooper. Tips: If the kid is youthful (for example younger than 4), feel free to put a wrap on teddy's bungle, and apologize to the messed-up trash can for sending it back home to be "fixed." More seasoned youngsters may relax because of animistic customs, in which the thing's soul is regarded and expressed gratitude toward the delight it brought and urged to go free before the said thing is reused. Attempt to abstain from utilizing terms like "discarded" or "hurled out," as these can infer relinquishment.

Instead, show how everything will increase new reason and new life, regardless of whether changed into different shapes. They Are Profoundly Irritated with Disturbing Film or Television Scenes. We've every single experienced second while sitting in front of the television or movies where something upsetting occurs, and we recoil away. For the more significant part of us, this inclination is transitory, and we can dismiss the experience as a positive response to a pretend scene. Not so for small empaths. They frequently feel for characters so profoundly that a disturbing scene will be profoundly upsetting to them. If it's awful enough, it may cause bad dreams, or gloom, or even continue frequenting them for quite a long time.

Tips: If you know their triggers, do look into before watching a film or Network program with them to check whether there are any upsetting scenes. Numerous children are especially vexed if creatures get injured onscreen, so maintain a strategic distance from motion pictures where there's any of that going on. Presently, a kid empath should create methods for dealing with stress after some time, so they don't conceal away from the whole world until the end of time. In that capacity, it's acceptable to open them to conceivably upsetting symbolism gradually, when you feel that they're prepared. You can begin with animation films, as it's simpler for them to comprehend that drawings are pretended and that nobody is getting injured without a doubt. The apparent truth of how much enduring goes on the planet can be genuinely overpowering for their little hearts, so delicacy truly is the request for the day, for whatever length of time that conceivable.

Love of Nature

Nature can be hugely recuperating for empaths for various reasons, so comprehend that it's doubly so for youngsters. Children are attracted to the natural world and love to investigate it. There's such an enormous amount to see! What's the more smell! Being out in nature is hugely quieting, and everybody can profit by more exercise out in the outside air and daylight, isn't that so?

Youngsters Who Invest A Ton of Energy Outside

Usually are attracted to natural stewardship, primary entitlements activism, and cultivating. They love to develop things, support life, and watch brilliant creatures in their natural environments. Empathic youngsters individually get energized by putting their hands in the soil, playing in the water, and any event, cuddling up to trees. Tips: Attempt to make outside experiences a customary event. If you have a lawn, help your children set up a mini veggie or herb garden only for them. Plant butterfly-and fowl cordial wildflowers, hang hummingbird feeders and set out water for frogs and amphibians.

In case you're an urban loft inhabitant, exploit kids' outside projects at neighbourhood parks and greenhouses. Escape the city for climbs or outdoors trips at whatever point conceivable, and get occupied with subjects your kid is keen on. Do they like to stargaze? Snatch a telescope and find out about groups of stars together. Is it accurate to say that they are regular healers? Take a kid agreeable homegrown medication course and do some mindful scrounging.

Energetic Peruses or Data Wipes

Is your kid keen on pretty much everything? Does the individual in question get intrigued by a subject and need to get the hang of everything there is to think about it? That is an exceptionally natural characteristic in empaths and begins when they can raise their heads all along. Everything is lovely, everything is impressive, and there's such a long way to go! Your youngster may begin perusing at a young age, and request visit library visits so they can drive through everything accessible regarding their matter of decision. On the other hand, particularly if they have a learning handicap, they may genuinely cherish nature or history narratives. Tips: Empower this at whatever point conceivable.

If the subjects that draw in them the most aren't crucial to you, that is alright: be straightforward with them about it, and urge them to investigate these alternatives all alone, or with peers (or potentially more distant family individuals) who have comparable premiums. They Need A Ton of Alone Time Much the same as grown-up empaths, kid-sized adaptations hunger for (and revel in) isolation. They're probably not going ever to get exhausted, because how would they be able to?! A considerable lot of these youngsters don't like merely being distant from everyone else; they need that by itself time for various reasons.

As referenced previously, if they've had emergencies or deadness due to tactile over-burden, calm alone time is utterly essential for them to energize. Consider it like the time skin takes to mend after a consume or a cut. Tips: Kindly don't blame them for being "solitary," or request that they be increasingly connected with others. You can't draw blood from a stone. Grown-ups who are depleted in the wake of nerve-racking days at work can communicate that they need quietness and isolation, and have their desires regarded. Children are fundamentally helpless before the grown-ups around them, and feel like they need to surrender to requests for social action or, more than likely they'll be rebuffed.

If it's not too much trouble regarding their requirement for isolation and perceive that it has nothing to do with you, and there's not all that much with them. You aren't being dismissed, and it's not undesirable for them to need alone time as opposed to playing with other kids. Odds are your children will welcome you significantly more for guarding their alone time.

Striking Visionaries

The striking – frequently clear – dreams that many empaths experience regularly start when they're exceptionally youthful. These may be extremely extraordinary, with extrasensory clairsentient angles, or may show as night dread. In any case, regardless of whether the fantasies are great or unnerving, they can influence empathic youngsters emphatically. Tips: Keeping a fantasy diary is an incredible route for children to process the symbolism they've seen, and they can think back after some time to see which topics or pictures have been repeating. Many empaths are likewise very claircognizant or perceptive, and it's not uncommon for their fantasies to work out as expected. This regularly starts in adolescence and can be captivating and startling to kids at turns. By keeping a diary, you can record dreams together and allude back to them if and when they happen.

On the off chance that they do work out as expected, if it's not too much trouble, promise the kid that there's nothing amiss with them, however, that they have a lovely blessing. Uplifting feedback, over and over. They Realize When Individuals Are Lying It is highly unlikely anybody can deceive these children: they know promptly when somebody's brimming with poop. They're profoundly intuitive, and can quickly figure your non-verbal communication out. Not merely yours, either: every one of those little "innocent exaggerations" that instructors and different grown-ups tell? They see directly through them. Tips: Be straightforward. Indeed (mainly) when it's troublesome – an express reality in language that is proper for their age and passionate turn of events.

Deceiving your kid, regardless of whether you accept that it's to their most significant advantage, will give them that they can never confide in you. If the topic isn't suitable for them, at that point, reveal to them that, though in a delicate way. Knowing reality, or even that it's a subject that they're not prepared for, will permit them to have significantly more confidence in you.

Masterful or Musically Slanted

Similarly, that small scale empaths will delight in nature and feeling. They're likewise regularly attracted to craftsmanship and music (both making it and getting a charge out of it). Empathic youngsters who battle to communicate in words may think that it's more straightforward to draw or paint. They may appreciate making comic books or bright artistic creations, or – mainly if they manage tension – they may discover it extraordinarily cleansing to work with the earth. Thus, various sorts of music may alleviate them, and they might be roused to figure out how to play an instrument. Tips: Support these tendencies at whatever point conceivable, without judgment. On the off chance that the kid shows you a riotously dynamic artistic creation, don't attempt to decipher the understandable importance: get some information about it. Have a go at making statements like, "I truly love the amazing way you utilized the shading green here. Would you be able to reveal to me how you felt when you painted this?"

Would you be able to assist me with understanding it so I can value it a similar way you do?" If your youngster needs to figure out how to play an instrument, cooperate to settle on one that they're keen on; however, it won't make you completely bonkers. A violin or cello may be more costly than a recorder, yet far less goading. The Sense that They Don't "Have a place" Numerous empaths understand very of a spot on this planet, and that feeling frequently starts in youth. Empathic children experience the world uniquely in contrast to "ordinary" kids, which can be fantastically estranging. They probably won't realize how to play appropriately, or get overpowered by game standards and disorderly conduct. Stylish points may not intrigue them, and they'll wind up being segregated by inner circles. Tips: Telling your children that they're unique won't cause them to feel vastly improved – they'll remain angry, and think that the primary individual who'll acknowledge them is you.

Invest More Energy

Moreover, kindly don't urge them to adjust, or to "invest more energy" to be something they're not, to fit in. This will squash their singularity and can show in some exceptional uneasiness and melancholy as they age. Attempt to assist them with finding their "clan," even at an early age. On the off chance that they have specific interests, search for nearby gatherings with different children their age so that they can associate with others of the like psyche. More established children can join online groups, or go to day camps that attention on their regions of intrigue. They are investing in energy with kids who are much the same as they will assist them with feeling less alone. They probably won't fit in with one specific gathering. However, they'll realize that there are others where they'll be acknowledged and acknowledged. Secretive Physical Manifestations Your little empath may experience the ill effects of regular stomach throbs, cerebral pains, or sore throats. Specialists probably won't discover anything amiss with them, yet that doesn't imply that the agony isn't genuine. Frequently, these issues can emerge from the exceptional feelings felt by the kid, which will genuinely show if the child can't communicate to discharge those emotions. Nervousness or upset will collect in the stomach area, causing distress. Strain and disappointment may cause a severe migraine, and so on. Tips: It's essential to not merely excuse these side effects as depression, or consideration chasing. Science has demonstrated that feeling and stress can show as physical agony, just as aggravation, and endocrine disturbance. Approve your youngster's side effects.

Tell them that you trust them, and promise them that you'll cooperate to assist them with feeling much improved. On the off chance that they're tormented with sore throats, and conditions like tonsillitis and strep have been excused, at that point, it may be a great subject matter. Do they sense that they're not being heard? Is it accurate to say that they are experiencing difficulty talking about their reality because of dread? Make some handcrafted, every single common popsicle, and assist them with communicating through composition or attracting until they're ready to verbalize. Do they have stomach hurts? That is generally identified with pressure or uneasiness. Peppermint tea or soda can be useful, and afterwards, non-critical profound paunch breathing and delicate yoga Once quieted, check whether you can work with them to make sense of where the steam is coming from, and check whether you can discover arrangements together— wrapping Things Up Empaths who are raising, working with, or encouraging empathic kids to have a prominent bit of leeway. We've been the place they are presently and can identify with them on a level that all can comprehend. Guardians, educators, and advisors who don't have empathic capacities can frequently battle with small scale empaths. They don't understand the extreme touchiness and attempt to get kids to toughen up, or be increasingly similar to the others. Their goals might be acceptable, in that they need to enable the children to stay away from shunning or humiliation. However, they can accomplish more harm than they understand.

Youngsters who are empaths experience the world uniquely in contrast to "customary" kids, and that must be recognized and bolstered. These youngsters are uncommon pearls and can make the world a beautiful, kind, and sympathetic spot. They need the assistance, direction, acknowledgement, and backing of people around them. You probably won't comprehend or identify with what these children experience, and that is alright: trust them, and be there for them. We need our children to be increasingly compassionate. She focuses on looking into that says youngsters are just about 50 per cent less sympathetic than they were decades prior, and that is an issue.

Being sympathetic makes it simpler for us to take part in seeing someone and permits us to feel associated with others. For a great many people, sympathy is a passage to a superior existence with improved correspondence. Notwithstanding, being an empath is on somewhat of an unexpected level in comparison to merely realizing how to understand. The street for empaths is increasingly confusing. Empaths are characterized as individuals who assume the sentiments of others – actually sympathizing with their tormentor feelings. Envision Teacher X from the X-Men funnies. He's a freak with the super intensity of clairvoyance, yet it could be contended that he is additionally an empath. His capacity to guess others' thoughts and experience their feelings drives his character in "X-Men: Long stretches of Future Past" to utilize medications to dull the tension and discouragement that join the entirety of the emotions he retains.

He begins the medications for different reasons yet remains on them to dull torment. This bodes well. Children who are empaths – otherwise called orchid kids or exceptionally delicate children – are bound to experience the ill effects of substance misuse issues and grief, conceivably because they retain the great and the terrible from others and have problems adapting thus go after different techniques to block out. To sympathize, individual needs to genuinely feel, and Sam can get high on the energy of a companion or end up in tears when somebody he adores is in any inconvenience. The issue is he doesn't have an off switch and can wind up a bundle of uneasiness just because he feels excessive.

Wired That Way

It's been known for quite a while that maniacs don't encounter sympathy. Investigations of prisoners who showed indications of psychopathic conduct uncovered a distinction when it came to feeling others' feelings. The individuals who were profoundly psychopathic felt no agony while envisioning terrible things transpiring, demonstrated by the way that the pieces of their minds wired for compassion didn't illuminate. Being equipped for compassion is acceptable. However, empaths are on the opposite finish of this range. They feel the torment of others, and they assimilate feelings like a wipe. It's depleting. However, it makes them great audience members and nurturers.

How Would We Acquaint Empaths with The World?

At the point when awful things occur on the planet, my significant other and I waver to impart subtleties to Sam. We need to instruct him that he can feel, help other people, and still endure. However, we dread him self-destructing as a result of how hard it is for him to disengage from another person's torment. We would prefer not to instruct children to be unempathetic; however, how would we prepare empaths to live in a flawed domain without remaining depleted, focused, and overwhelmingly miserable? Empath and MD Judith Orloff has a few hints:

Show Children Contemplation

Instructing empaths to ponder causes them delayed down, become mindful of their feelings, and work to manage their conduct. Empaths ought to have contemplation or quietness breaks sprinkled consistently. It might assist them with hitting the reset button before they are too overpowered. Empaths need to protect their vacation and know their cutoff points. They shouldn't join to be in a vast gathering of individuals for a whole day if they see the pressure from feeling a lot from others will deplete them. Help empaths draw lines and shield themselves from an excess of incitement when essential.

Instruct Them to Pick Companions Astutely

Great and terrible sentiments are infectious for empaths, with the goal that a hopeful companion who develops others and handles difficulties valuably will be useful for an empath. Orloff cautions that the inverse is valid if an empath is around "enthusiastic vampires." Being encompassed by allies loaded with dread, outrage, or other negative sentiments all the time is harming for empaths. They ingest the forceful feelings, and they can feel hurt by them. Instruct children to pick their nearest buddies carefully, and ensure they don't live in a house where unchecked outrage is the standard.

Guide Your Empath

The world is one of magnificence, yet it is additionally loaded with malevolence and agony. It generally will be, and empaths need to exist in this world without feeling the weight Teacher X did. We would prefer not to change empaths or instruct them to be hard. They aren't frail, and their capacities permit them to feel excellence and acknowledge goodness such that the vast majority of us can't. With a consistent hand, we can control them to utilize their empath powers and deal with themselves simultaneously.

Creator Donna Lynn Expectation poses a significant inquiry, "The empath helps other people by retaining a portion of their torment, yet who helps the empath?" The individuals who love them do by instructing them to grasp the superheroes they are. Tags addiction, culture and society, demise and biting the dust, sadness, compassion, Parent and Kid, character, Self-Consideration, the child-rearing experience

I saw something was diverse about my child when he was conceived. There was something in particular about how he took a gander at individuals; he gazed with a force I'd never observed an infant have. He had the option to centre, truly centre, and look at individuals without flinching, and there were times I felt such a solid feeling of the association from him. I got over it and disclosed to myself I was somewhat senseless. He was an infant all things considered; however, the inclination that he was retaining my feelings, just as the opinions of everyone around him, wouldn't leave me. At the point when he was a month and a half old, his father left on a 3-evening chasing excursion, and I recollect how frozen I was. I was hesitant to be distant from everyone else with a child and no back up even though he had recently started dozing longer stretches. We as a whole ability solid the "Mom Bear" nature is the point at which our children are that age, and I was a wreck. I was apprehensive somebody was going to break in, I was unable to loosen up regardless of how hard I attempted. I continued reminding myself what an extraordinary sleeper he was getting the chance to be, and we would be fine. We would have the option to get some rest and have additional cuddles.

In any case, what indeed occurred? Neither of us got any rest for three entire days, and it was my shortcoming. If I had recently had the option to unwind, he would have been fine. He realized his Mother was twisted tight, and I moved that worry to him, and he couldn't loosen up himself. I realize they state all youngsters feel our pressure and tension, and I trust it. However, I likewise believe a few children feel it more strongly than others, and my child is one of them. I've heard him inquire as to whether they were frantic at an extremely young age in a manner that sounded froze. It resembles he knows whether somebody is disturbed; he is going to feel it and necessities to get ready for it.

At the point when he was around 1, we were remaining in line at the supermarket, and he continued gazing at a man, a man who appeared to be splendidly ordinary and decent; however, he was frozen of him. He clung to me so tight and continued covering his head. At that point, it happened again with a lady when we were in line at a café. He disclosed to me he feared her. This turned out to be a piece of his life, and now at 14, I can determine what he is thinking, just by how he takes a gander at others. He is so mindful of his environment and can feel other's feelings, which can be acceptable on occasion, yet I realize he wishes he could turn it off. Calm his brain, and be. On the off chance that we go to a family assembling or gathering, he gets on things like pressure between two individuals or somebody feeling dismal then he needs to discuss it ("unload it") immediately because it causes him so much uneasiness.

I also am an empath, so I had the option to detect it in him immediately. I realize it very well may be debilitating, high, and befuddling all simultaneously. Judith Orloff M.D. composed a great article about raising an empath for Brain research. Today that is very useful. She clarifies an empathic youngster has a "sensory system which response all the more rapidly and firmly to outside upgrades including worry." From multiple points of view, this can be a lot for the kid to feel and can prompt "tactile over-burden" as they "see more, believe more, intuit more and experience feelings more." What some may believe is a youngster simply being excessively touchy or sensational, are they attempting to adapt to every one of these sentiments and feelings they are encountering.

Orloff says they may not appreciate certain fragrances or brilliant lights, and "their sensitivities can get ambushed by our coarse world." Since most children can't get expressive what is new with their feelings, it's our activity as guardians to assist them with comprehension and adapt to their sentiments and attempt to distinguish the things that may set them off. Orloff suggests perceiving the individuals or exercises that may overstimulate your youngster. Things like over-planned days, vicious network shows, and no alone time are regular triggers and can influence your kid's rest designs and their dispositions. It's imperative to take note of your youngster is absorbing others' feelings, particularly those of dear loved ones, and they don't have "indistinguishable components from non-empath kids to screen out the light, commotion, and the tumult of groups," says Orloff. Empathic kids can regularly be named as "modest," or "touchy" and are once in a while misdiagnosed with misery. (Even though empathic kids can positively be discouraged, this isn't generally the situation.)

It's simple for our empathic kids to feel misconstrued, and Orloff says first we should draw out the best in our youngsters by supporting their "sensitivities as a statement of greatness, empathy, and profundity." There's nothing amiss with being so in line with others that their feelings and emotions come off on you; truth be told, I think it is a superpower. Be that as it may, it very well may be disappointing for our children, just as for their parent, to oversee. Significantly, our empathic children acknowledge there is nothing amiss with them, and being more delicate and natural than others is not an awful thing. In essence, you cannot help how you feel about specific individuals or circumstances. You can, in any case, oversee them or avoid individuals or occasions that cause you an excess of stress. Self-care, and realizing when to look at, is essential for empathic children (and grown-ups as well). Empaths feel things on the other level. We can't resist. It's what our identity is. I am glad to be one, I am pleased to raise one, and on the off chance that you solicit me, the world needs a more considerable amount of them.

Practical Exercises for Empaths.

Clairvoyance – this is one of the least indicated characteristics, as being besieged with feelings and energies and emotions, for the most part, mists different capacities from appearing. I've just encountered this a couple of times, automatically. I've been doing the exercises I found since I was around 11, which is the point at which my compassion came through full power and put me in hellfire. If I can recall right, it, for the most part, happens when I'm practically snoozing, and my cerebrum is showing "beta" waves. I feel that is what they call it. You'll have the option to tell if it's your considerations or not because when it transpired, it wasn't my voice. She stated, "I think they have them at PetSmart." Sounded unmistakable and like there was somebody close to me. This one I have not created anything to create it additionally, cause heck, we Empaths have enough to manage as of now.

The following levels have more to do with the Empath's condition. Empaths are signs of a passionate flight or battle reaction, so they should consistently know about their health. Our watchmen are always up, continually watching individuals, watching the climate, everything to know about potential perils, physical and profound. Creature correspondence – Presently, this isn't caring for motion pictures where creatures speak up and begin talking English. This is the place a touch of clairvoyance, clairsentience, and Claircognizance combine. When addressing the beast, it's more than a "knowing" as present-day agnostics depict it. The Empath feels a surge of feeling, unmistakably, not human. With this surge comes sentiments of the bodies that aren't our species and comprehension of the character of the creature. Empaths won't slaughter an animal or living thing. It took me everlastingly to have the option to weed my nursery without feeling blame, by turning a few "stations" off not to get those signs.

Flor apathy – as I call it, is the capacity to peruse and speak with plants, which is far not the same as talking with creatures. I address the herbs that I develop. The signs I get aren't surges of energies; progressively like spikes that ascent and fall on outlines. The powers I get while doing so reveal to me the state of mind of the plant and what it needs right now, i.e., water, less sun, and so on. This can likewise incorporate having the option to share the memory of a plant. Science currently realizes they are fit for the mind with a "cognizance" that we can impeccably characterize yet. At the point when my plants' leaves begin kicking the bucket, I register to perceive how much vitality they are attempting to provide for that leaf. If they are placing a ton of spirit into the perishing leaves to try to fix them, there's not a great deal of enthusiasm going to enable the plant to sprout and develop. When finely tuned, the correspondence is more close to home and dissimilar to a vitality radio broadcast; this is the point at which the need "sexual orientation" of the plant is resolved, and you can talk with the real soul of the plant as opposed to merely the physical and enthusiastic byways of the living being.

Geomancy – this is the capacity to peruse the land. This likewise incorporates feeling ley lines, underground springs, and so on. Empaths likewise get amazingly unhinged before catastrophic events. Alongside these levels, the Empath's physical faculties are likewise touchy. They read non-verbal communication and outward appearances like perusing a book and can hear and fathom feelings that spill from another's tongue like it's a melody they've been tuning in again and again for quite a long time. This is the reason you can't mislead an Empath. I mean you can, because we won't generally get down on you about it, however, be careful. The principle issue with Empaths is we are fundamentally a break in universes. We are focused on where the profound and physical domains float and meet. Empaths are continually going about as a capacity for energies. As a result of this, Empaths are become ill effectively and consistently have a youth loaded up with affliction. My first birthday celebration, I had a twofold ear infection. At the point when I was 8, I had influenza, pneumonia, a cold, and more ear infections across the board summer. I've had pneumonia and bronchitis a higher number of times than I can check. Thus, we should continually watch and ground some of the time each hour.

Empaths get vitality continually, however with preparing, we can perform the reason for these blessings: send energy. We can get the feelings of another, and venture feelings also. This is the reason. Empaths make such extraordinary healers. We get information on torment since we can take care of business. Doing this, we become genuine chemist of vitality and feelings. We can transform suffering into comfort, worry into harmony, and so forth. From birth, Empaths are continually aware of others. While we may not comprehend the idea of what we do, we move our vitality (rings, as I call them) around the vitality fields of others. We generally do so naturally and unwittingly to comprehend what is around us, ensure we are sheltered, see all sides of an occasion, and so forth. The individuals who are not prepared past simply feeling and establishing are only wipes for energies; we frequently don't have the foggiest idea where we stop, and someone else starts. While this is incredible is connections once in a while, it's total damnation in a market or shopping centre. You're essentially conveying the entire *** town around with you while doing tasks. Most can't be in broad daylight for over 60 minutes if that much. However, with control, the Empath can figure out how to avoid and divert energies, can deliberately decide to open up to just a single individual at once, and know when they can securely allow their gatekeeper to down. While most Empaths display these practices, some don't work by any means. I mean by any stretch of the imagination.

These are individuals who mostly appear to be numb to everything, they scarcely show outward appearance, unreservedly open up, and have a high resistance for torment. This is the Disassociated Empath. Rather than feeling, they don't. Rather than getting or anticipating, their passionate and otherworldly frameworks are indeed closed down or stopped up. More often than not, this outcome from some awful experience that was excessively hard on the empathic nature so it "left." Right up 'til today, I have not discovered how to turn around this. The following will be the finish of this post, yet ideally, the exercises to come will help you in building up your inclinations and will ideally help in tidying up this wreckage of a world a few. I'm not going to incorporate the "characteristics" of an Empath as those are shown by pretty much every individual. On the off chance that you're a genuine Empath, at that point, you've managed the equivalent I have. You'll know.

Exercises for The Troubled and Creating Empath

Establishing

This is the most basic method each individual ought to learn, particularly the Empath. Each father's vitality as they go about existence. Empaths gather 5x the measure of vitality others do. Keep in mind; we are a verge in the gravity between domains, so we're fundamentally sitting in the vivacious channel, getting a lot of stuff that doesn't go down. Close your eyes and, with your physical faculties, feel the earth underneath you. Geomancy is utilized here to contact the earth. Dive as deep into the soil as you can, feeling the worms and stones underneath your feet. Presently broaden the vitality of your body down, starting from the tips of your toes. These are your "underlying foundations." I additionally push life from the give of my feet down to turn into a tapped base of sorts. At the point when your underlying foundations are sufficiently profound, name their reason to deplete any vitality that isn't your own, so you're not clutching it. You'll see the shade of energy that leaves. This will be the shade of outside vitality for you. Do this each morning and night. Some should do this on an hourly premise.

Protecting

This is the following procedure I saw as accommodating to my compassion. Close your eyes, and envision a shield of white vitality around you. See the surface of this shield. Life isn't static, so you'll see the energy whirling and turning. Concentrate on this shield for as long as possible, filling it with enough vitality to last. Name its motivation: to allow healthy life from the earth in and to consume off all remote energy. Do this until you're ready to deal with positive vitality from others securely. Snap your fingers multiple times to "take care of business." This should be done during that time as you feel it wear off. Furthermore, you'll know; my state of mind transforms, I get drowsy, and so forth. It's like being hit with a medication you're attempting to keep away from.

Clearing

An atmosphere of the Empath is likely the hardest spot to get energies that don't should be there out. It resembles driving around for something in a gallon container of nectar. Tears can be made in the emanation by terrifying encounters, medication and liquor use, and awful physical wellbeing decisions. These gaps need fixing by applying nonstop flows of vitality to the spot until its "settles" or "gets" into the draw of your air. There are various levels that I won't talk about here; however, individuals state there are commonly 5-7 layers. In any case, that doesn't make a difference to the Empath; what is essential if we get most of the entirety of the garbage out.

Hold your hand out from you, palms confronting you. Slowing being your palms internal. Stop when you feel shivering or "push" on your palm. This means when you've hit one of the layers. Tenderly push through and allow your hands to go where they have to, going about as a magnet in gathering all the negative vitality that didn't go during the establishing procedure. At the point when you feel that you've gotten as much as possible without anyone else, slowly run your hands in cold water to wash the energies off. Some additionally prefer to poke their hands down into the earth to ground the energies out and afterwards wash their hands with just water. Next, you should wipe the "dust" off your air by feeling for the first layer as in the past and delicately cleaning the vitality field of anything sticking to it. End a similar way: soil or water, or both.

Contemplation

Ordinary contemplation rehearses basic in adjusting the idea of the Empath. Chakra exercises are incredible here also. Turning it down, Envision your sympathy as a lively radio. The volume is the brilliance of your external vitality field, which attracts different energies to you. Inside you, see the dial in the centre of your chest. Turn this dial to diminish the lights and crank the volume down along these lines turning your affectability down with it. You'll increase better control with training. At the point when you do this, notice your present affections for the following hour and check whether they are your own or somebody else's. Turn it up and see the changes. This will lead you to recognize your vitality and that of others.

Not A Chance

I like this one best, as I use it when out in the open. It's equivalent to protecting, except it's the shield is named to push every single remote vitality away once they get so close (around 5 feet).

Mostly, as you stroll out in the open, you'll be strolling in an air pocket that is by all accounts in a bog of vitality, merely pushing everything off the beaten path as you go. Which is the reason I call this "Probably not." Not today.

Water

Water is the most exceptional partner of the Empath, with stone coming next. At the point when the Empath is overly sensitive, getting into a hot shower will ground you once again into your physical faculties and parity out your energies, even the remote ones, so they are simpler to deal with. Empaths are delicate to vitality like the skin is to fire: water alleviates the torches and cools you. Life is vibration, and with enough, it becomes heat. Water chills off the energies by slowing their waves along these lines slowing down the procedure and their effect on the Empath's framework.

Become Acquainted with You

Empaths are continually interfacing with things and individuals, to such an extent, the free light of themselves. Practice strategies of feeling how your feet and hands twist, feeling your chest rise, and fall with the breath, feel the torment you experience while stepping on hot cement. Ground yourself into you. This will help in grasping the suffering of others, so you don't turn out to be wholly enmeshed into their frameworks. With training, this will give you the power over your faculties to "step out" when you pick and how far you wish to go.

Mindfulness

Sit alone someplace and essentially become mindful of your environment, genuinely and enthusiastically. Feel the individuals in different places in the house, the trees outside, and so forth. This will develop the Empathic cognizance, so you are increasingly mindful of the things affecting you, the energies in your condition, the wellbeing of the spot, and so forth. This will likewise heighten different endowments usually, for example, geomancy, mediumship, and so forth. Following quite a while of training, these exercises will turn out to be natural. You'll need to turn up your affectability and mindfulness to utilize your compassion. You presently have what you have to at long last get your and the of others, together. You're not insane, just blessedly screwed. Deal with yourself, know yourself and be sheltered.

Essential Oil Recipes for Anxiety

Fragrant healing is the act of breathing in the aroma of essential oils to improve your prosperity. One hypothesis of how they work is that by animating the smell receptors in your nose, they can send messages to your sensory system. They are additionally thought to affect the body's compound and vitality frameworks subtly. Along these lines, fragrant healing is regularly utilized as an appropriate solution for ease tension and stress. The U.S. Nourishment and Medication Organization (FDA) doesn't control essential oils, so be tireless in your training. You should utilize remedial evaluation oils that don't contain engineered aroma. Essential oils must be weakened with a bearer oil before they're applied to the skin. This decreases your danger of bothering. For grown-ups, every 15 drops of essential oil ought to be weakened with 1 ounce of transporter oil. The utilization of essential oils in youngsters ought to be under the supervision of their human services supplier. For kids, the blend is substantially more weakened with a proportion is 3 to 6 drops of essential oil to 1 ounce of transporter oil. Some famous bearer oils are almond, coconut, and jojoba. Essential oils ought to never be ingested, despite cases on the web that propose something else. There's insufficient research on any one essential oil to demonstrate it's protected to swallow. Every essential oil is altogether different, and some are poisonous. Continue perusing to get familiar with the essential oils you can use to diminish your side effects of uneasiness.

Lavender Essential Oil

One of the most well-known essential oils for unwinding is Lavender. Lavender essential oil is an unquestionable requirement have if you consistently experience pressure and nervousness. It has been demonstrated to reestablish the sensory system by bringing down pulse and pulse. It can assist with quieting the nerves, conciliate fretfulness, and improve rest quality. Utilize a lavender rollerball to apply to your sanctuaries and wrists, or consolidate with a transporter for a loosening up knead oil.

Rose Essential Oil

Rose essential oil is removed from rose petals, and its fragrance is eminent for alleviating feelings, cerebral pains, and adjusting hormones. Rose is known for fortifying the heart in times of high pressure, sorrow, and sadness. Use in a steaming shower or apply straightforwardly on the skin to help with mind-set swings, hormones, and feelings.

Bergamot Essential Oil

Bergamot essential oil is delivered from the strip of the fragrant citrus organic product. It is frequently utilized in conventional Chinese medication to improve the progression of vitality, battle bacterial contaminations, and bolster stomach related wellbeing. It is a viable energizer because of its mind-set improving characteristics, advancing sentiments of delight, newness, and vitality. Bergamot essential oil improves blood flow, invigorates hormonal emissions, and stomach related wellbeing, carrying equalization to the body.

German Chamomile Essential Oil

On the off chance that you love chamomile tea, you will value the quieting impacts of Chamomile essential oil. Chamomile advances inward quiet, lessens uneasiness, and quiets the sensory system. It can likewise be utilized to decrease the aggravation of the stomach related tract, managing state of mind, and feelings of anxiety. For stress help, join chamomile essential oil with a transporter oil, and apply to the sunlight-based plexus and midsection button.

Melissa Essential Oil

Lemon Analgesic, additionally generally known as Melissa, has been utilized for a long time. Known for its therapeutic and inspiring characteristics, it has additionally been given the name "solution of life." Melissa essential oil quiets the brain, helps invulnerability, and fortifies the sensory system. It can go about as a stimulant and discharge sentiments of bitterness and stress. Add to a hot shower or back rub straightforwardly on the skin to advance profound unwinding, diminishing pressure, and uneasiness.

Jasmine Essential Oil

Jasmine essential oil is generally utilized in parts of Asia as an appropriate solution for tension, stress, a sleeping disorder, and melancholy. In China, Jasmine has been regularly used to detox and clear the respiratory framework. It goes about as a characteristic calming just as effects affecting the cerebrum improving temperament and vitality levels. Apply straightforwardly to your wrists or neck to advance unwinding or add a couple of drops to a hot shower.

Clary Sage Essential Oil

With a beautiful natural smell, Clary Sage is compelling in quieting pressure and uneasiness. The oil goes about as an upper by advancing sentiments of prosperity and inward harmony. Clary Sage is additionally referred to go nearly as an incredible hormone balancer and helps decrease the side effects of PMS. Apply straightforwardly to feet or heartbeat focuses on improving balance hormones. On the other hand, consolidate with a couple of drops of chamomile to appreciate in a hot shower.

Neroli Essential Oil

Gotten from the citrus product of a similar name, Neroli can be utilized for a scope of afflictions, including uneasiness help. Old Egyptian clerics utilized Neroli essential oil to mend their bodies, brains, and spirits. It goes about as a soothing, which controls the metabolic framework and discharges sentiments of outrage, crabbiness, and stress. It loosens up both body and soul. Add a couple of drops to a hot shower or back rub straightforwardly on the skin to alleviate pressure and uneasiness.

Basil Essential Oil

One of the lesser-known essential oils, Basil, is a standout amongst other essential oils to lessen tension and improve the state of mind. Thought about the sovereign of herbs in India, it is revered and treated as sacrosanct because of its exceptionally advantageous properties. Basil essential oil has a quieting impact on the sensory system, decreasing tension, exhaustion, mental strain, and wretchedness. It additionally goes about as a characteristic energizer, advancing harmony and clearness of the brain. Add a couple of drops to your diffuser, and appreciate the alleviating and loosening up the fragrance. Still can't choose which essential oil to pick? Attempt our Quiet and Destress essential oil mix. It joins orange, patchouli, and sandalwood essential oils to help dissolve away pressure and quiet and calm psyche and body.

Lavender

Lavender is one of the most well-known fragrance-based treatment oils. As indicated by 2012 research, lavender scent-based treatment is thought to quiet uneasiness by affecting the limbic framework, the piece of the cerebrum that controls feelings. The most effective method to utilize: Appreciate a loosening up the lavender shower by consolidating a few drops of lavender oil with a teaspoon of transporter oil or an unscented shower gel. Mix the blend into warm bathwater not long before entering.

Sweet basil

Sweet basil essential oil originates from a similar herb that you use to make marinara sauce. In fragrant healing, it's ideal for helping quiet the mind and eases the pressure. As per a 2015 study trusted Source on mice, the phenol mixes in sweet basil oil alleviated nervousness. These mixes were seen as less calming than the tension medicine diazepam. Step by step instructions to utilize: Include a few drops of sweet basil oil to a room diffuser or breathe in through an inhaler tube.

Chamomile

Chamomile is notable for its unwinding and calming properties and inebriating fragrance. There isn't a lot of research on chamomile essential oil for tension. Research Trusted Source has appeared, in any case, that chamomile enhancements may profit individuals with mellow to direct summed up uneasiness issue. The most effective method to utilize: Backrub weakened chamomile oil into your skin or added it to a steaming shower.

Yang

Flower scented yang is utilized in fragrance-based treatment to advance unwinding. As indicated by a recent report on medical attendants, breathing in a mix of yang, lavender, and bergamot brings down pressure and tension levels, circulatory strain, pulse, and serum cortisol. Step by step instructions to utilize: Apply weakened yang to your skin, add to a room diffuser, or breathe in legitimately.

Frankincense

Frankincense oil is produced using the gum of the Boswellia tree. It has a musky, sweet smell that is thought to ease tension. As per a recent report, a fragrance-based treatment hand kneads utilizing a mix of frankincense, lavender, and bergamot improved stress, sadness, and torment in individuals with terminal malignancy. Step by step instructions to utilize: Backrub weakened frankincense oil onto your hands or feet. You can likewise add frankincense to a diffuser.

An anxiety condition isn't created or brought about by a single factor; however, a blend of things. Various components assume a job, including character factors, troublesome educational encounters, and physical wellbeing. A few people who experience anxiety conditions may have a hereditary inclination towards anxiety, and these conditions can here and there run in the family. Be that as it may, having a parent or close relative experience anxiety or other emotional wellness condition doesn't mean you'll naturally create fear. Research recommends that individuals with certain character qualities are bound to have a concern. For instance, kids who are fussbudgets, effortlessly bothered, bashful, hindered, need confidence, or need to control everything, now and then create anxiety during youth, puberty, or as grown-ups. While a few people may encounter an anxiety condition without anyone else, others may meet numerous anxiety conditions or other emotional wellbeing conditions. Despondency and anxiety conditions frequently happen together. It's essential to check for and get help for every one of these conditions simultaneously. A few people who experience anxiety may utilize liquor or different medications to assist them in dealing with their situation.

At times, this may prompt individuals to build up a substance use issue alongside their anxiety condition. Liquor and substance use can disturb anxiety conditions, especially as the impacts of the substance wear off. It's imperative to check for and get help for any substance use conditions simultaneously. Anxiety and sadness are on the ascent among America's childhood and, regardless of whether they buy and by experience the ill effects of these conditions or not, seven-in-ten teenagers today consider them to be severe issues among their friends. Worry about psychological wellness cuts across sex, racial and financial lines, with generally equivalent portions of adolescents across segment bunches saying it is a noteworthy issue in their locale. Fewer teenagers, however, still considerable offers, voice worry over harassing, illicit drug use, and liquor utilization. More than four-in-ten states these are serious issues influencing individuals their age in the region where they live, as indicated by a Seat Exploration Center study of U.S. teenagers ages 13 to 17.

Extracurricular Exercises

Regards to the weight's youngsters face, scholastics best the rundown: 61% of teenagers state they feel a ton of strain to get passing marks. By examination, around three-in-ten states, they think a great deal of pressure to look great (29%) and to fit in socially (28%), while about one-in-five feel also forced to be engaged with extracurricular exercises and to be acceptable at sports (21% each). And keeping in mind that about portion of youngsters see chronic drug use and liquor utilization as serious issues among individuals their age, less than the one-in-ten state they buy and by feeling a great deal of strain to utilize drugs (4%) or to drink liquor (6%). The weight youngsters think to do well in school is tied in any event to some extent to their post-graduation objectives. Around six-in-ten youngsters (59%) state, they intend to go to a four-year school after they finish secondary school, and these adolescents are more likely than the individuals who have different designs to state they face a great deal of strain to get passing marks. Young ladies are almost certain than young men to state they intend to go to a four-year school (68% versus 51%, individually), and they're likewise bound to state they stress much over getting into their preferred school (37% versus 26%). Current examples in school enlistment among 18-to 20-year-olds who are no longer in secondary school mirror these sex elements. In 2017, 64% of ladies right now who were no longer in secondary school were tried out school (counting two-and four-year universities), contrasted, and 55% of their male counterparts. In numerous ways, be that as it may, the long-haul objectives of young men and young ladies don't very necessarily.

Around nine-in at least ten in each gathering state having an occupation or profession they appreciate would be amazingly or imperative to them as a grown-up (97% of young ladies and 93% of young men state this). Also, equal portions of young ladies and young men see getting hitched (45% and half, individually) and having kids (41% and 39%) as needs for them, by and by, when they grow up. In any case, young men are impressively almost certain than young ladies to the state. Having a great deal of cash would be amazingly or imperative to them (61% versus 41%). While young men and young ladies face vast numbers of similar weights – for instance, they're about similarly liable to state they feel strain to get passing marks – their day by day encounters vary in different manners. Young ladies are almost certain than young men to state they face a ton of strain to look great: About 33% of young ladies (35%) state this is the situation, contrasted, and 23%

of young men. Also, a more significant portion of young ladies than young men state they frequently feel tense or anxious about their day (36% versus 23%, individually, state they think along these lines each day or consistently). Simultaneously, young ladies are bound to state they routinely get excited about something they learn at school: 33% of young ladies say this happens each day or consistently, versus 21% of young men. And keeping in mind that little portions of young ladies (7%) and young men (5%) state they get in a tough situation at school every day or practically day by day, young ladies are more probable than young men to state this never transpires (48% versus 33%).

In an expansion to these sexual orientation contrasts, the study additionally discovers a few differences in the encounters and desires of teenagers across salary gatherings. Around seven-in-ten adolescents in family units with yearly wages of $75,000 or increasingly (72%) state they intend to go to a four-year school after they finish secondary school; 52% of those in families with livelihoods somewhere in the range of $30,000 and $74,999 and 42% in families with earnings below $30,000 state the equivalent. Among youngsters who intend to go to a four-year school, those in families with livelihoods below $75,000 express undeniably more worry than those with higher wages about having the option to manage the cost of college. And while a generally small portion of adolescents by and large state they face a great deal of strain to help their family monetarily, teenagers in lower-salary families are bound to state they probably face some weight right now. There are likewise contrasts by family pay in the issues adolescents states exist in their networks. Teenagers in lower-pay-family units are bound to state adolescent pregnancy is a significant issue among individuals their age in the zone where they live: 55% of youngsters in families with salaries below $30,000 state this, versus 38% of those in the centre pay gathering, and a considerably littler offer (22%) of those in family units with livelihoods of $75,000 or more. Contrasted and youngsters in the higher-pay gathering, those in family units with livelihoods below $30,000 are additionally bound to refer to harassing, illicit drug use, neediness, and possess as serious issues.

Various Evaluations

Youngsters in lower-salary family units additionally have various evaluations of the measure of time; they go through with their folks. Four-in-ten youngsters in family units with salaries below $30,000 state they invest too little energy with their people, contrasted and around one-in-five adolescents in families with higher wages. These are among the critical discoveries of an overview of 920 U.S. adolescents ages 13 to 17 directed online Sept. 17-Nov. 25, 2018.1 All through the report, "youngsters" alludes to those ages 13 to 17. About six-in-ten teenagers (59%) state they intend to go to a four-year school after they finish secondary school; 12% arrangement to go to a two-year school, 5% plan to work all day, 4% plan to try out a specialized or professional school and 3% plan to join the military. Another 13% of teenagers state they don't know what they'll do after secondary school. Young ladies are more likely than young men to state they intend to go to a four-year school in the wake of completing secondary school: 68% of young ladies state this, contrasted and about a portion of young men (51%). Contrasts in the shares of young men and young ladies who say they intend to go to a two-year school, take a crack at a specialized or professional school, work all day, or join the military after secondary school is little or no critical. Among teenagers with, at any rate, one parent with a four-year college education or higher, just as those in family units with yearly earnings of $75,000 or progressively, around seven-in-ten state, they intend to go to a four-year school after secondary school. By examination, about a portion of adolescents whose guardians don't have a four-year college education or with family earnings below $75,000 state the equivalent. Some 65% of teenagers who state they intend to go to a four-year school after secondary school says they stress probably some over having the option to manage the cost of school.

Natural life merchants at business sectors like Huanan need a "supported and solid source" of supply, so domesticated animals' homesteads to breed the creatures fit the bill, he says. Be that as it may, another outcome of China's exchange untamed life for the feasting table is creatures that don't typically live respectively in the wild are put together in confines, regularly in restricted, unsanitary conditions. That makes for a dangerous potential pool of virus blends, says Timothy Sheahan, an associate educator of the study of disease transmission at the College of North Carolina, Church Slope. At the point when that marvel hits the human natural pecking order, the outcome can be lethal, says Erasmus Clinical Center's Koopmans. The WHO says 70 per cent of infection-causing pathogens found in the previous 50 years originate from creatures.

Yet, researchers attempting to follow the sources of the new coronavirus still can't conclusively say it made a move from a creature to a human at the Huanan advertise because the beast and patient zero – the principal individual to be tainted – haven't yet been distinguished. It's conceivable the connection may never be indisputably found. Helps or AIDS was named all things considered in the US in 1982, and in the next year, the virus that causes it, HIV, was found, as per the non-benefit Helps Establishment in the US. It wasn't until 1999, or after 17 years, that a chimpanzee subspecies in Focal Africa was named as the feasible wellspring of the virus, most likely tainting people who chased it for meat and changing into HIV inside human hosts. The most particular known instance of contamination was found in a blood test taken from a man in 1959 in Kinshasa, in then-Belgian Congo, the foundation says. It takes note of that it's as yet not known how that man got tainted, yet Helps at that point spread across Africa for a considerable length of time before discovering its way to the US and different nations.

In like manner with Sirs. The WHO has said the sickness is "believed to be" a creature virus that spread from an "up 'til now unsure" creature like bats, which at that point moved to people in China from civet felines. Another analysis on the wellspring of the new coronavirus has gone to the likelihood that it might not have originated from a creature in the Huanan showcase. This referred to distributed clinical records appearing in the most particular case admitted to the medical clinic. The contaminated individual had no known relationship with the market. That has prompted theory it came into the city from another course, perhaps going between has unnoticed as it transformed. Different hypotheses propose the virus "got away" from the Wuhan Organization of Virology, which constructed one of the world's biggest databases of viral strains found in bats. The lab and one of its driving bat virus scientists have dismissed that hypothesis.

The proof in following Guides and Sirs shows that conclusively wedding a virus to its unique host, demonstrating how it arrived, and afterwards how it bounced to a recognized human patient zero is inexact science, best case scenario. Be that as it may, when it "broke out" in Wuhan, the way of SARS-CoV-2 could then be found in the path of the sickened and the dead, moving among its new human has and going with them as they took transports, prepares and flights inside China and onwards to abroad occasion goals in Thailand, conferences in Germany and excursions on journey boats to Japan. In any case, pursuing it the other way, withdraw the evolved form of life, back through the spit or blood that could have caused cross-species viral exchange between two animals, and go into the ranch or backwoods that was home to the contaminated animal leaves no such noticeable path, just a hereditary one.

The path of that "ultra-visible, ultra-filterable substance" alluded to by German bacteriologists over 100 years prior. What made the following of the virus conceivable is the work done by China's analysts at establishments that crunched the pathogen in hereditary sequencers. By January 12, the virus' genetic code had been transferred by those analysts into a worldwide open-get to the database and imparted to the WHO. "It's presumably the most punctual, quickest turn out of a genome in relationship with an episode we've at any point seen," says virologist Ian Mackay, a partner teacher at the College of Queensland in Australia. "Also, it's so fundamental to our comprehension of what's going on," the virologist says, disclosing that it assists with distinguishing the source creature and for chip away at immunization to start. Investigation of the hereditary make-up likewise uncovered an at no other time seen highlight right now coronavirus: clingy sugar atoms that may permit it to conceal itself from assaults by the invulnerable human framework.

It additionally yielded a waitlist of potential creature supplies – key suspects are among China's 147 known types of bat. The horseshoe bat (Rhinolophus affine) conveys a strain with 96 per cent closeness to the new coronavirus, distinguished in January by famous bat coronavirus specialist Shi Zhongli of the Wuhan Foundation of Virology. That 4 per cent contrast demonstrates another creature likely interfered with the bat and a human, with the virus reshuffling its hereditary make-up to all the more likely tie to cells in the new host, and afterwards again when it bounced into people. The flaky pangolin has shown up on the potential line-up of go-between creatures after analysts found a viral strain with up to 99 per cent hereditary comparability to the novel coronavirus inside one of the warm-blooded creatures. There is a full scope of animals that could correspondingly convey related viruses," says irresistible sickness master Eddie Holmes of the College of Sydney. This issue likely won't be settled until we have done significantly increasingly creature testing," he says.

Also, 70% express probably some worry about getting into their preferred school. Psychological wellness is a global issue. Dysfunctional behaviour influences individuals of each race, class, and nationality. Access to emotional well-being assets is a worldwide emergency. That entrance is influenced and traded off (or encouraged) by factors from all degrees of society: authoritative, therapeutic, network, business, relational, person. The disgrace that psychological sickness isn't a particular disease, or that it just influences the frail, or that it is despicable, those marks of shame penetrate every one of those levels. This incorporates governments defunding emotional well-being care, therapeutic experts rejecting or staying away from issues of dysfunctional behaviour in their patients, networks who walk out on their most in danger individuals, and families who shroud behind dividers of secrecy. The Mayo Center has some accommodating exhortation concerning how we can help understand our psychological wellness emergency.

To begin with, get treatment from any place you are agreeable and capable (be that a companion, a book, or an expert), and understand that doing so is an extraordinary, beneficial thing. As the Center notes, don't let disgrace make self-uncertainty and disgrace. Disgrace doesn't only originate from others. You may erroneously accept that your condition is an indication of individual shortcomings or that you ought to have the option to control it without assistance.

Instructing yourself about your condition

Looking for mental directing, instructing yourself about your condition, and associating with others with psychological maladjustment can assist you with increasing confidence and beat damaging self-judgment. The following significant activity is to keep away from segregation, as this regularly worsens the issue. This could begin with something straightforward, for example, routinely going out for a walk or joining a networking club, or include some progressively devoted work, for example, entering a care group. What's more, something that we would all be able to do is take a stand in opposition to disgrace. The Center proceeds, consider communicating your feelings on occasions, in letters to the manager or on the Web. It can help impart fortitude in others confronting comparable difficulties and teach the general population about dysfunctional behaviour. Maybe, of course, worries about managing schools are increasing every day among youngsters in lower-pay-family units. Among teenagers who state they intend to go to a four-year school, around seventy-five per cent (76%) in family units with salaries below $75,00to state they stress probably some over having the option to bear the cost of it, contrasted and 55% of those in families with livelihoods or $75,000 or more.

Looking ahead, virtually all adolescents state they seek to have a vocation or profession they appreciate: 63% state this would be critical to them, by and by, as grown-ups, and another 32% state it would be significant. Most teenagers additionally state helping others who are in need would be incredibly (42%) or (39%) essential to them when they grow up. Youngsters give a lower demand for marriage and children. About half (47%) state getting hitched would be incredibly or critical to them as grown-ups, and 39% say the equivalent regarding having youngsters. With regards to fortune and acclaim, 51% of teenagers state having a great deal of cash would be incredibly or critical to them, while generally few (11%) say the equivalent regarding getting renowned. Typically, young men and young ladies have comparative yearnings. Usually, equivalent portions of young men and young ladies state getting hitched, having children, and having a vocation or profession they appreciate would be amazingly or critical to them as grown-ups. Be that as it may, young men (61%) are almost certain than young ladies (41%) to the state having a ton of cash when they grow up would be amazingly or critical to them.

Incidental anxiety is an ordinary piece of life. You may feel on edge when confronted with an issue busy working, before stepping through an exam or settling on a significant choice. In any case, anxiety issue includes more than transitory stress or dread. For an individual with an anxiety issue, the anxiety doesn't leave and can deteriorate after some time. The sentiments can meddle with day by day exercises, for example, work execution, school work, and connections. There are a few distinct kinds of anxiety issues. Models incorporate summed up anxiety issues, alarm issues, and social anxiety issues. Anxiety UK propelled an understudy manual for anxiety. Here are some self-improvement tips: On the off chance that you feel yourself begin to freeze, let yourself know: don't freeze; you can do this. Self-talk can lessen anxiety. Work on controlling your relaxing. Have a go at taking in through your nose for four seconds, holding for two seconds, at that point, breathing out through your mouth for six seconds.

How to Identify Negative Thoughts Patterns When They Present Themselves?

On the off chance that you discover huge occupied talk rooms an issue, start by sitting close to the exit. Record addresses so you can tune in back to any bits you missed. Break coursework and papers into little lumps. This takes a touch of arranging and means not leaving everything to the latest possible time, yet it fights off anxiety. The most investigation into youngsters' abilities to focus proposes a cutoff of 40 minutes, so work fifty-fifty hour pieces with brief breaks between for a beverage or a much-needed refresher. Stalling can be the restless individual's greatest foe. Persuade yourself to work for only five minutes. When you've begun, you might have the option to continue onward. If not, at any rate, you have accomplished five minutes of work. Be thoughtful to yourself, however, trained. It is anything but difficult to turn into the cause of all your problems. Acknowledge that things are intense at present and consider how you can function with your cerebrum to get things going. Moderate your caffeine and liquor admission.

Exorbitant caffeine builds indications of anxiety, and even though liquor is a relaxant, it may not support the following day. Recall you are not the only one. Every other person may look as though they are adapting fine, yet a significant number of them are battling as well. Converse with individuals. Follow a healthy everyday practice of eating, resting, and work out. Indeed, even 30 minutes strolling a day can lessen anxiety. Upset dozing and consumption are exemplary backups to stress and can make an endless loop. If this is going on, look for help. Essential consideration doctors and therapists analyze somebody as having an anxiety issue if manifestations happen for a half year on a more significant number of days than not and fundamentally meddle with the individual's capacity to work at home, work, or school. Specialists perform physical and mental assessments to preclude different reasons for the manifestations of anxiety. Cardiovascular infection, thyroid issues, menopause, substance misuse, and additionally tranquillize reactions, for example, from steroids, may cause events like those of an anxiety disorder. There are commonly two kinds of medicines that appear to be similarly powerful: psychological conduct treatment (CBT) and particular serotonin reuptake inhibitor (SSRI) prescriptions. The best examination that looked at them straightforwardly in kids discovered one is no superior to the next, and that consolidating the two works excellent to utilizing either alone. Intellectual, social treatment is an extremely brilliant treatment, yet the specialist must have some experience conveying it.

Replace Your Poor Coping Strategies with Good Ones

Explicit systems should be followed. There are not unreasonably numerous advisors in the US who are promptly accessible to apply those methods. Generalized Anxiety Issue (Stray) is a misrepresented anxiety and strain that endures for a considerable length of time and influences around 6.8 million Americans or about 3.1 per cent of the populace. Stray makes individuals foresee calamity and stress too much over numerous things, from more significant concerns, for example, wellbeing, cash, or work to increasingly routine matters, for example, vehicle fixes or arrangements. Stray influences twice the same number of ladies as men, and the anxiety turns out to be so extreme, typical life and connections become impeded.

Physical manifestations can join it, for example, weariness, cerebral pains, muscle strain and hurts, trouble swallowing, trembling, jerking, peevishness, sweating, and hot flashes. The turmoil ordinarily grows step by step and may start whenever during life, even though the hazard is most elevated among youth and middle age. It is analyzed when somebody goes through, at any rate, a half year stressing exorbitantly without a particular focal point of the dread and powerlessness to control the anxiety. Obsessive-Enthusiastic Turmoil (OCD) is an anxiety issue set apart by disturbing thoughts and formal practices. Fixations are monotonous musings or motivations, for example, a dread of getting contaminated from another person's germs or harming a friend or family member. These fixations make unnecessary anxiety and worry for the individual influenced. Even though the musings are nosy and undesirable, the individual with OCD can't stop them. Impulses are tedious practices individuals with OCD feel constrained to actively trying to control or diminish the anxiety made by the fixations. This can incorporate things like continually watching that a stove is set for forestall a fire, or regular cleaning or hand-washing to evade pollution. Frenzy issue is portrayed by startling and rehashed scenes of extreme dread joined by physical side effects that may incorporate chest torment, heart palpitations, the brevity of breath, unsteadiness, or stomach trouble. Unexpected assaults of terror describe it, generally joined by a beating heart, dampness, shortcoming, faintness, or dazedness.

During these assaults, individuals with alarm issues may flush or feel cooled; their hands may shiver or feel numb; and they may encounter sickness, chest torment, or covering sensations. Fits of anxiety, for the most part, produce a feeling of illusion, a dread of approaching fate or terror of losing control. Fits of stress can happen whenever, in any event, during rest. Post-Awful Pressure Issue (PTSD) is an anxiety issue that can create after a presentation to a frightening occasion or experience in which grave physical damage happened or was compromised. After horrendous mishaps, for example, demise, a seismic tremor, war, auto collisions, floods, or flames, it isn't extraordinary for individuals to encounter sentiments of elevated dread, stress, bitterness or outrage. On the off chance that the feelings endure, notwithstanding, or become severe, or the individual gets activated into remembering the occasion in their day by day life, this can influence the individual's capacity to work and might be an indication of PTSD. Social Fear, or Social Anxiety Issue, is an anxiety issue described by overpowering anxiety and extreme hesitance in normal social circumstances. Social fear can be restricted to just one sort of thing, for example, a dread of talking informal or casual events, or eating or drinking before others. In its most serious structure, social fear might be ample to such an extent that an individual encounters side effects nearly whenever they are around different people.

Short & Long-Term Rewards

Stress is a normal physical reaction to occasions that cause one to feel compromised or that irritated one's equalization somehow or another. At the point when the body detects threat genuine or envisioned—the body's protections get going in a fast, programmed process known as the 'battle or flight' response, or the pressure reaction. The sensory system reacts by discharging a surge of pressure hormones, including adrenaline and cortisol, that stir the body for crisis activity. Worry during improvement has frequently been viewed as a possibly problematic power, equipped for instigating sickness states if excessively drawn out or exceedingly exceptional. It can likewise, notwithstanding, favour versatility and versatile preparation that is significant to exploring a human life.

Incalculable examinations have demonstrated that severe disregard during outset, both in people and in research facility creatures, brings about strange long-haul advancement of organic frameworks engaged with the guideline of feelings. However, the reaction to push is likewise a key driver to singular improvement. The natural structure answerable for physical responses to a stressor facilitates prompt replies to extreme difficulties as well as capacities as an instrument that empowers the portrayal of a situation as ideal or undermining. Therefore, the pressure reaction framework advances long haul versatile procedures that set up the person to adapt to explicit outside difficulties. Youth everything being equal, yet particularly more youthful youngsters may think that it is hard to perceive and verbalize when they are encountering pressure. For youngsters, stress can show itself through changes in conduct. Necessary changes can incorporate touchiness, withdrawal from some time ago pleasurable exercises, routine articulation of weights, over the top grievances about the school, visit crying, a show of astonishing dreadful responses, detachment anxiety, dozing excessively or excessively little, or eating too or overly low. With teenagers, while investing more energy with and trusting in peers is a typical piece of growing up, fundamentally staying away from guardians, surrendering long-term fellowships for another arrangement of friends, or communicating casual threatening vibe toward relatives may demonstrate that the youngster is encountering enormous pressure.

Stop Absorbing Negative Energies

Taking on others' feelings could be the most significant test profoundly touchy individuals face. We can retain feelings from nearly anybody whenever: a relative we live with, the market assistant, an associate, or a much more peculiar. We increase a great deal from this one of a kind capacity—like having the option to understand others—however, we additionally follow through on a substantial cost for it. Engrossing others' feelings can make it difficult to tell which sentiments are genuinely our own. We may even feel constrained by this attribute. It can impact everything from what sort of conditions we hang out in, to who we let into our lives, to what kind of occupation we do. For instance, on the off chance that somebody is consistently feeling awful, we'll maintain a strategic distance from that individual because their negative emotions cut us down. Moreover, if we get terrible vibes from a spot, we won't go there any longer. Be that as it may, there is another approach to live. We can figure out how to flourish on the planet with our exceptional blessing, on the off chance that we have the correct devices. So here are four different ways to assist you with halting engrossing others' vitality.

Toward the day's end, it is essential to perceive both the endowments and difficulties of being an empath. In reality, as we know it where such a significant number of individuals battle to recognize and communicate feelings, compassion can appear to be a superpower. Do you regularly feel profoundly checked out the sentiments of individuals around you? Do swarms make you awkward? OK (or the individuals nearest to you) depict yourself as a touchy individual? Provided that this is true, you might be an empath. Dr Judith Orloff, a pioneer in the field, portrays empaths as the individuals who assimilate the world's delights and stresses like "enthusiastic wipes." In her book "The Empath's Survival reference: Life Methodologies for Delicate Individuals," she proposes empaths come up short on the channels a great many people use to shield themselves from excessive incitement and can't resist the urge to take in encompassing feelings and energies, regardless of whether they're acceptable, awful, or something in the middle.

Kim Engel, a San Diego-based advisor, grows this further: "Empaths have a higher affectability to outside upgrades, for example, sounds, huge characters, and wild conditions. They bring a great deal of heart and care to the world and feel things profoundly." Sounds natural? Here are 15 different signs you may be an empath. You have a great deal of compassion. The term empath originates from empathy, which is the capacity to comprehend the encounters and sentiments of others outside of your point of view. State your companion lost their canine of 15 years. Compassion is the thing that permits you to comprehend the degree of agony she's experiencing, regardless of whether you've never lost an adored pet. Be that as it may, as an empath, you make things a stride further. You sense and feel feelings as though they're your very own piece of understanding. As it were, another person's torment and bliss become your torment and satisfaction. Closeness and closeness can overpower you. Empaths regularly find visit close contact troublesome, which can make sentimental connections testing. You need to associate and build up an enduring organization. Yet, investing a lot of energy with somebody prompts pressure, overpower, or stresses over losing yourself in the relationship. You may likewise see tactile over-burden or a "frayed nerves" feeling from a lot of talking or contacting. Yet, when you attempt to communicate your requirement for time alone, you retain your accomplice's and feel considerably increasingly troubled. Be that as it may, setting substantial, clear limits can help decrease trouble, Engel recommends.

Get Grounded

This is the most significant thing we can do toward the beginning of the day—or whenever. It's an undeniable fact profoundly touchy individuals experience difficulty staying grounded because we feel everything so sharply and live in our minds. In any case, establishing ourselves is the initial step to take if we would prefer not to haul around others' feelings and vitality as though they were our own. Establishing causes, us to tune into our bodies and the current second and spotlight less on the inward exchange going through our minds. It takes just five minutes to do one of these things: Imagine uncovers developing the base of your feet. The roots venture profound into the ground. Picture this until your feet feel weighted down. Run fresh water on your wrists. Or, on the other hand, unite the wrists, one on the other, with the sides going in inverse ways. Hold for five minutes.

Go through five minutes, reflecting, concentrating on deep inward breaths and exhalations. State the word OM, drawing out the name gradually and rehashing it for five minutes. Feel the vibration of the word in the body. Sit on or contact the earth/ground. Stroll on the land in exposed feet. Embrace a tree. Nature can have a ground-breaking purifying impact since it causes us to centre around a world outside ourselves.

Imagine

Perception is hugely successful for keeping others' vitality separate from our own. To do this, we can picture ourselves in a crate. This crate has four dividers encompassing us, with a top on our head. This container permits positive vitality to enter, yet it repulses life we don't need. Individuals can't tell we put it there. We despite everything sense what others are feeling and thinking, be that as it may when we have perceived their vitality, it remains with them. The spirit doesn't get trapped with our own

Clear

This is exceptionally valuable after we have assimilated undesirable vitality. While alone and in a calm spot, begin to wipe away the life encompassing your body. Cup your hands and start over your head. Utilizing two sides, slice through the vitality in a snappy, swiping activity, pushing it away and imaging your hands clearing your head region, at that point descending to your neck, chest, stomach area, etc. Proceed with right down to the feet. At the point when you're set, imagine yourself in a white air pocket—others' vitality can't enter this ensured space.

Accomplish the Work

This progression is more unpredictable than the others; however, it can't be disregarded. We take on others' feelings, contemplations, and sensations effectively, yet have we at any point halted and wondered why we do this? There might be an inclination for us to be unknowingly pulled in to aiding and mending others. One way we do this is by retaining others' harmful (or unfavourable) vitality. At the point when we ingest this vitality, they leave the communication feeling much improved, while we leave feeling more awful. Be that as it may, regardless of whether we're mindful of it or not, we're despite everything getting something out of this exchange. This is the point at which we have to accomplish some inward work. We should look at our centre convictions and sincerely ask ourselves what the result is. Who might we be without this attribute? What would we be able to do with our lives? How would we feel when we help recuperate others? How would we help mend ourselves? What is our opinion about the limits? Does value assume a job?

These are, for the most part, addresses we can investigate while accomplishing our internal work. At the point when we reveal unhelpful shrouded convictions, we can release them and supplant them with new ones. The best method to manage antagonistic vitality and to prevent others' negative life from advancing into your body is to know about it and see how it influences you.

Engel concurs, including that "empaths can be effortlessly overpowered by feeling everything all the more seriously." On the off chance that you can without much of a stretch sense how others feel, you'll likely make some hard memories taking care of the enthusiastic "commotion" from a group, or even a little gathering of individuals, for an all-inclusive timeframe. At the point when you're getting on adverse feelings, vitality, or even physical pain from individuals around you, you may become overpowered or genuinely unwell. Accordingly, you may feel generally high all alone or in the organization of only a couple of individuals, one after another. You make some hard memories, not caring. An empath doesn't merely feel for somebody — they think with somebody. Taking in others' feelings so profoundly can make you need to take care of them. "Empaths need to help," Susskind says. "In any case, this isn't constantly conceivable, which can disillusion an empath." You may think that it's hard to watch somebody battle and follow up on your common tendency to help facilitate their misery, regardless of whether that implies retaining it yourself. People will, in general, reveal to you their issues. Touchy, empathic individuals will, in general, be awesome audience members. Your friends and family may feel consoled by your help and connect with you first at whatever point they experience trouble. Caring profoundly can make it difficult to tell individuals when you approach the purpose of overpowering. In any case, it's imperative to discover a parity. Without limits, unchecked generosity and affectability can prepare for "feeling dumps" that might be a lot for you to deal with on the double. Empaths may likewise be progressively powerless against control or dangerous practices. Your sincere want to help individuals in trouble can leave you ignorant of indications of harmfulness. You may have a more profound comprehension of the agony energizing their conduct and need to offer help. In any case, it's essential to recollect you can't do much for somebody who isn't prepared to change. You have a high affectability to sounds, scents, or sensations. An empath's expanded affectability doesn't merely identify with feelings. There's a ton of cover among empaths and individuals who are profoundly delicate, and you may find that you're likewise progressively touchy to your general surroundings. This could mean: Aromas and scents influence you all the more unequivocally. Bumping sounds and physical sensations may influence you all the more firmly.

You want to tune in to media at low volumes or get data by perusing. Certain sounds may trigger a passionate reaction. You need time to energize "Uplifted affectability to others' torment can be depleting, so empaths may wind up effectively exhausted," Susskind says. Indeed, even an over-burden of positive sentiments may deplete you, so it's essential to require some investment you have to reset. On the off chance that you can't circumvent overpowering feelings and rest your faculties, you're bound to encounter burnout, which can negatively affect prosperity. Requiring time alone doesn't mean you're a thoughtful person. Empaths can likewise be outgoing individuals or fall anyplace on the range. Perhaps individuals invigorate you — until you arrive at that purpose of overpowering. Outgoing empaths may need to take additional consideration to find some harmony between investing energy with others and reestablishing their passionate stores. You don't care for struggle. In case you're an empath, you likely fear or effectively maintain a strategic distance from strife. Higher affectability can make it simpler for somebody to offend you. Indeed, even spur of the moment, comments may cut all the more profoundly, and you may think about analysis all the more literally. Contentions and battles can likewise cause more misery since you're not just managing your sentiments and responses. You're additionally engrossing the feelings of the others in question. At the point when you need to address everybody's harmed except don't have the foggiest idea of how even minor contradictions can get more diligently to adapt to. You frequently feel like you don't fit. Despite being exceptionally sensitive to the sentiments of others, many empaths think that it is hard to identify with others. Others probably won't comprehend why you become depleted and focused so rapidly. You may battle to understand the feelings and emotions you ingest or feel like you aren't "ordinary." This may lead you to turn out to be increasingly private. You may abstain from discussing your sensitivities and sharing your instincts, so you learn about less of the spot.

Looking Good!

At the point when you perceive those emotions, you can change your condition, scrub down, or begin dealing with some breathing activities to pull together and pull together your considerations. Keeping yourself shielded from negative vitality is significant because it can deplete you and make you substantially less gainful than you could be throughout everyday life. Avoid it by and large on the off chance that you can oversee it. Negative vitality is a whole lot of nothing for anybody.

Get Clear on What You are Eager to Grasp in Your Life

When you conclude that you're not putting an adverse individual out of your life for good, you have to figure out how to oversee them and their pessimism in your life. This implies you have to get clear on what you are happy to endure and what you won't endure. You don't need to mention to individuals what these limits are, yet you have to know them and submit to them yourself. You may conclude that you won't talk about specific themes, for example, cash, around adverse individuals since it generally leaves you feeling remorseful about how much cash you make or have.

Don't Respond to Others' Antagonism, react such That Serves You

As opposed to attempting to address somebody who is being antagonistic, advise yourself that you get the chance to conclude how to react to that individual, and you don't have to take care of into their cynicism. A ton of times, basically damaging them with a positive reaction is sufficient to get them to sit up and focus on their cynicism. However, it's not your business to attempt to transform them. Concentrate on how you need to appear for the discussion and adhere to that.

Having a go at Looking at Something Different That Doesn't Burdeno

On the off chance that you find that the discussion is transforming into an antagonism fest, at that point, take a stab at changing the subject and looking at something that everybody can appreciate. Raise your main tune or movement or far superior, request that the antagonistic individual educate you regarding something they appreciate. It'll help move their concentrate away from whatever it is that they are grumbling about and will assist you with having the option to all the more likely deal with the experience.

Adopt an Arrangements Based Strategy

It's a by and large settled upon the idea that adverse individuals will, in general, have an issue for each arrangement. So, on the off chance that you wind up within sight of somebody who just keeps setting up detours, at that point, you may need to strike them with vast amounts of answers for their issues. Even though it's not in every case enough to get them to adjust their perspective, it will at any rate permit you to leave the experience feeling like you don't detest everything and everybody.

Recall That Others' Assessments of You Aren't Significant

Somebody who is very negative always will have some things to state about you and your life. You'll have to get a tough skin on the off chance that you are going to keep on having this pessimistic individual in your life and let the remarks move away from you. Recollect that the things this individual says are not about you by any stretch of the imagination, however, that they are discovering something in you that they don't care for about themselves, so they are anticipating that onto you. It's not you; it's them.

Quit Attempting to Change How Contrary Others Are Throughout everyday life

A most baffling aspect regarding adverse individuals is that they gripe about everything and keeping in mind that it is plain as day to you that they should simply change a couple of things about their life. They wouldn't be so pessimistic always; the contrary individual can't see the advantage of that approach. Along these lines, it's primarily significant that you remember that it isn't your duty to fix this individual. They need to choose. They need to appear as something else.

Be simply the Best Form You Can Be

Recollect that you can't change somebody's cynical point of view. You must be a superior form of yourself than you were yesterday; maybe, that may motivate the antagonistic individuals throughout your life to get it together and quit acting like a primary child. Be that as it may, if not, you can just stress over yourself, so put your concentration there as opposed to agonizing over how you can help the antagonistic individuals on the planet. In case you're searching for explicit moves you can make to carry on with a more joyful life, look at our top of the digital line book on essential Buddhist lessons). Is it true that you are an Antagonistic Individual? Here Are 12 Different Ways to Tell Cynicism can take a superbly decent life and ruin it. Drag it through the mud. Flip around your own. If you locate that a more significant number of individuals are leaving you than toward you, it may be an ideal opportunity to consider that you are an antagonistic individual.

In any event, when you realize that you are the issue here, you can begin to take a shot at the things that are shielding you from carrying on with your best life. What's more, diminishing the measure of negative vitality in your life will surely assist you with carrying on with a more joyful life. That is the universe's method for attempting to get you to see the antagonism in your own life. Focus.

You Battle with Individuals a Ton

Maybe you start ruckuses in any event when you don't intend to begin inconvenience. Possibly you generally have a chip on your shoulder or have a comment to individuals when they haven't requested your supposition. Focus on how you raise issues with individuals and check whether you are beginning discussions on a negative note.

Individuals Don't Look at You Without Flinching

Individuals who don't regard you won't look at you without flinching. On the off chance that you radiate antagonistic vibes, individuals may attempt to shield themselves intuitively by maintaining a strategic distance from eye to eye connection with you. If you find that individuals don't look at you without flinching, this is because they don't care for your antagonism, and they are attempting to abstain from getting whatever it is you have to go on.

Companions Drop Plans

On the off chance that your companions are continually dropping plans with you, something is presumably off-base. This is a decent time to inquire as to whether it's them or if it's you. Newsflash: it's quite often you. Also, your companions may have just attempted to reveal to you how negative you are. Nevertheless, you are excessively up to speed in your show to understand that they've been advising you to take off for some time.

Individuals Genuinely Get Some Distance from You

Likewise, to maintaining a strategic distance from eye to eye connection, individuals will dismiss their bodies from your body when they are conversing with you since they are attempting to shield themselves from your cynicism. They may likewise fold their arms to mirror blocking antagonism, and they will be moving ceaselessly from you like the discussion proceeds.

Somebody Is Continually Asking You, "What's Up?"

On the off chance that you simply appear as though something isn't right always, that is bad. Cheerful individuals don't stroll around with a negative demeanor all over. Here and there, individuals intuitively need others to get some information about their sentiments or ask about a distressed look. Hence, they play it up and afterwards snap-down somebody's throat when they get the very thing they needed. Everything so negative.

No One Approaches You for Help

If you have a feeling that you are, to a greater extent, a dumping ground for harmful data than somebody who can lift the spirits of companions, it may be because your loved ones as of now consider you to be as a rule so contrary that somewhat more won't hurt. The distinction here, however, is that they don't request you to help fix things: they simply dump all their psychological trash on you.

The Family Maintains A Strategic Distance from You

On the off chance that your family is headed toward shop without you, or if everybody unexpectedly gets peaceful when you stroll in the room, it can get extremely awkward. In any case, consider that they weren't discussing you when you strolled in the room; maybe they simply don't need you to participate in the discussion since, you know, you're negative.

You Feel Tired, Always

Pessimism can burden us in a sensible manner, not merely in our psyches. On the off chance that you have an inclination that you are worn out regularly and don't appear ever to feel alleviation, it may be that your antagonism has shown itself in a manner that is keeping you down throughout everyday life. This is because of a physical weight to convey.

You Are Incredibly Disorderly

Strangely enough, individuals who will, in general, be extremely harmful make some hard memories getting and remaining sorted out. This is for various reasons including negative musings, for example, "why trouble?", "it'll simply get wrecked again in any case," and "no one wants to think about it."

You Don't Begin Any New Ventures

If you haven't begun anything new in some time, it's a smart thought to wonder why not? Antagonistic individuals don't see the purpose of attempting to improve things and, consequently, don't participate in exercises that could help push things ahead. Or on the other hand, surprisingly more terrible, they don't accept things that can show signs of improvement, so they never attempt.

At the point when we quit retaining awkward feelings, we are allowed to concentrate on different things. We can utilize our freshly discovered vitality to achieve the fantasies and objectives we set out for ourselves. We are entitled to travel through the world in another, engaging way. A way that permits us to utilize this one of a kind blessing to our advantage—which at last will profit the world. If you've at any point invested some energy with a pessimistic individual, you know how rapidly you can begin to take on that negative attitude. Have you at any point felt that you wish you had realized how to shield yourself from negative vitality? Now and again, it happens that individuals don't understand they have gotten contrary because of being around antagonistic individuals. Furthermore, opposite individuals are the most exceedingly awful. On the off chance that you are feeling overpowered from assuming the negative vitality of others, there is an approach to prevent it from occurring.

Here are how to shield yourself from engrossing others' negative energy so you can continue ahead with living a progressively positive and beneficial life. 1) Recognize Whose Feeling is Available At the point when negative feeling assumes control over, it's critical to distinguish the source. Is it your negative feeling, or did you get it from another person? On the off chance that it is yours, at that point you can manage it and work through those feelings, yet if it is somebody else's, you have to perceive that it's not your weight to convey and release it. Put Some Separation Among You and the Antagonism Head outside, go for a stroll, have lunch in your vehicle: whatever you need to do to part with yourself some space from the antagonism and the antagonistic individuals, do it. Here and there, all you need is a couple of moments to refocus your considerations and advise yourself that their pessimism isn't your cynicism. Know Your Cutoff Points With regards to managing pessimism and negative vitality, it's imperative to comprehend what triggers that feeling in you. At the point when you can distinguish an inclination related to cynicism, you can recognize it sooner and manage it quicker. If that antagonism is associated with an individual, you can see it originating from a mile away and begin strolling the other way. Relax On the off chance that you incline that you are getting overpowered by negative feelings, vitality, or another person's antagonistic feeling or vitality, at that point, take a couple of moments to manage your breathing and reset your considerations.

Reflect On the off chance that negative emotion and energy are streaming over you, take a couple of moments to sit unobtrusively in your head and ruminate. Square the negative contemplations and account for the positive feelings and vitality in your life. (To figure out how to think, look at our manual for consideration here Get Clear with Individuals With regards to overseeing pessimistic energy and adverse individuals, in some cases you need to lay down the law and state "no." The word no has a ton of intensity that we regularly underestimate. It can leave somebody speechless when it is utilized effectively. If somebody is attempting to take your daylight, defining cutoff points and limits with that individual can go far to changing the tune of their tune when they are around you. Imagine Yourself Resistant to Pessimism Perception has become an essential and useful asset that individuals can use to improve their lives from numerous points of view, including, indeed, shutting out negative vitality.

On the off chance that you pause for a moment to envision yourself invulnerable to negative energy, your body will have the option to shut it out of your life. This can set aside some effort to rehearse. However, it is justified, despite all the trouble, to spare yourself the difficulty of managing outside pessimism, and it's exceptionally flawless how it functions after some time to ensure you. Put it Out of Your Body At the point when negative vitality makes its way into your life, and you can return it directly out of your life by utilizing representation to push it from your physical self. Envision seeing the negative vitality leave your body and imagine occupying the space with a positive spirit. Wash it Off On the off chance that you feel genuinely and intellectually depleted from a negative experience or have been hauling around negative energy throughout the day, clean up, or a shower. They will assist you with feeling like you are genuinely washing the negative vitality endlessly. Also, a hot bath or shower will help you with feeling revived and loose. On the off chance that you scrub down not long before bed, your muscles will be warm and free, and you'll have a peaceful night's rest as opposed to hurling and turning stressing over the adverse vitality in your body.

Ending Perfectionist Thinking

Prescriptions help, however right now, they can't fix anxiety issues, treat their manifestations. For specific individuals, the way toward finding a medication that works with their body's one of a kind science can be a wellspring of stress all its own. As per the NAMI, a few drugs can take a long time to start working and cause undesirable symptoms. In the wake of breaking down the logical writing that has been delivered in peer audit articles through the span of the last 50 years, Whitaker saw that some mental prescriptions show up as compelling over the present moment, yet that these medications eventually increment the likelihood that an individual will turn out to be constantly sick over the long haul.

This doesn't imply that drug doesn't work (it accomplishes work, and for many individuals). Or maybe, what it means is that our present medications have various issues and don't work (or don't function admirably) for all individuals. Right now, we are gaining ground. However, we have a great deal of work that, despite everything, should be finished. Wellbeing frameworks have not yet satisfactorily reacted to the weight of the mental issues.

How to Stop Inhibiting Yourself?

You can stop inhibiting yourself by necessarily constraining yourself to supersede your indiscreet inclination to permit your restraints to govern, and they will slowly scatter. The more occasions you prevail with regards to doing this... and wind up accomplishing something which in any case your restraints wouldn't have permitted you to do, the simpler it will become to do it once more. Inevitably of doing this, they will leave totally, and you'll be allowed to do whatever you like! On the off chance that that sounds more difficult than one might expect... you understand it appropriately. In any case, despite being troublesome, there is no more straightforward, nor increasingly powerful, the method for doing it. Coarseness your teeth, summon your dauntlessness, and stroll with certainty... Open the entryway which drives outside of your customary range of familiarity, and make only one little stride out. Utilize your psyche to get to that courage and truly power your foot to make that initial step... If anxiety gets through and you retreat, that is alright. Try not to thrash yourself about it. Attempt again later on, yet make two strides when you do it. Continue doing this, trying to continue expanding the means.

PART 2

Vagus Nerve

Vagus Nerve

The vagus nerve is a mixed nerve. It is the most extended and most widely distributed group of nerves in the human brain. It contains sensory, motor, and parasympathetic nerve fibres. The vagus nerve exits the medulla oblongata, and after passing through the cranial crest, along both sides of the oesophagus, through the neck and thoracic cavity, into the abdomen through the oesophagal hiatus at T10 height above the diaphragm; it controls most of the respiratory system, digestive system, heart and other organs Sensation, movement and glandular secretion; therefore vagal nerve damage can cause dysfunction of circulation, breathing, digestion, etc.

From the bottom of the vagus nerve in the medulla of the vertebral beam and the cerebellar peduncle between (referred to as the ambiguous nucleus configuration), then we will drill the jugular foramen, into the carotid sheath being, along the internal carotid artery and the internal jugular vein in the middle of Down to the neck, chest, and abdomen, innervating the visceral nerves. 80-90% of the vagus nerve is composed of afferent nerve fibres, which can transmit sensory information to the central nerve fibres.

In the carotid sheath, the vagus nerve will descend first between the internal carotid artery and the external carotid artery, and after reaching the junction of the two highways, it will then go to the posterolateral side of the common carotid artery. The general visceral afferent nerve (GVA) cell bodies of the vagus nerve will gather in the inferior vagus ganglia on both sides.

The right vagus nerve will branch into an ascending branch called the right recurrent laryngeal nerve. The right recurrent laryngeal nerve bypasses the right subclavian artery and goes up to the trachea and oesophagus. The right vagus nerve continued to descend, passing in front of the right subclavian artery and falling along the superior vena cava. After that, it gives behind the right main bronchus and branches into the nerve plexus of the heart, lungs, and oesophagus. After the right vagus nerve passes through the lower part of the throat, it will form the posterior vagus nerve trunk, and then enter the oesophagal hiatus of the diaphragm

The left vagus nerve also passes between the left common carotid artery and the left subclavian artery and is attached to the aortic arch. The left vagus nerve also separates the recurrent laryngeal nerve, but unlike the right side, the left recurrent laryngeal nerve bypasses the aortic arch and travels to the trachea and oesophagus through the left side of the arterial ligament. The left vagus nerve will also branch into the plexus of the heart, lungs, throat and other organs, and form the anterior vagus nerve trunk in front of the throat, enter the oesophagal hole into the diaphragm, enter the abdominal cavity to control the liver, kidney, intestine, stomach and other organs.

What Is the Role of the Vagus Nerve?

The walking nerve is the 10th pair of cranial nerves. It is the longest and most widely distributed pair of cranial nerves. It contains sensory, motor, and parasympathetic nerve fibres. The vagus nerve innervates most organs of the two systems of breathing and digestion, such as the sensation, movement, and glandular secretion of organs such as the heart. Therefore, vagus nerve injury can reduce circulatory, digestive and respiratory dysfunction.

The vagus nerve is a mixed nerve and contains four types of fiber. The individual visceral motor fibres originate from the suspicious nucleus of the medulla oblongata and dominate the striated muscles of the pharynx and larynx. Generally, visceral motor fibres originate from the dorsal nucleus of the medulla oblongata, and the parasympathetic nerve fibres emitted from this nucleus are exchanged for neurons in the parasympathetic ganglion in or near the organ. Organs that control the activities of smooth muscle, heart muscle and glands.

Generally, the cell body of visceral sensory fibres is located in the inferior ganglion below the jugular foramen, in which the central process stops at the nucleus of the solitary tract, and the surrounding processes are also distributed in the organs of the chest and abdominal cavity. Generally, the number of somatosensory fibres is the smallest. The cell body is located in the superior ganglion within the jugular foramen. The central process stops at the spinal nucleus of the trigeminal nerve ridge.

The vagus nerve is the nerve with the most extended stroke and the most extensive distribution in the cranial nerve. It enters and exits the brain from behind the medullary olive under the root filaments of the glossopharyngeal nerve, and exits the cranial cavity through the jugular foramen. Afterwards, descend into the internal carotid, behind the common carotid artery and the internal jugular vein, and enter the chest cavity through the upper thorax. On the chest, the left and right vagus nerves have different movements and positions.

The left vagus nerve descends to the front of the aortic arch between the left common carotid artery and the left subclavian artery. After passing through the remaining lung root, a small branch is divided into the left pulmonary plexus, and then divided into several small chapters in front of the oesophagus to form the Anterior oesophagus plexus, and continued down into the anterior trunk of the vagus nerve.

The right vagus nerve descends along the right side of the trachea through the front of the right subclavian artery and then divides several branches behind the right lung root to participate in the right pulmonary plexus, and then distributes the department behind the oesophagus to form the posterior oesophagal plexus after the vagus nerve is synthesized at the lower end of the oesophagus dry. The anterior and posterior trunks of the vagus nerve go down into the abdominal cavity through the throat with the throat to the abdominal cavity, and the anterior and posterior trunks are divided into terminal branches.

Anatomy of the Vagus Nerve

The vagus nerve is the largest nerve in the autonomic nervous system and one of the most critical nerves in the human body. The vagus nerve helps to regulate many critical aspects of human physiology, including heart rate, blood pressure, sweating, digestion and even speaking. For this reason, the medical community has been looking for ways to regulate vagal function.

Anatomy of the vagus nerve

The vagus nerve (also called the tenth cranial nerve or CN X) is a very long nerve that originates in the brain stem and extends down through the neck and into the chest and abdomen. If you carry both motor and sensory information, and it provides nerve innervation for the nerves, major blood vessels, airways, lungs, oesophagus, stomach, and intestines.

Although there are two vagus nerves (left and right), doctors usually refer to them as "vagus nerves". The vagus nerve helps control several muscles in the throat and speech box. It plays an essential role in regulating heart rate and keeping the gastrointestinal tract functioning usually. The vagus nerve also brings sensory information from the internal organs back to the brain.

The Function of the Vagus Nerve

The enormous significance of the vagus nerve may be that it is the main parasympathetic nerve of the human body, providing parasympathetic nerve fibres for all major organs of the head, neck, chest and abdomen. The vagus nerve is responsible for gag reflex (causing a cough reflex when stimulating the ear canal), slowing the heart rhythm, controlling sweating, regulating blood pressure, stimulating gastrointestinal motility and controlling blood vessel tension.

Vagal Reflex

Sudden stimulation of the vagus nerve produces a so-called "vascular vagal reflex", which consists of a sudden drop in blood pressure and a slowing of the heart rhythm. Gastrointestinal diseases or reactions to pain, fear, or unexpected stress may trigger this reflex. Some people are particularly prone to vasovagal reflexes, whose changes in blood pressure and heart rate can cause loss of consciousness-a disease called "vasovagal syncope".

Under certain medical conditions, especially when the autonomic nerve function is abnormal, the vagus nerve is also over-activated. Stimulating the vagus nerve can produce therapeutic effects (such as stopping supraventricular tachycardia (SVT) or playing ic attacks) and can help doctors diagnose specific types of heart murmurs. Vagal nerve stimulation can be easily achieved by using Valsalva manoeuvres.

Vagus Nerve and Heart

The right vagus nerve provides the sinus node, and its stimulation can produce sinus bradycardia. The left vagus nerve provides power to the atrioventricular node, and its stimulation can create some form of heart block. By creating a short heart block, Valsalva action can terminate multiple SVTs. Why do people faint?

Vagus Nerve in Medical Treatment

Because the vagus nerve has many vital functions, the medical community has been interested in the idea of using vagal nerve stimulation or vagal nerve block in medical treatment for decades.

For decades, vagotomy (cutting of the vagus nerve) has been the primary treatment for peptic ulcer disease because it is a way to reduce the amount of digestive acid produced in the stomach. However, vagus neurotomy has some adverse effects, and with the use of more effective treatments, it has become less and less frequent.

Nowadays, people are very interested in using electronic stimulators (radically modified pacemakers) to stimulate the vagus nerve for a long time to treat various medical problems. Such devices (often referred to as vagal nerve stimulation devices or VNS devices) have been successfully used to treat patients with severe epilepsy who are challenging to treat with medication. VNS therapy is sometimes used to treat refractory depression.

Because everything looks like a nail when you hold a hammer, the company that makes VNS equipment is studying its use in several other situations, including high blood pressure, migraine, tinnitus, fibromyalgia and weight loss. There is indeed hope in such applications of VNS. However, once the hype is replaced by reliable clinical evidence, the true potential of VNS will emerge.

Vagus Nerve Stimulation Dramatically Reduces Inflammation

Inflammatory reactions play a central role in the development and persistence of many diseases and may lead to debilitating chronic pain. So, in many cases, inflammation is your body's response to stress. Therefore, biological markers that reduce the "fight or flight" response in the nervous system and reduce stress can also reduce inflammation.

Usually, doctors prescribe medicine to fight inflammation. However, there is increasing evidence that another way to fight inflammation is to engage the vagus nerve and improve the "vagal tone". This can be achieved by using daily habits such as yoga and meditation, or in more extreme inflammatory conditions (such as rheumatoid arthritis (RA)) by using an implanted vagus nerve stimulation device (VNS).

The vagus nerve is known as "wandering nerve" because it has various branches that branch from two thick stems planted in the cerebellum and brainstem and move along the abdomen to the lowest internal organs of the stomach, thus touching the heart and most of the main organ. Vagus means "wandering" in Latin. The words vagabond, vague and vagrant all originate from the corresponding Latin root.

In 1921, the German physiologist named Otto Loewi found that stimulation of the vagus nerve would trigger the release of the Vagusstoff substance ("Vagus substance" in German) he created, resulting in a decrease in heart rate. And the "vagus substance" was later identified as acetylcholine. And became the first neurotransmitter discovered by scientists. Vagusstoff (acetylcholine) is like a sedative, and you only need to exhale a few deep breaths for a long time to manage yourself. Consciously using the power of the vagus nerve can establish an internal sedation state while suppressing the inflammatory reflex.

The vagus nerve is the main component of the parasympathetic nervous system, which regulates the "rest and digestion" or "tends to be friendly" responses. On the other hand, to maintain homeostasis, the sympathetic nervous system drives the "fight or flight" response.

Healthy vagal tone is part of the feedback loop related to positive emotions.

The heart rate slightly increased when inhaling, and decreased when exhaling, indicating healthy vagal tone. Diaphragm deep breathing-slow expiration for a long time is the key to stimulating the vagus nerve and slowing the heart rate and blood pressure, especially when expressing anxiety. A higher vagal nerve tension index is closely related to physical and mental health. In contrast, low vagal tone index is associated with inflammation, depression, depressed mood, loneliness, heart attack and stroke.

A study published in "Psychology" in 2010 "How Positive Emotions Build Physical Health: Perceived Positive Social Relationships Explains a Spiral Rise between Positive Emotions and Vagal Tension". In this study, Barbara Fredrickson and Bethany Kok of the University of North Carolina at Chapel Hill trained on the vagus nerve. They found that the high vagal sentiment index is part of the feedback loop between positive emotions, physical health, and positive social relationships. Their research shows that positive emotions, healthy social relationships and physical health can affect each other, which is a self-sustaining upward spiral dynamic and feedback loop that scientists have just begun to understand.

In this experiment, Frederickson and Kok used love meditation (LKM) technology to help participants better self-positive emotions. However, they also found that merely thinking about positive social connections and trying to improve close interpersonal relationships can also improve vagal tone. In 2014, based on the findings of Swiss researchers, I wrote the blog post of "Psychology Today" "How does the vagus nerve convey intestinal intuition to the brain?" The researchers determined how the vagus nerve conveys the "gut sensation" of anxiety and fear of the brain. Clinical and experimental studies have shown that stress and depression are related to the upregulation of the immune system, including increased production of pro-inflammatory cytokines. When administered to patients or experimental animals, cytokines have been found to induce typical symptoms of depression. Therefore, some low mood, low energy and lack of motivation may be caused by increased levels of cytokine protein.

Vagus nerve stimulation (VNS) significantly reduces inflammation of arthritis

Recently, a team of international researchers from Amsterdam and the United States conducted a clinical trial that showed that using a small implanted device to stimulate the vagus nerve can significantly reduce inflammation and improve the prognosis of rheumatoid arthritis patients by inhibiting the production of cytokines. According to researchers, RA is a chronic inflammatory disease that affects about 1.3 million people in the United States and costs tens of billions of dollars in treatment each year.

The neuroscientists and immunologists involved in this research used the latest technology to map the neural circuits that regulate inflammation. In a course called "inflammatory reflex", the action potential transmitted in the vagus nerve suppresses the production of pro-inflammatory cytokines. The July 2016 study "Vaginal nerve stimulation inhibits cytokine production in rheumatoid arthritis and reduces the severity of the disease" was published online in the Proceedings of the National Academy of Sciences (PNAS) and will be published in an upcoming print edition.

This is the first human study to reduce the symptoms of rheumatoid arthritis by stimulating the vagus nerve with a small implanted device. The device triggers a chain reaction, which diminishes cytokine levels and inflammation. Although the focus of this study is rheumatoid arthritis, the results of the trial may affect patients with other inflammatory diseases, including Parkinson's, Crohn's, and Alzheimer's. Paul-Peter Tak, a principal international researcher and lead author of the paper, in the Department of Clinical Immunology and Rheumatology at the Academic Medical Center of the University of Amsterdam, said in a statement, "This is the first research to evaluate whether implanted electronic devices can directly stimulate inflammatory reflexes to treat human RA. We have previously shown that targeted therapy for inflammatory reflexes can reduce inflammation in RA and animal models. It is also possible Related to other immune-mediated inflammatory diseases. "

These findings suggest a new way to fight diseases that are currently being treated with relatively expensive drugs that have many side effects. VNS provides healthcare providers with a potentially more effective way to improve the lives of people with chronic inflammatory diseases.

Conclusion:

"This is a real breakthrough in our ability to help patients with inflammatory diseases. Although we have previously studied animal models of inflammation, so far, we have no evidence that electrical stimulation of the vagus nerve can indeed suppress the production of cytokines and reduce the severity of the disease. Degree. I believe this research will change the way we look at modern medicine and help us understand that with a little help, our nerves can make the medicines needed to help our body heal itself. "

The emerging field of bioelectronics integrated traditional Chinese and western medicine uses advanced neuromodulation devices to target various diseases traditionally treated with drugs. Stimulating the vagus nerve provides significant advantages for drug use-for example, lower cost and fewer side effects.

Vagus Nerve and Anxiety

The vagus nerve is one-tenth of the twelve cranial nerves, the longest in the human body. The word "vagus nerve" means "trombone" in Latin, which perfectly illustrates the path of this nerve extending in various organs of the human body. The vagus nerve was born in the box of the skull, just in the spinal cord, and fell into the neck developed on the two branches, and passed through various organs of the path to the abdomen.

The vagus nerve interferes with the sensitivity of the mucosa of the respiratory tract and transmits the rhythm, intensity and frequency of breathing. It affects the pharynx, larynx, oesophagus, trachea and bronchi, and applies nerve fibers to the heart, stomach, pancreas and liver. But it also performs anti-tasks. In other words, it receives signals from internal organs and sends them to the brain for processing.

Although perhaps the most interesting is the relationship between the vagus nerve and anxiety because it also transmits signals of nervousness or calmness, anger or relaxation. To understand the connection between the vagus nerve and anxiety, we need to know that the nervous system is composed of two "opposite" systems that continuously send information to the brain.

The sympathetic nervous method prepares us for action, so it mainly feeds hormones such as adrenaline and cortisol. The parasympathetic nervous system interferes with relaxation. Both systems can be used as accelerators and reducers. The sympathetic nervous system accelerates and activates us. Because the parasympathetic nervous system helps us relax and slow down, it uses neurotransmitters such as acetylcholine, which lowers heart rate and blood pressure, which slows down the work of organs.

The Function of the Vagus Nerve

The vagus nerve manages the parasympathetic nervous system. It interferes with many features from mouth movement to the heartbeat. Similarly, when infected, it may cause various symptoms. Some of the vagal tasks in our body are:

- It helps to regulate heartbeat, control muscle movement and maintain breathing rhythm.
- Maintain the function of the digestive tract, contract the stomach, and intestinal muscles to digest food.
- It is easy to relax under stressful conditions or to show that we are in danger; we do not have to lower our vigilance.
- Send sensory information about the state of organs to the brain.

Vagus Nerve and Anxiety

When we are under pressure, the sympathetic nervous system is activated. If tension persists, and we cannot turn off the physiological response that triggered it, then it will not cause problems for a long time. At the brain level, this involves the activation of two pathways: the hypothalamic-pituitary-adrenal axis and the brain-gut axis.

The brain responds to stress and anxiety by increasing the production of hormones (CRF) from the hypothalamus to the pituitary, where they induce the release of another hormone (ACTH), which is then transmitted to the adrenal glands through the bloodstream to stimulate cortisol and Induction of adrenaline, they are inhibitors of the immune system and inflammatory precursors, which is why when we feel stressed and anxious, we are prone to illness. We will eventually suffer from depression, which is a kind of inflammation Diseases related to brain response.

It seems that this is not enough. Chronic stress and anxiety can lead to an increase in glutamate in the brain, which is an over-produced neurotransmitter that can cause migraine headaches, depression and anxiety. Also, high levels of cortisol reduce the volume of the hippocampus, which is the part of the brain responsible for forming new memories.

Vagus involvement can cause dizziness, gastrointestinal problems, arrhythmia, difficulty breathing, and uneven emotional response. Because the vagus nerve cannot activate relaxation signals, the sympathetic nervous system remains active, which will cause an impulsive reaction and suffer anxiety. Surprisingly, a study accompanied by the University of Miami found that vagal tone was passed from mother to child. Women who suffer from anxiety, depression, or anger during pregnancy have low vagal activity, their children have low vagal activity, and low levels of dopamine and serotonin.

Can Strengthening the Vagus Nerve Become the Secret to Eliminating Anxiety?

Anxiety can be a real addiction. It is impossible to complicate, esoteric individual, and difficult to predict. Sometimes, we think our anxiety has passed, and we have finally taken a step forward, but then some things have changed, and we stand up again and try to return to peace and tranquillity. We are all students with anxiety disorders, which is why it is incredible to understand exactly how the nervous system works and the measures we can take. But what does it really mean to calm the nervous system? Many people describe it as slowing the heart rate, deepening breathing and relaxing different muscles-but what the real connection between these feelings and the brain is? Okay, let us introduce you to the vagus nerve, which is part of the body, and it seems to explain how our minds control our bodies, how our bodies affect our thoughts and may provide us with what we need to calm the two. Tool.

What is Vagus, and Why Should I Care?

The vagus nerve passes through the neck from the bottom of the brain and then branches off the chest, extending all the way to the abdomen. The word "vagus nerve" actually means "wandering" in Latin. This is exactly what the vagus nerve does. It wanders in the body, touching the heart and almost all major organs. For a long time, this nerve has been regarded as the "superior internal sensory system" because it can regulate breathing, heart rate, muscles, digestion, circulation and even vocal cords. Are you interested?

If you have not heard of vagus nerves, then you are not alone. This may be because, although scientists know that it has many functions, they are not sure exactly how this nerve actually works. What we know is that it is the main regulator of the peripheral nervous system, and because of its ability to slow our pulse and lower blood pressure, it is also known as the "rest and digestion" response. The vagus nerve also plays a central role in the gut-brain axis, which has become quite important in the health field.

How Does the Vagus Nerve Affect my Health?

In 1921, a German physiologist first discovered that stimulation of the vagus nerve would trigger the release of what he called Vagusstoff (vagus nerve material), resulting in a slower heart rate. It was later discovered that the substance was actually acetylcholine, which is an important neurotransmitter in our nervous system. Since then, researchers have discovered more information about the vagus nerve and its role in various diseases and important systems in the body. For example, electrical stimulation of this nerve has been shown to reduce the rate of seizures and help relieve depressive symptoms. The strength of the vagus nerve or vagus nerve is related to inflammation, immune system regulation, metabolism and mood regulation, and we can all consider this important.

So, what does the vagus nerve mean to mental health? Low vagal tone can cause poor mood, and attention regulation, inflammation, depression, and even be used to measure people's sensitivity to stress. At the same time, healthy vagal emotions are related to the opposite emotions: positive emotions and psychological balance. Some studies even suggest that increasing vagal tone may help treat addiction and certain cravings. Knowing this, it may be time-to commemorate Mental Health Month-let we all study this very important part of the body.

Can I Enhance the Vagus by Myself?

Wondering if you can enhance the vagal tone to improve your health? you're very lucky! Many psychologists, neuroscientists and general health experts say that we can use the power of the vagus nerve to improve our mental health. Christopher Bergland of Psychology Today wrote: "Vagstov (acetylcholine) is like a sedative; you only need to take a deep, deep breath of the diabetes muscle to manage yourself." In other words, the vagus nerve is closely related to breathing-no wonder connecting breathing is the basic principle of yoga and meditation. In addition to breathing, there are many other ways to give the vagus nerve much-needed exercise. So, here are the five ways to help you relieve anxiety and stress at the neurobiological level.

1. Sing and Music

Studies have shown that singing has a biologically soothing effect, which is related to the vagus nerve. From slow spells to chanting, to making your favourite 90s song, it's all-inclusive.

2. Laughter

One of the side effects in the study that tested the effects of vagal nerve stimulation on children with epilepsy was uncontrollable laughter. Although this is not an ideal side effect in a clinical setting, it does indicate that laughter is associated with increased vagal stimulation. So smile often; there are many proven benefits!

3. Intermittent Fasting.

Some studies have shown that fasting and dietary restrictions can activate the vagus nerve, and considering all other health benefits of fasting, it is definitely something to consider.

4. Biofeedback.

Biofeedback, especially heart rate variability biofeedback, is an amazing technology that works by visually showing what is happening in the body. Although in this way, one can better understand the physiological role of deep breathing or relaxation techniques. The vagus nerve plays a major role in respiratory regulation and heart rate variability, so this may be an interesting exercise.

5. Cold Exposure.

Studies have shown that cold exposure can cause changes in the activity of the parasympathetic nervous system, which is known to be regulated by the vagus nerve. Therefore, if you have never tried the benefits of hot and cold showers, the vagus nerve may be a good reason to start.

6. Probiotics.

We already know that the vagus nerve plays a major role in the gut-brain axis, but for scientific reasons, we now know that gut microbe can actually activate the vagus nerve. As you can imagine, this plays an important role in our brain and behaviour- in case you need other reasons to invest in effective probiotics.

Are you looking for more anti-anxiety skills? These are our 13 favourite foods that can help relieve anxiety and stress, and provide an article to help you identify unexpected habits that may make you moody, anxious and depressed.

Vagus Nerve Stimulation Technology: How to Maintain the Vagus Nerve?

Vagal tension is an internal biological process that represents vagal activity. Increased vagal tone activates the parasympathetic nervous system, which means that we can relax more quickly under stressful conditions, which will have a positive effect on our emotional balance and overall health.

Various vagal stimulation techniques exist:

1. Exposed to the Cold

It has been found that exposure to cold activates the vagus nerve because it stimulates cholinergic neurons that pass through these innervations. The survey conducted by the University of Oulu revealed that frequent exposure to weather helps reduce the angry response that triggers the sympathetic nervous system.

A cold shower of 30 seconds a day or a cold towel on the face is sufficient. Some people lie on the abdomen and put a block of ice on the nape of the neck. Others like to down a glass of cold water.

2. Dia Muscle Breathing

Most people inhale air 10 to 14 times per minute, which means they have shallow breathing. The ideal situation is to inhale air six times per minute. Therefore, another very effective vagal stimulation technique is deep breathing.

In particular, the breathing of the diaphragm muscle activates the vagus nerve, and the brain thinks it is necessary to calm itself down, even if the nerve does not explicitly specify the order. The mechanism is the same. If you close your eyes and pat with your finger on the eyelid, you will feel a short flash of light, because the brain will explain it this way. Breathing through the diaphragm allows us to take deeper breaths to introduce air into the lower chest, use the membrane properly and promote relaxation.

3. Meditation, Yoga and Tai Chi

Meditation can increase vagal tone. Researchers at the University of Oregon have proven this. They have seen that mindfulness meditation can promote a positive feeling for themselves in only five days, which leads to activation of the vagus nerve and regulates the activity of the parasympathetic nervous system, which is better than traditional relaxation techniques. Much more.

Even exercises like yoga and tai chi are ideal for stimulating the vagus nerve. A Boston University study showed that yoga could increase GABA neurotransmitters and promote a feeling of calm and tranquillity by helping to fight anxiety and stress. On the other hand, researchers from the National Medical College of Yongming University say that Tai Chi can balance the heart rhythm, which means it can stimulate the modulation of the vagus nerve.

9 Fascinating Facts About the Vagus Nerve

The vagus nerve is so described because it "wanders" like a tramp, sending sensory fibers from the brainstem to the internal organs. The vagus nerve is the longest intracranial nerve, and it controls your internal nerve centre-parasympathetic nervous system. It is responsible for supervising various vital functions, transmitting motion and sensory impulses to every organ of the body. New research shows that it may also be the missing link in the treatment of chronic inflammation and the beginning of an exciting new therapeutic field for the treatment of severe, incurable diseases. These are nine facts about this powerful nerve bundle.

1. The Vagus Nerve Prevents Inflammation

A certain degree of inflammation after injury or illness is reasonable. However, from sepsis to autoimmune disease rheumatoid arthritis, too many diseases are associated with many diseases and conditions. The vagus nerve manipulates a vast network of fibers, distributed across all organs like a spy. When it receives a signal of early inflammation (the presence of cytokines or substances called tumour necrosis factor (TNF)), it reminds the brain. It extracts anti-inflammatory neurotransmitters that regulate the body's immune response.

2. It Helps You Remember

A study conducted at the University of Virginia in rats showed that vagal stimulation stimulates memory. This action releases the neurotransmitter norepinephrine into the amygdala, thereby consolidating memory. Related studies in humans have shown that the treatment of Alzheimer's disease and other diseases has broad prospects.

3. It Can Help You Breathe.

The neurotransmitter acetylcholine caused by the vagus nerve tells your lungs to breathe. This is one of the reasons why botulinum toxin, which is often used in cosmetics, may be dangerous because it interferes with the production of acetylcholine. However, you can also stimulate the vagus nerve by doing abdominal breathing or holding your breath four to eight times.

4. It is Closely Related to Your Heart.

The vagus nerve is efficient for controlling the heart rhythm by electrical pulses on specialized muscle tissue in the right atrium (the heart's natural pacemaker), and the release of acetylcholine slows the pulse. By measuring the time between each heartbeat and then plotting it on a chart, the doctor can determine your heart rate variability or HRV. This data can provide clues about the elasticity of your heart and vagus nerve.

5. It Initiates Your Body's Relaxation Response.

When you keep a vigilant sympathetic nervous system to speed up wrestling or escape reactions, pour the stress hormones cortisol and epinephrine into the body, and the vagus nerve will tell your body to relax by releasing acetylcholine. The vagus tendrils extend to many organs, just like optical cables, giving instructions to release enzymes and proteins (such as prolactin, vasopressin, and oxytocin) to calm you down. People with more robust vagal responses are more likely to recover faster after being stressed, injured or sick.

6. It Switches Between Your Internal Organs and Brain.

Your intestine uses the vagus nerve like a walkie-talkie to tell the brain how you feel with electrical impulses called "action potentials." Your gut feels very real.

7. The Movement of the Vagus Nerve is the Most Common Cause of Hair Loss.

If you tremble or feel uncomfortable when you see blood or flu shots, you are not weak. You are experiencing "vagal syncope". Your body's response to stress can overstimulate the vagus nerve, which can cause a drop in blood pressure and heart rate. During periods of extreme syncope, blood flows to your brain, causing you to lose consciousness. But most of the time, you only need to sit down or lie down to relieve symptoms.

8. Electrical Stimulation of the Vagus Nerve can Reduce Inflammation, and can Completely Suppress Inflammation.

Neurosurgeon Kevin Tracey was the first to prove that stimulation of the vagus nerve can significantly reduce inflammation. The results for rats were so successful, he replicated the experiment in humans and obtained amazing results. Electronic implants are used to create vagus nerve-stimulating implants, which are significant in rheumatoid arthritis (no cure and often treated with toxic drugs), hemorrhagic shock, and other equally severe inflammatory syndromes. The reduction in magnitude or even ease.

9. Vagus Nerve Stimulation has Created a New Field of Medicine.

Under the stimulation of vagal nerve stimulation therapy to successfully treat inflammation and epilepsy, the emerging medical research field (called bioelectronics) may become the future of medicine. Scientists and doctors hope to use implants that can deliver electrical pulses to various parts of the body to treat diseases with fewer drugs and fewer side effects.

Vagus Nerve Stimulation and Depression

Vagus nerve stimulation has often been used to treat epilepsy. The US Food and Drug Administration (FDA) Trusted Source approved VNS in 2005 as an option for patients with drug-resistant depression. This process involves the stimulation of the vagus nerve by electric shock. This stimulation seems to change the brain wave pattern and help reduce or eliminate depression symptoms.

How Does VNS Work

There are two main vagus nerves, one on each side of the body. Both start at the bottom of the neck and extend from the brain stem to the chest. VNS involves implanting a pacemaker-like device called a pulse generator in the chest cavity. The device is slightly larger than a one-dollar silver coin. And it is connected to the left vagus nerve through a thread that runs under the skin. The pulse generator is programmed to deliver current continuously. It stimulates nerves for a certain period of time. Then pause for a few minutes before sending the next pulse.

The doctor is not entirely sure how the stimulation of the vagus nerve relieves the symptoms of depression. It seems that VNS may help to reset the chemical imbalance in the emotional centre of the brain. Many medical experts have compared it with electroconvulsive therapy (ECT). Although ECT is a treatment that involves stimulating parts of the brain with electrical pulses.

Who is VNS Suitable For?

Vagal stimulation has only been used to treat depression in recent years. Research on how it works is still ongoing. It is usually considered a last resort. Doctors usually recommend that you try different types and combinations of drugs and psychotherapy before trying VNS.

This treatment is recommended only for adults 18 years and older with antidepressants. The FDA also recommends that you continue other forms of treatment with VNS. Other treatments include drug therapy and cognitive behavioural therapy. People who are pregnant or have other neurological diseases may not be eligible for VNS. Your doctor can help you determine if vagal nerve stimulation is right for you. Many health insurances plans do not cover VNS. This process may cost thousands of dollars.

Possible Side Effects and Complications

Vagal nerve stimulation involves major surgery to implant a pulse generator. Complications may occur during and after the operation. Common risks associated with surgery include:

- Infection
- Pain
- Breathing problems
- Vagus nerve injury

Another risk of VNS surgery is the possibility of vocal cord paralysis. This will happen if the device moves after implantation. You may also need to stop taking certain medicines a few days before the operation.

People who have undergone VNS surgery may experience a variety of side effects. These can include:

- Chest pain
- Sore throat
- Hard to swallow
- Difficulty breathing

Depression may also worsen in some people. In some cases, the pulse generator may be interrupted or need to be adjusted, which requires another operation.

The Importance of Vagus Nerve to Health

Have you ever questioned why some people feel full after eating a small amount of food, while others are hungry until they take a large portion?

The answer may be the sensitivity of the vagus nerve. The vagus nerve is the nerve that connects the intestine to the brain and is an essential part of the parasympathetic nervous system (the "rest and digestion" reaction is basically the opposite of "fighting or running away").

The signals transmitted by the vagus nerve from the intestine to the brain can affect your activation of hunger and fullness, emotional and stress levels, and inflammatory stress responses. The signal travels from the vagus nerve of the brain to the intestine, affecting digestion, secretion of digestive enzymes, and gastrointestinal motility.

This is a significant way. The activation of the vagus nerve is related to obesity, gastrointestinal diseases, cardiovascular diseases, low mood (such as depression) and various other chronic health problems. This is why the vagus nerve is so important, and how diet improves health by affecting vagal signals in the gut. The vagus nerve controls your hunger.

The signal of hunger and fullness is a significant way of communication running up and down the vagus nerve. E.g....

A large amount of food in the stomach transmits satiety signals to your brain through the vagus nerve. This is how your mind knows that you will no longer feel hungry after a meal. Nutrient sensors and neurotransmitters (such as serotonin and ghrelin) produced in the gut can also send hunger and satiety signals to the brain through the vagus nerve.

Obesity is associated with reduced sensitivity of the vagus nerve to fullness signals, and there is a lot of evidence that this is caused by diet. Obesity diets can actually change the vagus nerve's sensitivity to fullness signals, so the brain needs more food to get the "immediate fullness" signal. As you might expect, stimulation of the vagus nerve (which makes the satiety signal "increase the volume") often leads to weight loss in experimental animals- although it is worth noting that the results of human studies are uneven.

Vagus Nerve and Other Health Problems

Hunger is a significant cause of vagus nerve. However, if you study PubMed in-depth, you will find that vagal dysfunction is actually related to various other problems. This is because the vagus nerve also helps regulate inflammation, and inflammation involves almost all chronic diseases. Stimulating vagal nerve signals into the brain has an anti-inflammatory effect-it can reduce the brain's stress response and reduce the production of inflammatory cytokines.

Upset Stomach

Because the vagus nerve is a two-way path, and there are many complex feedback loops between the brain and the intestine (remember, the vagus nerve operates bidirectionally!), The effect here is challenging to unravel. But for those who only care about improving their health, the exact mechanism may not be as important as a result, which is absolutely impressive:

Vagal control inflammation can affect cardiovascular health, and vagal stimulation may help prevent cardiovascular events. In patients with Crohn's disease, an inflammatory bowel disease, the vagal nerve signal disappears, and a small preliminary study found that vagal nerve stimulation helps treat symptoms.

The vagus nerve may also be associated with irritable bowel syndrome, and vagal nerve stimulation may help reduce IBS pain. This study is fascinating: using vagus nerve stimulation to treat diabetes-prone rats can prevent depression and insulin resistance. This is enormous evidence that depression and diabetes may both originate in the intestines.

If a poor diet affects the sensitivity of the vagus nerve, then it may also have second-hand effects on all of these diseases. So, this may be one of the purposes of why gut health plays such an essential role in overall health.

Maintain and Feed the Vagus Nerve

So far, we know that obesity "cafeteria diet" (high-fat, high-carbohydrate junk food) will reduce the sensitivity of the vagus nerve, and vagal nerve stimulation will offset this situation, which is a great benefit to weight ... and All other aspects. Unfortunately, the "vagus nerve stimulation" in these studies is not something you can do at home; it is a device that allows the subject to be surgically implanted into the body. However, if poor eating habits can reduce the sensitivity of the vagus nerve, then good eating habits can help it recover. In addition to "don't eat junk food", here are some more specific studies. This study found that dietary fat reduces inflammation through its effect on the vagus nerve. The author concludes: "High-fat nutrition has a therapeutic effect on various inflammatory diseases (such as sepsis and inflammatory bowel disease (IBD)), which is characterized by an inflammatory response, in which ... intestinal barrier function is impaired."

The link between a ketogenic (very high fat, low carbohydrate) diet and vagal stimulation is supported. Vagal stimulation is two effective treatments for drug-resistant epilepsy. The ketogenic diet may suppress hunger and reduce inflammation by stimulating the vagus nerve.

The study also found that probiotics can activate the vagus nerve. Probiotics improve the stress signal of the intestines and brains of students taking stress tests and inhibit the release of the stress hormone cortisol. This suggests that probiotics may be able to disrupt the intestinal-gut-gut-brain feedback loop above and below the vagus nerve that causes psychological problems caused by intestinal problems, thereby sending more hormonal stress signals to the brain, causing more bowel problems. Aerobic exercise may also help.

For immediate satisfaction, you can also use the Valsalva action for vagal stimulation. Sit down because it makes you dizzy. Take a deep breath, then close your mouth and pinch your nose so that the air cannot escape. Then pretend as if you want to breathe, but don't open your nose or mouth, you should feel the pressure of the air. Continue for 15 to 20 seconds, then let the air expel and breathe normally. (If any weight lifting is performed, this is a breath-holding motion that stabilizes the spine during squats and deadlifts.)

The Valsalva exercise will not have a long-term impact but may be helpful in emergencies, such as before testing or during commuting. There is nothing to continue-very little research on diet and vagus nerves. But this is the beginning thing; it does support all the essential connections of the intestine, brain and the rest of the body. Understanding the vagus nerve helps explain why gut health, mental health, and general health are intertwined with each other, and why good gut health is so essential for things beyond digestion.

Vagus Nerve Stimulation and its Many Benefits

Inflammation is the source cause of most diseases because the immune system sends out an inflammatory response to protect cells when it senses danger. However, discovering the initial cause of inflammation may prove to be a more significant challenge. The vagus nerve is connected to a multi-body system and has a significant impact on systemic inflammation and overall health.

Explore the vagus nerve and its functions

Why the vagus nerve is necessary and how it promotes health, including:

- Why the vagus nerve is important
- How the vagus nerve affects health
- Signs and symptoms of vagal dysfunction
- Vagus nerve stimulation and its benefits
- Important note about gluten and vagus nerve

Why the Vagus Nerve is Important

"Vagina" is derived from the Latin word "vagus" (vagus), which means "drift", and its name is true and correct. The vagus nerve extends from the roots of the cerebellum and brainstem, meanders through the body, and branches multiple times to innervate all the following major organs:

- Pharynx
- Throat
- Heart
- Oesophagus
- Stomach
- Small intestine and
- Large intestine until its splenic flexure

The extended range causes the vagus nerve to play a role in functions such as taste, swallowing, speech, heart rate, digestion and excretion. The vagus nerve is an irreplaceable member of the parasympathetic nervous system (PNS). It is related to physiological activities classified as "rest and digestion."

As the name suggests, PNS is correctly used to calm the body and digest food to restore the body's energy supply and other functions. To achieve this goal, the vagus nerve communicates with its related organs by releasing a neurotransmitter called acetylcholine, which helps regulate blood pressure, blood sugar balance, heart rate, taste, digestion, breathing, crying, sweating,

Kidney function, bile release, saliva secretion, female fertility and orgasm.

Hormones throughout the body also come into contact with the vagus nerve. Insulin reduces the release of glucose in the liver, which stimulates the vagus nerve, while the thyroid hormone T3 stimulates the vagus nerve, which increases appetite and ghrelin production. Ghrelin also stimulates the vagus nerve to increase hunger.

The vagal function is essential for the release of oxytocin, testosterone and vasoactive intestinal peptide. The activation of parathyroid hormone, which produces growth hormone-releasing hormone GHRH, and converts vitamin D3 into active vitamin D, also depends on the vagus nerve.

How the Vagus Nerve Affects Mental and Physical Health

Although the vagus nerve affects the central nervous system composed of the brain and spinal cord or organs other than the central nervous system, it is essential to remember that the vagus nerve is rooted in the brain stem and cerebellum. The best vagal function or "high vagal tone index" is associated with secure social connections, positive emotions and better physical health. People with low vagal tone index will feel depressed, heart attack, loneliness, negative emotions and stroke. Brain health and gut health affect each other, and the vagus nerve is precisely the link between the two. The vagal tone index can be regarded as the human body's "intuition", which is directly transmitted to the brain and produces more positive or negative feedback loops.

Emerging research shows that the vagal tone index is determined by the signals (called cytokines) released by the immune system. In order to better understand the potential of vagal stimulation to treat inflammatory diseases (such as rheumatoid arthritis) without the use of drugs, research is ongoing.

Signs and Symptoms of Vagal Dysfunction

In view of the extensive connection between the brain and the intestine via the vagus nerve and its branches, many areas are prone to dysfunction. These areas can be divided into three main areas:

- Communication in the brain
- Communication from the brain to other organs
- Communication between different organs and brain

Depending on the affected area, vagal dysfunction may manifest as:

- Aggression
- Anxiety
- Brain fog
- Chronic inflammation
- Delayed gastric emptying

- Depression
- Hard to swallow
- Dizziness or syncope
- Fatigue
- Heart rate changes (big or low)
- Heartburn
- Irritable bowel syndrome (IBS)
- Vitamin b12 deficiency
- Weight gain

Without diagnosis or treatment, vagal dysfunction can lead to more severe diseases, including:

- Alcohol addiction
- Autism
- Bulimia
- Cancer
- Chronic heart failure
- Fibromyalgia
- Heart disease
- Intestinal leakage syndrome
- Memory impairment or Alzheimer's disease
- Migraine
- Mood disorder
- Multiple sclerosis (MS)
- Obesity

- Obsessive-compulsive disorder (OCD)
- Poor blood circulation
- Tinnitus

Avoiding diseases and lifestyle choices that damage the vagus nerve is essential to maintaining the aforementioned signs and symptoms. These include alcoholism, anxiety, diabetes, fatigue, physical damage to the vagus nerve, poor posture and stress.

Vagus Nerve Stimulation and its Benefits

Vagal nerve dysfunction is usually caused by a low vagal tone index, so stimulation of the vagus nerve can be used as a treatment for the above symptoms, signs and diseases. Many of these treatments represent lifestyle changes, which means that it is safe to use more than one of the following practices to increase the vagal tone index.

- Add seafood to your diet: EPA and DHA found in seafood stimulate the vagus nerve, increase heart rate variability and decrease heart rate. These effects can also be obtained from fish oil supplements.
- Be a yogi: Yoga can not only improve mood and reduce anxiety but also increase the activity of the vagus nerve and parasympathetic nervous system. Slow, deep breathing associated with yoga activates the highly sensitive baroreceptors in the heart and neck, called baroreceptors, which send signals to the brain to activate the vagus nerve.

- Build a social relationship: Studies have shown that social relationships bring individuals closer to others, a feeling that stimulates the vagus nerve.
- Chewing gum: Chewing gum can promote the release of the hormone CCK in the intestinal tract, which helps to improve the communication between the vagus nerve and the brain.
- Cough or contract abdominal muscles: The vagus nerve produces a sensation of coughing or defecation, so resuming these activities will stimulate the vagus nerve.
- Eat more fibre: Fibre increases GLP-1. GLP-1 is a hormone that supports communication between the vagus nerve and the brain. It slows the emptying of the stomach and prolongs the fullness of the body.
- Joint throat: Activities such as singing, gargle, and even activating gag reflex will attract the throat and stimulate the vagus nerve. To help activate the gag reflex, use a tongue depressor or spoon.
- Exercise regularly: Exercise stimulates the vagus nerve and stimulates intestinal flow, thereby benefiting the vagus index and faecal matter.
- Intermittently fast: Intermittent fasting can reduce the number of calories consumed. The reduction in calories will cause the heart rate variability to soar and the

metabolism to drop sharply. These are two events that trigger vagal nerve function.
- Find an acupuncturist: Traditional acupuncture therapy, especially ear acupuncture, stimulates the vagus nerve.
- Direct sunlight: UVA rays increase the body's level of stimulating melanocytes (MSH), which is another hormone that stimulates the vagus nerve. UVB rays increase the number of MSH receptors throughout the body, making it possible for more MSH to bind.
- Daily prayer: Studies have shown that prayer increases diastolic blood pressure and heart rate variability, thereby stimulating the vagus nerve. These effects enhance overall cardiovascular health.
- Smile more: The connection between laughter and vagus sounds has initially been due to people fainting due to events involving body droop, such as coughing, laughing, bowel movements, swallowing, and urination. Fainting is caused by other syndromes related to the vagus nerve, but in healthy individuals, laughter can enhance cognitive ability while preventing heart disease.
- Learn to love the cold: Adjusting to a temperature lower than the average body temperature will trigger PNS function through vagal nerve stimulation. The best results can be achieved by drinking cold water, immersing your face in cold water or washing cold water.

- Meditate every day: Meditation to promote love and friendliness within the spirit will increase the vagal tone index. Chanting is another method of meditation that produces the same effect.
- Practice Tai Chi: Studies have shown that Tai Chi increases heart rate variability, indicating that it can be achieved by activating the vagus nerve.
- Regular massage: Neck and foot massage stimulates the vagus nerve while simultaneously reducing the risk of seizures and heart disease, respectively. Whole-body pressure massage stimulates intestinal function and indirectly activates the vagus nerve.
- Sleep on the right: Lying on the back will reduce activation of the vagus nerve, but sleeping on the right side will show greater vagal stimulation than sleeping on the left side.
- Spend some time with Nervana: Nerves are a form of technology designed to stimulate the vagus nerve with radio waves synchronized with music. It can be used as a single-sided generator or a double-sided headset. Nervana triggers the release of neurotransmitters in the brain and causes physical and mental peace.
- Supplement zinc and serotonin (5-HTP): Zinc is essential for the function of the vagus nerve, and many people unknowingly lack this mineral. Serotonin activates the vagus nerve through several different receptors in the

body. Taking probiotics to optimize intestinal health is the ideal choice to maximize vagal stimulation. Taking probiotics can ensure this, especially the probiotic Lactobacillus rhamnosus, which improves the GABA receptor function of the vagus nerve in animal studies.
- Try enema: Accelerating bowel movements enlarges the bowel and activates vagal activity.
- Treatment with pulsed electromagnetic field (PEMF): Research has confirmed that the magnetic field stimulates the vagus nerve by increasing heart rate variability. Using a device that stimulates pulsed magnetic field waves directly on the intestine, head and neck will target the vagus nerve.
- Perform vocal cords: Recitation, humming, singing, speaking, and other harmony exercises increase heart rate variability, thereby activating the vagus nerve.

Anatomy and Function of the Vagus Nerve

The word "blur" means wandering in Latin. This is a very suitable name because the vagus nerve is the longest cranial nerve. It extends from the brain stem to a part of the colon.

The sensory function of the vagus nerve is divided into two parts:

- Somatic cell composition. These are the sensations felt on the skin or muscles.
- Internal organs. These are the sensations felt in human organs.

The sensory functions of the vagus nerve include:

- Provides somatosensory information on the skin behind the ear, the outside of the ear canal and certain parts of the throat
- Provides visceral sensory details on the larynx, oesophagus, lungs, trachea, heart and most of the digestive tract
- Plays a small role in the sense of taste near the base of the tongue

The motor functions of the vagus nerve include:

- Stimulates the muscles in the pharynx, larynx and soft pa, which is the fleshy area near the back of the top of the mouth
- Stimulates the muscles of the heart and helps lower the resting heart rate
- Stimulates involuntary contractions of the digestive tract, including the oesophagus, stomach, and most intestines, allowing food to pass through the digestive tract.

Vagus Never Test

To test the vagus nerve, the doctor may check the vomiting reflex. During this part of the examination, the doctor may use a soft cotton swab to itch the throat on both sides. This should cause the person to get sick. If the person is not nauseous, it may be caused by the vagus nerve.

Vagus Problem

Nerve injury

Damage to the vagus nerve may produce a series of symptoms because the nerve is very long and affects many areas.

Potential symptoms of vagus nerve damage include:

- Difficulty speaking or unclear voice
- Hoarseness or wheezing
- Drinking water trouble
- Loss of vomiting reflex
- Earache
- Abnormal heart rhythm
- Abnormal blood pressure
- Reduced gastric acid production
- Nausea or vomiting
- Bloating or abdominal pain
- Someone's symptoms may depend on where the nerve is damaged.

Gastroparesis

Experts believe that damage to the vagus nerve may also cause gastroparesis. This situation will affect the involuntary contraction of the digestive system, thereby preventing the regular emptying of the stomach.

Symptoms of gastroparesis include:

- Nausea or vomiting, especially food that has not been digested for hours after eating
- Loss of appetite or fullness soon after a meal
- Acid reflux
- Abdominal pain or bloating
- Unexplained weight loss
- Blood sugar fluctuations

Some people develop gastroparesis after a vagal nerve cut operation, which removes all or part of the vagus nerve.

Vagal Syncope

Sometimes the vagus nerve overreacts to specific stress triggers, such as:

- Exposure to extreme heat
- Fear of physical harm
- See blood or draw blood
- Nervousness, including trying to defecate
- Standing for a long time

Remember, the vagus nerve stimulates specific muscles in the heart, which can help slow down your heart rate. Overreaction can cause a sudden drop in heart rate and blood pressure, which can cause syncope. This is called vasovagal syncope.

Vagus Nerve Stimulation

Vagus nerve stimulation involves placing the device inside the body, which uses electrical pulses to stimulate the nerves. It is used to treat epilepsy and depression that do not respond to other therapies. The device is usually placed under the skin of the chest and connected to the left vagus nerve by wires. After activating the invention, it will send a signal to your brainstem through the vagus nerve, and then transmit the information to your brain. Neurologists usually program the device, but people typically receive a handheld magnet, which they can also use to control the device.

It is believed that vagal stimulation may help treat a range of other diseases in the future, including multiple sclerosis, suspicious sources, Alzheimer's disease, trusted sources, and cluster headaches.

How to Stimulate Your Vagus Nerve for the Better Mental Health

Over the years, vagal stimulation has played a crucial role in controlling anxiety and mental health. What is the vagus nerve? The vagus nerve is the largest cranial nerve in your body. It connects your brain to many vital organs of the body, including the intestines (gut, stomach), heart and lungs.

The word "vagus nerve" means "the wanderer" in Latin, and it accurately represents how the nerve wanders throughout the body and reaches each organ. The vagus nerve is also a crucial part of the parasympathetic "rest and digest" system. It will affect your breathing, digestive function and heart rate, all of which will have a significant impact on your mental health.

However, what you need to pay special attention to is the "tone" of the vagus nerve. Vagal tension is an internal biological process that represents vagal activity. Increasing vagal tone activates the parasympathetic nervous system, and a higher vagal sound means that your body can relax more quickly after stress. In 2010, researchers discovered that vagal tone is high, and there is a positive feedback loop between positive emotions and good health. In other words, the more you increase the vagal tone, the better your physical and mental health, and vice versa.

"It's almost like yin and yang. The vagus nerve response reduces stress. So, it lowers our heart rate and blood pressure. So, it changes the function of certain parts of the brain, stimulates digestion, and all these things that happen when you relax." Interestingly, research has even shown that vagal tone is passed from mother to child. Frustrated during pregnancy, anxious and angry mothers have low vagal activity. Once they have a baby, the neonatal vagal event is shallow, and the levels of dopamine and serotonin are also small.

Vagal nerve tension can be measured by tracking specific biological processes such as heart rate, respiration rate, and heart rate variability (HRV). When your HRV is high, your vagal tone is also high. They are interrelated. You can use the EmWave2 device to increase HRV. Some researchers use EmWave2 in their research to measure vagal tone.

If your vagus nerve is lowered, rest assured you can take steps to enhance the vagus nerve by stimulating it. This will enable you to respond more effectively to the emotional and physical symptoms of brain and mental illness.

Stimulation of the vagus nerve and enhancement of vagal tone have been shown to help treat a variety of brain and mental health conditions, including:

- Depression
- Anxiety
- Alzheimer's disease
- Migraine
- Fibromyalgia
- Tinnitus
- Alcohol addiction

- Autism
- Bulimia nervosa
- Personality disorder
- Heroin seeking behaviour
- Poor memory
- Elderly emotional disorders
- Multiple sclerosis
- Obsessive-compulsive disorder
- Severe mental illness
- Traumatic brain injury
- Chronic fatigue syndrome

For people with treatment-resistant depression, the FDA even approved a surgically implanted device that regularly stimulates the vagus nerve. And it works. But you don't have to go that way.

Follow the 13 steps below, and you can naturally enjoy the benefits of vagal stimulation.

1. Cold Exposure

Acute cold exposure has been shown to stimulate the vagus nerve and activate cholinergic neurons through the vagus pathway. Researchers have also found that regularly placing yourself in the cold will reduce your sympathetic "fight or flight" response and increase sympathetic nerve activity through the vagus nerve.

I often wash in cold water and go out wearing the least clothes in cold weather. Try to end your next shower with at least 30 seconds of cold water, and then see how you feel. Then work your way longer. This is painful, but the lingering effect is worth it. You can also simply stick your face in cold water to relax.

2. Deep Breathing and Slow Breathing

Deep breathing and slow breathing are another way to stimulate the vagus nerve. Studies have shown that it can reduce anxiety and increase the parasympathetic nervous system by activating the vagus nerve.

Most people breathe about 10 to 14 times per minute. About six breaths in one minute is an excellent way to relieve stress. You should breathe deeply from the transverse diaphragm. Although when you do this, your stomach should expand outward. Your breath should be long and slow. So, this is the key to stimulating the vagus nerve and achieving relaxation.

The best way to know if you are on the right track is to use the EmWave2 device. This is a biofeedback device that helps you adjust your breathing rate. I have previously written about the benefits of using this device here.

3. Sing, hum, Sing and Gargle

The vagus nerve attaches to your vocal cords and the muscles in the back of your throat. Singing, humming, chanting and gargle can activate these muscles and stimulate the vagus nerve. It turns out that this increases heart rate variability and vagal tone. I often rinse my mouth before swallowing. Dr Datis Kharrazian's book "Why doesn't my brain work?"

4. Acupuncture

Acupuncture is another alternative therapy that can stimulate the vagus nerve. I like the ear acupuncture very much. Ear acupuncture refers to inserting a needle into the ear. I suggest that you try to find a doctor who can provide medical staff in your area, especially when you want to quit psychiatric drugs. The first time I took antidepressants helped me. I'm surprised.

Studies have shown that ear acupuncture stimulates the vagus nerve, increases vagal activity and vagal tone, and can help treat "neurodegenerative diseases caused by vagal regulation". In my experience, ear acupuncture is extra effective than ordinary acupuncture. I am not sure why. I have personally noticed that ear acupuncture has more benefits.

At the end of each appointment, my practitioners will fix these small black seeds on my ears. I also use this acupuncture pad at home to relax before bed.

5. Yoga and Tai Chi

Yoga and Tai Chi are two "body and body relaxation" techniques that work by stimulating the vagus nerve and increasing the activity of the "rest and digest" nervous system of the parasympathetic nerve. Studies have shown that yoga increases

GABA. The researchers believe that this is achieved by "stimulating vagal afferent", which increases parasympathetic nervous system activity.

The researchers also found that yoga stimulates the vagus nerve, so people who deal with depression and anxiety should practice yoga. Despite many excellent studies, I do not like yoga. Many people swear, but this is not for me. I like Tai Chi. Tai Chi has also been shown to improve heart rate variability, which researchers believe means it can "enhance vagal modulation".

6. Probiotics

For researchers, it is becoming increasingly clear that intestinal bacteria can improve brain function by affecting the vagus nerve. Although in one study, animals were given the probiotic Lactobacillus rhamnosus, and the researchers found positive changes in GABA receptors in their brains, reduced stress hormones, and reduced depression and anxiety-like behaviour.

The researchers also concluded that the vagus nerve promotes beneficial changes between the gut and the brain. When the vagus nerves of other mice were excised, the addition of Lactobacillus rhamnosus to its digestive system failed to reduce anxiety, stress and improve mood. Another study found that the probiotic Bifidobacterium Longum works through the vagus nerve to normalize anxiety-like behaviour in mice.

Both Lactobacillus rhamnosus and Bifidobacterium longum are included in Optimal Biotics supplements. I have written some other methods before that can increase the beneficial bacteria in the intestines. You can read about it here. Seven other probiotic strains that can help treat anxiety disorders.

7. Meditation and Neurofeedback

Meditation is my favourite relaxation technique, and it can stimulate the vagus nerve and increase vagal tone. Studies have shown that meditation can increase vagal mood and positive emotions and promote a sense of friendliness. Another study found that meditation reduced sympathetic "fight or escape" activity and increased vagal modulation. The "OM" chanting frequently performed in meditation stimulates the vagus nerve. I can't find any research to prove this, but in my experience, neurofeedback has significantly increased the heart rate variability and vagal tone measured by my wave.

Now that I have completed neurofeedback, I now use the Muse headband for meditation. Similar to neural feedback, it can provide you with real-time feedback about brain waves. I have written here before; you can get it through Amazon or Muse website.

8. Omega-3 Fatty Acids

Omega-3 fatty acids are essential fats that the body cannot produce. They are mainly found in fish and are necessary for the normal electrical function of the brain and nervous system. They often appear in most of my posts because they are essential for brain and mental health and affect many aspects of health.

They have been shown to help people overcome addiction, repair "leaky brains", and even help reverse cognitive decline. But the researchers also found that omega-3 fatty acids increase vagal tone and vagal activity. Studies have shown that they reduce heart rate and increase heart rate variability, which means they may stimulate the vagus nerve.

A large number of fish consumption is also related to "enhancing vagal activity and parasympathetic advantage". This is why I have to eat a lot of wild salmon, and this krill oil supplement.

9. Exercise

I have discussed how use increases the brain's growth hormone, supports the brain's mitochondria and helps reverse cognitive decline. But it can also stimulate the vagus nerve, which may explain the beneficial effects of the vagus nerve on the brain and mental health. Many brain health experts recommend exercise as the first recommendation for optimal brain health.

This is my daily exercise:

- Weightlifting 1-4 times a week
- High-intensity interval sprints 1-2 times a week
- Do my best (ideal walk 30-60 minutes a day)

Walking, weight lifting and sprinting are the best ways to exercise, but you should choose your favourite exercise or daily exercise method so that you can always stick to it.

10. Zinc

As I discussed earlier, zinc is an essential mineral for mental health, especially if you have a chronic anxiety disorder. One study showed that zinc could increase vagal stimulation in zinc-deficient rats. And it is estimated that 2 billion people worldwide lack zinc, and six different studies have shown that subclinical zinc deficiency can impair brain function in children and adults.

Therefore, if you have a brain disease or mental illness, it is likely that you will collapse. Best food sources of zinc include oysters, grass-fed beef, pumpkin seeds, cashew nuts, mushrooms and spinach. However, I still recommend at least a short-term supplement to ensure that you consume enough. I created and took the best zinc supplements to ensure that my zinc level is optimal. If you are interested in discovering more steps to increase the zinc content, please check my previous articles on zinc and copper.

11. Massage

Studies have shown that massage can stimulate the vagus nerve and increase vagal activity and vagal tone. The vagus nerve can also be stimulated by pressing certain areas of the body.

Foot massage (foot reflexology) has been shown to increase vagal modulation and heart rate variability, and reduce the sympathetic response to "fight or escape". Massaging the carotid sinus near the right side of your throat can also stimulate the vagus nerve to reduce seizures. I get a massage from a registered massage therapist every two months.

12. Socialize and Laugh

I have discussed how socializing and laughing can reduce the body's primary stress hormones. Now, I understand that they are likely to do this by stimulating the vagus nerve. Researchers have found that reflecting on positive social relationships can improve vagal tone and increase positive emotion.

Laughter can increase heart rate variability and improve mood. Vagus nerve stimulation usually causes laughter, indicating that they are connected and influence each other. Therefore, my suggestion is to hang out with your friends and laugh as much as possible. Although I should probably listen to my ideas here, I am introverted and often avoid socializing too full.

13. Intermittent Fasting

On most days, I don't eat breakfast at all, and then eat my first meal at 2 or 3 pm every day to "rest". This means that all the food I eat in a day is within 8 hours. This has many health benefits. As I discussed earlier, intermittent fasting can increase growth hormone in the brain, improve mitochondrial function, and may help some people overcome brain fog and cognitive decline.

Studies have also shown that fasting and calorie restriction increase heart rate variability, which suggests that it increases parasympathetic nerve activity and vagal tone. The best ways to start fasting is simply to eat dinner at around 6 o'clock, do not eat anything before going to bed, and then eat a regular breakfast the next day. That should give you about 12-14 hours of fasting time.

Conclusion

You do not have to be controlled by body and mind. You have the right to tell them what to do. By stimulating the vagus nerve, you can send a message to the body; it is time to relax and reduce stress, which can improve mood, health and elasticity for a long time. The enhancement of vagal emotions allows me to overcome anxiety and depression, and to manage better when anxiety and depression occur. Overall, I hope you apply some of the above steps to daily life and make your life more ideal.

How to Overcome Fear and Anxiety

Fear is one of the important emotions. And it has a powerful effect on your body and mind. When we are in a state of emergency, for example, if we are caught in a fire or attacked, fear will send a strong reaction signal. It will also take effect when you encounter non-dangerous events (such as exams, public speaking, new jobs, appointments and even parties). This is a natural response to perceptible or real threats.

Anxiety is a word we use to express some kind of fear, usually related to threats or ideas of specific issues in the future rather than the present. Fear and anxiety can last a short time and then disappear, but they can also last longer, and you may fall into it. In some cases, they may take over your life, thereby affecting your ability to eat, sleep, focus, travel, enjoy life, and even leave home or go to work or school. This will prevent you from doing what you want or need to do, and also affect your health.

Some people are overwhelmed by fear and want to avoid situations that may make them feel fearful or anxious. Breaking this cycle may be difficult, but there are many ways to do it. You can learn to reduce fear and cope with anxiety so that it will not stop your life.

What Scares You?

Many things scare us. Fear of things like fire may keep you safe. Fear of failure will make you try to do well so that it will not fail, but if you feel too intense, fear will also prevent you from doing well. What you worry about and how you behave when you are afraid will vary from person to person. Just know what makes you feel frightened and why it becomes the first step in solving the fear problem.

What Makes You Anxious?

Since anxiety is fear, the fear we described above also applies to stress. The term "anxiety" is often used to describe the anxiety or to express fear and persistence. Use it when you are worried about what is going on in the future rather than what is happening now. Anxiety is a word that health professionals often use when describing persistent fear. Because the underlying emotions are the same, when you feel fear and anxiety, you feel very similar.

How Do Fear and Anxiety Feel?

When you feel fear or severe anxiety, your body and mind will move quickly. These are some things that can happen:

- Your heart beats fast – maybe it feels irregular
- You breathe quickly
- Your muscles are weak
- You sweat a lot
- Upset stomach or bowel movements

- Find it difficult to focus on anything else
- Are you dizzy?
- You feel frozen
- You can't eat
- You sweat
- Your mouth is dry
- Your muscles are tight

These things happen because your body feels fear and is preparing you for unexpected needs, so that your blood flows to muscles, increases blood sugar, and gives you the mental ability to focus on your body being Things considered threatening. In the long run, when suffering from anxiety disorders, you may have some of the above symptoms and a greater sense of fear, and you may become irritable, have difficulty falling asleep, have headaches, or have difficulty performing work and planning for illness. In the future; you may encounter problems in making love and may lose your confidence.

Why am I Doing this? When I am Not in Any Real Danger?

Early humans needed quick, powerful reactions caused by fear because they were often in a dangerous situation. We no hard face the same threats in modern life. Nonetheless, our mind and body still work in the same way as our early ancestors, and we have the same reaction to modern concerns about bills, travel, and social conditions. However, we cannot escape these challenges, nor can we actually attack them!

The physical sensations of fear can be intimidating in itself- especially if you are experiencing anxiety, and you don't know why, or they look out of proportion to the situation. In addition to alerting you to danger and preparing for coping, your fear or anxiety can provoke any possible imaginary or minor threat.

Why Won't my Fear Disappear and Let me Return to Normal Again?

When you face something strange, anxiety may be a one-time feeling. But it may also be a long-standing daily problem, even if you are not sure why. Some people are continually feeling anxious without any particular trigger.

There are many causes of fear in daily life, and you cannot always figure out exactly why you might be frightened or hurt. Even if you can see the proportion of doubt, the emotional part of the brain will continue to send danger signals to your body. Sometimes, you need physical and mental ways to cope with fear.

What is a Panic Attack?

Panic disorder is when you feel overwhelmed when you are physically and psychologically afraid-what are the symptoms listed under "What do you feel about fear and anxiety?" People with panic disorder say they have difficulty breathing, and they may worry that they are having a heart attack or will lose control of their bodies. If you need help with emergency panic, please refer to the "Support and Information" section at the end of this manual.

What is Phobia?

Phobia is an extreme fear of a specific animal, thing, place or situation. People with phobias need to avoid any contact with particular causes of anxiety or fear. The idea of exposure to hatred makes you feel anxious or panic.

How do I know if I Need Help?

Fear and anxiety affect us all from time to time. Only in difficult and long-lasting situations will doctors classify it as a mental health problem. If you have been feeling anxious for weeks, or feel that fear is affecting your life, then it is best to ask your doctor for help or try using one of the website or phone number brochures listed later in this method. The same is true if phobias cause problems in your daily life, or if you experience panic disorder.

How Can I Help Myself?

If you ever avoid situations that scare you, you may stop doing what you want or need to do. You won't be able to test whether the job is always as bad as you expected, so you missed the opportunity to formulate fears and reduce anxiety. If you fall into this mode, anxiety problems will increase. Exposing yourself to fear can be an effective way to overcome this anxiety.

Knowing Yourself

Keep anxiety diaries or thought records to keep a record of when and what happened. You can try to set some small, achievable goals to deal with your fears. You can carry a list with you, and these lists can sometimes be helpful when you become fearful or anxious. This may be an effective way to solve the underlying beliefs behind anxiety.

Exercise

Increase the amount of use. Practice requires concentration, which can free you from fear and anxiety.

Relax

Learning relaxation techniques can help you ease the psychological and physical feelings of fear. It can help you hang your shoulders and breathe deeply. Or imagine yourself in a relaxing place. You can also try to learn knowledge such as yoga, meditation, massage, or listen to the happiness podcast of the Mental Health Foundation.

Healthy Diet

Eat more fruits and vegetables and try to avoid overeating sugar. A drop in blood sugar can cause you anxiety. Avoid drinking too much tea and coffee because caffeine increases anxiety levels.

Avoid Drinking or Drinking in Moderation.

It is common for people to drink when they are nervous. Some people call alcohol "Dutch courage", but the sequelae of alcohol can make you feel more afraid or anxious.

Complementary Therapy

People find that complementary therapies or exercises or such as relaxation techniques, meditation, yoga or tai chi, can help them relieve anxiety.

Faith / Spirit

If you are religious or spiritual beliefs, this can make you feel connected to something bigger than yourself. Faith can provide a way to cope with daily stress, and attending churches and other faith groups can provide you with a valuable support network.

Speech Therapy

Speech therapy, such as counselling or cognitive behavioural therapy, is beneficial for people with anxiety disorders, including computerized cognitive behavioural therapy, which can guide you through a series of on-screen self-help exercises. Visit your GP for more information.

Medication

Medications are used to provide short-term help instead of focusing on the root causes of anxiety. When used in combination with other treatments or support, the remedy may be most useful.

Support Group

By asking people who have experienced anxiety, you can learn a lot about managing stress. Local support groups or self-help groups bring people with similar experiences together so that they can listen to each other's stories, share skills and encourage each other to try new self-management methods. Your doctor, library, or local civic advisory board will provide you with detailed information about nearby support groups.

Secrets About Stress and Health

Everyone knows that "life stress events" such as unemployment, death of loved ones and divorce (or marriage) increase the risk of illness. Various other life events can also cause stress, and the adverse health effects can range from a cold to severe depression, or even a fatal heart attack. Of course, understanding the link between Stress and illness will only cause you other troubles and may even increase Stress. If you value your health, maybe you should stop reading immediately. Think twice, don't. Most of the claims that stressful events damage health are correct, but some studies are reassuring. Not all secrets about the stress-disease relationship are bad.

If you have read psychology, psychiatry and medical science literature in the past few decades, you may have realized these "secrets". If not, they will be well summarized in a paper and appear in the next issue of the Annual Review of Psychology, which includes Sheldon Cohen and Michael LM Murphy (Michael LM Murphy and Aric A. Prather analyze (in no particular order) what they call the "ten" surprising facts about stressful life events and disease risks. "

Experts Disagree on What is Pressure

No one thinks that certain events can cause severe psychological (and physical) Stress. There is no doubt that the death of a spouse is diagnosed as having a terminal illness and (parent) separating the child from the parent is a "significant stressful life event". However, no clear rules have been established to define the characteristics that classify events into this category (this complicates stress studies, and the results are often unclear).

Some researchers believe that the amount of stress depends on how much "adaptation" is needed to adapt (this is why marriage can be considered particularly stressful). The second theory is to measure Stress based on the degree of threat or injury caused by the event. Some experts believe that pressure is a mismatch between demand and resources. (If you have enough resources (for example, money) to solve and control the difficult situation, the pressure will not be so high; if the boss wants you to complete a three-person project alone within an impossible deadline, then you will feel Stress.) The fourth view holds that "target interruption" is the main feature of life stress events; morbidly, one of the most frequently interrupted goals is to be mentally healthy.

Of course, these theories about stress event guidelines are not mutually exclusive. "There is a clear overlap between these methods," Cohen and colleagues wrote. Overall, they believe that the "threat or harm" view is the most generally accepted view.

For recent examples of stressful life events (primary and secondary), psychologists may ask how to measure a person's stress level. This includes everything from the death of a spouse, to a mortgage, to obtaining a speeding ticket. The life events usually included in a stress questionnaire may be objectively good or bad, primary or secondary. These include the death of spouse, divorce, unemployment or even great achievements. Some stress lists focus more on traumatic events such as attacks. Others asked about events that occurred last year. These changes have brought major or minor changes to daily life and need to be adjusted or adjusted, even if these changes seem to be beneficial (get promoted). Some critical events related to the disease are those that affect social status, self-esteem, identity and physical health.

Not everyone's effects are equal, and there are many differences in how people react.

Stress Can Affect Many Diseases

Depression and heart disease are usually associated with stressful events, but the effects of Stress also extend to other health problems. Many (or even most) conditions can be related to life Stress in some way. Stress can increase anxiety, confuse your hormones and discourage healthy practices such as exercise and diet. At the same time, Stress can trigger bad behaviours, such as smoking and drinking. All of these reactions may have a negative impact on vital organs (brain, heart, liver), and may cause various health problems by triggering disease onset or accelerating disease progression. Stressful events reduce resistance to infection, and even cancer may be related to Stress. But the evidence about cancer is unclear. Stress may affect the development of cancer, but the most potent research shows that the more likely effect of Stress is to reduce the survival rate of disease, rather than cause cancer.

Stress Does Not Mean You Will Get Sick

There is no doubt that trauma and stress events can damage your health. But not always. Cohen and colleagues wrote: "Overall, most people who experience stressful events do not get sick." Experiments that exposed stressed and non-stressed people to the common cold virus found that compared to non-stressed people, they suffer from Stress There are more people than colds, but in spite of this, half of the stressed people remain healthy. Even depression is not an inevitable result of significant life stress. People are more resilient than others. And positive self-image and sense of control are signs of resilience. Negative attitudes and excessive reflection can make the balance frustrating.

Stress Events Will Not Happen Arbitrarily.

With the exception of relatively rare natural disasters, fatal accidents, and other nasty limitations, stressful events are not equal-opportunity attackers. Your personal characteristics and situation and the environment you are in are more or less at risk of life stress. Communities with low socioeconomic status are places where stress events are above average. People with low socioeconomic status are more likely to suffer violence, child death and divorce. Even personality can increase your stress risk (for some reason, neuropathy, people who are not severe and unhappy are more likely to divorce). A study found that "people characterized by negative attribution styles" (i.e., assholes) will encounter more "interpersonal conflicts", thereby increasing the risk of stressful events. In addition, a stressful event (such as unemployment) may lead to other activities (such as loss of income, relocation or divorce). There is ample evidence that stressful events can worsen the disease you already have.

The Disease May be Earlier than Stress

Although some evidence supports the idea that Stress may cause various diseases, it may not be accurate for genuinely healthy people. "Instead, the event may affect the risk of the disease by inhibiting the body's ability to resist invading pathogens or aggravating the progress of the ongoing pre-morbid process," Cohen and colleagues wrote. It looks like a stress-triggered disease, "it may actually be a previously undiscovered disease that is triggered by stress." Therefore, in some cases, Stress may not be the cause of the disease itself, but only to cause the previous condition found worsened.

Some Stressful Situations are More Powerful than Others

The magnitude of the pressure event depends largely on the nature of the pressure. Studies have shown that the most destructive is the "threat to threaten one's ability or status", which is hitting people's "core identity." Loss of identity, loss of work, and interpersonal conflicts with a spouse or close friend can all exacerbate health problems, from increasing the risk of depression to increasing hypertension and reducing resistance to respiratory infections.

Generally, Chronic Stress is More Severe Than Acute Stress

It is not necessarily obvious that long-term, persistent or repeated Stress is worse than a one-time stress event. May adapt to constant stress-once you get used to Stress, and it may not cause you too much trouble (or damage your health). On the other hand, continuous Stress may be detrimental to health, because Stress is always present, and may occur when the body is vulnerable for other reasons at any time. Overall, chronic Stress may be worse because it may have a continuing adverse effect on the body's anti-disease immune system. Like a single traumatic event, acute stress may trigger a rapid deterioration of existing diseases such as heart disease. In this case, a sufficiently strong stress event can cause a fatal heart attack.

Perhaps Many Stress Events are Worse than Fewer Stress Events

The effects of stressful events may add up over time; a simple checklist to check how many stressful events a person has experienced in the past year indicates that experiencing more events will herald a deterioration in health. However, it is too complicated to state the exact reason, even in general. (The checklist method for collecting data may be wrong.) In fact, if the intensity of a single event is sufficient to seriously increase the health risk, other events do not necessarily increase the risk further. Therefore, it is unclear how the incident should be calculated; Cohen and colleagues pointed out that changing residence and reducing income after divorce may count as one of three things. This may not be the number of events, but the number of "life areas" where you are under pressure is more important. (Work, family life, medical issues, and financial issues all represent different areas where Stress can occur.)

A study looked at how people's self-reported stress experiences affected their ability to resist exposure to a common cold virus, rhinovirus. Those who report more stressful events are more likely to have a biologically proven cold, but even for those who are stressed, infection is inevitable: about half of stressful people are not sick.

The Impact of Stressful Events Depends on Your Life

Just as certain events can make people feel stressed, so are some non-events. These things don't happen during normal life. People usually expect to graduate from school (high school or university), find a job, get married, have children, and then retire. If you cannot graduate, cannot find a job or refuse to propose, then in life, if you expect to succeed in these areas, these pressures will be great. It may also be that different periods of life are more vulnerable to the adverse effects of stress than others. For example, childhood trauma is associated with a higher risk of chronic disease in later life. Such trauma may lead to lasting biological changes, which can be the cause of future diseases. In addition, Cohen and co-authors wrote: "Adversity in childhood may make a person face more pressure in life."

Stress Does Not Affect Men and Women Equally

Men and women respond differently to stress in behaviour and physiological response. Moreover, women are obviously more likely to experience stress than men. Part of the reason may be because "men often only report stress events that occurred directly on them," while women believe that when actual events happen to people around them, they also feel stressed. Men and women may also vary in their vulnerability to stress-induced diseases. For example, women seem to be more likely to develop depression related to Stress.

Health Problems Related to Stress That You Can Fix

Need another thing to reduce stress? Your stress may make you sick. "Stress not only gives us feel bad emotionally," said Jay Winner, M.D., the author of Life Without Stress and the head of the Sansum Clinic stress management program in Santa Barbara, California. About any health condition, you can think of. "

The study found many stress-related health problems. Stress seems to increase or increase the risk of diseases such as obesity, heart disease, Alzheimer's disease, diabetes, depression, gastrointestinal diseases and asthma.

Health Problems Related to Stress

What are the most important health issues related to stress? This is a sample.

Heart disease. For a long time, researchers have suspected that stress is high, and type A personality is at a higher risk of hypertension and heart disease. We don't know why. Stress directly increases heart rate and blood flow and causes cholesterol and triglycerides to be released into the blood. Stress may also be related to other problems-the increased likelihood of smoking or obesity-indirectly increases the risk of heart disease.

Doctors do know that sudden emotional stress can cause serious heart problems, including heart attacks. People with chronic heart disease need to avoid acute stress as much as possible and learn how to successfully manage the inevitable stress in life.

Asthma. Many studies have shown that stress can make asthma worse. Some evidence suggests that chronic stress by parents may even increase the child's risk of asthma. One study investigated how parental stress affects the incidence of asthma in young children who are also exposed to air pollution or whose mother smoked during pregnancy. Children whose parents are stressed are at a much higher risk of developing asthma.

Obesity. Excess fat in the abdomen seems to have a greater health risk than fat in the legs or buttocks-unfortunately; this is where people with high stress seem to store. Wenner said: "Stress leads to increased levels of the hormone cortisol, which seems to increase the amount of fat deposited in the abdomen."

Diabetes. Stress can worsen diabetes in two ways. First, it increases the likelihood of bad behaviour, such as an unhealthy diet and excessive drinking. Second, stress seems to directly increase blood sugar levels in patients with type 2 diabetes. Headache stress is considered to be one of the most common causes of headaches-not only tension headaches, but also migraines.

Depression and anxiety. It is not surprising that chronic stress is associated with an increased prevalence of depression and anxiety. A survey of recent research found that people who are related to work stress (such as those who require high salaries and rarely get paid) are 80% more likely to suffer from depression within a few years than those who are less stressed.

Gastrointestinal problems. This is one thing that stress does not work-it does not cause ulcers. However, this makes them worse. Wenner said that stress is also a common factor in many other gastrointestinal diseases, such as chronic heartburn (or gastroesophageal reflux disease, GERD) and irritable bowel syndrome (IBS).

Alzheimer's disease. An animal study found that stress may worsen Alzheimer's disease, causing its brain lesions to form faster. Some researchers speculate that reducing stress may slow the progression of the disease.

Accelerate ageing. In fact, there is evidence that stress can affect your age. One study compared the DNA of high-stress mothers (who take care of a chronically ill child) with the DNA of inanimate women. The researchers found that specific regions of the chromosome show an effect of accelerating ageing. Stress seems to accelerate ageing for about 9 to 17 years.

Die young. One study looked at the effects of stress on health by studying the spouses who cared for the elderly. They naturally suffered a lot. The study found that caregiver's mortality rate was 63% higher than that of people without a caregiver's age.

Vagus Nerve Stimulation

Vagus nerve stimulation involves using the device to stimulate the vagus nerve with electrical pulses. Currently, the FDA has approved implantable vagus nerve stimulators for the treatment of epilepsy and depression. There is a vagus nerve on each side of the body, running from the brain stem through the neck to the chest and abdomen.

In traditional vagus nerve stimulation, a device is surgically implanted under the skin of your chest, and a thread is placed under your skin to connect the device to the left vagus nerve. Although when activated, the device sends electrical signals to your brainstem along the left vagus nerve, and then sends signals to certain areas of your brain. The right vagus nerve is not used because it is more likely to carry fibers that supply nerves to the heart. The new non-invasive vagal nerve stimulation device does not require surgical implantation and has been approved in Europe for the treatment of epilepsy, depression and pain. Although the US Food and Drug Administration lately approved a non-invasive device that stimulates the vagus nerve to treat cluster headaches.

Why Do

About one-third of epilepsy patients do not fully respond to antiepileptic drugs. Vagal stimulation may be an option to reduce the frequency of seizures in people who are not controlled by drugs. Vagus nerve stimulation may also be helpful to those who do not respond to depression, such as antidepressants, psychological counselling (psychotherapy) and electroconvulsive therapy (ECT).

The U.S. Food and Drug Administration (FDA) has approved vagus nerve stimulation for use in:

- Four years old and above
- Have partial (partial) epilepsy
- Poor seizure control

The FDA has also approved vagal stimulation to treat depression in adults who have:

- Suffering from chronic refractory depression (refractory depression)
- Try four or more drugs or electroconvulsive therapy (ECT) or neither
- Continue standard depression treatment and vagal stimulation

In addition, researchers are investigating vagal stimulation as a potential treatment for a variety of diseases, including headache, rheumatoid arthritis, inflammatory bowel disease, bipolar disorder, obesity and Alzheimer's disease.

Risky

For most people, vagal nerve stimulation is safe. But it does have some risks, both in the operation of implanting the device and the risk of brain stimulation.

Surgical Risk

Surgical complications of implanted vagus nerve stimulation are rare and similar to the risks of performing other types of surgery. They include:

- Make a cut (incision) to implant the pain of the device
- Infection
- Hard to swallow
- Vocal cord paralysis, usually temporary, but can be permanent

- Side effects after surgery

Some side effects and health issues associated with implanted vagus nerve stimulation may include:

- Voice change
- Hoarse
- Sore throat
- Cough
- Headache
- Shortness of breath
- Hard to swallow
- Skin stinging or puncture
- Insomnia
- Increased sleep apnea

For most people, side effects are tolerable. Over time, they may lessen, but as long as you use implanted vagus nerve stimulation, some side effects may still be troublesome. Adjusting electrical pulses can help minimize these effects. If the side effects are unbearable, the device can be turned off temporarily or permanently.

How Do You Prepare

Before deciding to perform this procedure, it is important to carefully consider the pros and cons of implanting vagus nerve stimulation. Make sure you know what all other treatment options are, and you and your doctor think that implanting vagus nerve stimulation is the best option for you. Ask your doctor what you should expect during the procedure and after the pulse generator is installed.

Food and Medicine

You may require to stop taking certain medications early, and your doctor may ask you not to eat the night before the operation.

What Can You Expect?

Before the program

Before the operation and your doctor will perform a physical examination. You may need a blood test or other tests to make sure you do n't have any health problems. Your doctor may require you to start taking antibiotics before surgery to prevent infection.

In the program

Surgery to implant a vagus nerve stimulation device can be performed in an outpatient clinic, although some surgeons recommend overnight. The surgery regularly takes an hour to an hour and a half. And you may still be awake, but there are drugs that numb the surgical area (local anaesthesia), or you may lose consciousness during the operation (general anaesthesia).

The surgery itself does not involve your brain. Make two incisions, one in your chest or underarm (armpit) area and the another on the left side of the neck. The pulse generator is implanted in the upper left of your chest. The device was originally a permanent implant so, but it can be removed if necessary.

The pulse generator is about the size of a stopwatch and relies on battery power. The wire is connected to the pulse generator. The wire extends from the chest to the neck under the skin and connects to the left vagus nerve through a second incision.

After the Program

The pulse generator is turned on when you visit your doctor's office a few weeks after the operation. It can then be programmed to deliver electrical pulses to the vagus nerve at various durations, frequencies and currents. Vagal stimulation usually starts at a low level and then gradually increases, depending on your symptoms and side effects. The stimulus is programmed to turn on and off at specific cycles, such as turning on for 30 seconds and turning off for 5 minutes. When nerve stimulation is enabled, you may experience some tingling or mild neck pain and temporary hoarseness.

No symptoms of seizures or depression were detected by the stimulus. When turned on, the simulator will turn on and off at the interval selected by the doctor. You can use a hand-held magnet to start stimulation at other times, for example, if you feel an impending attack. Magnets can also be used to temporarily turn off vagus nerve stimulation, which may be necessary when you perform certain activities (for example, public speaking, singing or exercising), or when you have meals when you have difficulty swallowing.

You need to see a doctor regularly to ensure that the pulse generator is working properly and is not displaced. Please consult your doctor before performing any medical examinations (such as magnetic resonance imaging (MRI)) that may interfere with the device.

Result

Implantation of vagus nerve stimulation does not cure epilepsy. Most patients with epilepsy will not stop the seizure completely or take the epilepsy medication completely after the operation. But many people will have fewer seizures, up to 20% to 50%. Seizure intensity may also be reduced.

You may need several months or even a year or more of stimulation to notice any significant reduction in seizures. Vagus nerve stimulation can also shorten the recovery time after a seizure. People with vagal nerve stimulation to treat epilepsy may also improve mood and quality of life.

Research on the benefits of implanted vagus nerve stimulation for depression is still mixed. Some studies have shown that the benefits of vagus nerve stimulation for depression will gradually increase over time, and it may take at least a few months to find that the symptoms of depression have improved. Implanted vagus nerve stimulation is not effective for everyone, nor is it intended to replace traditional therapies. In addition, some health insurance companies may not pay for this procedure.

Implantation of vagus nerve stimulation as a treatment for Alzheimer's disease, headache, and rheumatoid arthritis is too little to draw any clear conclusions about its efficacy on these issues. More research is needed.

Does the Vagus Nerve Affect Sleep?

Seizures are very sensitive to sleep patterns. Some people have their first and only episodes after "overnight all night" at the university or after long periods of poor sleep. If you have epilepsy, a lack of "good sleep" will make most people more likely to have seizures. It can even increase the intensity and duration of seizures.

In this month's case article about epilepsy patients treated with a vagus nerve stimulator, we studied the relationship between sleep and epilepsy and how vagal nerve stimulator treatment affects the patient's condition. This study provides an opportunity to review the abnormal brain electrical activity, vagal nerve stimulants' understanding of sleep patterns and sleep breathing, as well as the complex factors of neurological complications and multiple drugs leading to excessive daytime sleepiness.

What is Vagal Stimulation?

Vagus nerve stimulation (VNS) is a method used to treat epilepsy. So, it involves implanting a pacemaker-like device that generates electrical pulses to stimulate the vagus nerve. The vagus nerve is one of the twelve cranial nerves. It transmits pulses between the brain and other parts of the brain and various body structures (mainly in the head and neck). The vagus nerve-the longest cranial nerve-also extends to organs in the chest and abdomen. And it serves many organs and structures, including the larynx (speech box), lungs, heart and gastrointestinal tract.

How Vagal Nerve Stimulation Affects Sleep and Sobriety

Vagus nerve stimulation has many effects on sleep and wakefulness, including improving daytime alertness and changes in sleep structure, reducing REM sleep and increasing wakefulness, waking up after falling asleep, and NREM stage 1 sleep. Stimulation is also associated with reduced airflow and efforts consistent with VNS activation. Please note that before implanting VNS in a patient, a sleep study suspected of sleep apnea should be performed.

Anti-Inflammatory Diet

Inflammation helps the body fight disease and protects it from harm. In most cases, this is an essential part of the recovery process. However, some people's physical conditions prevent the immune system from working correctly. This failure may result in persistent or recurrent low-level inflammation.

Chronic inflammation can occur with many diseases or such as psoriasis, rheumatoid arthritis, and asthma. And there is evidence that dietary choices may help control symptoms. Anti-inflammatory diets favour fruits and vegetables, foods containing omega-3 fatty acids, whole grains, lean protein, healthy fats and spices. It does not encourage or restrict the consumption of processed foods, red meat and alcohol.

The anti-inflammatory diet is not a specific eating habit but a way of eating. And the Mediterranean diet and the DASH diet are examples of anti-inflammatory foods.

What is an Anti-Inflammatory Diet?

Some foods contain ingredients that can cause or exacerbate inflammation. Sugary or processed foods can do this, and fresh whole foods are unlikely to produce this effect. The focus of the anti-inflammatory diet is on fresh fruits and vegetables. Many plant foods are good sources of antioxidants. However, certain foods trigger the formation of free radicals—for example, people fried food in cooking oil that was repeatedly heated.

Antioxidants in the diet are molecules in food that help the body scavenge free radicals. Free radicals are natural by-products of specific body processes, including metabolism. External factors such as stress and smoking may increase the number of free radicals in the body. Free radicals can cause cell damage. So, this damage increases the risk of inflammation and can cause many diseases.

The body produces some antioxidants to help remove these toxic substances, but antioxidants in the diet also help. Anti-inflammatory diets favour foods are rich in antioxidants rather than those that increase free radical production. Omega-3 fatty acids present in oily fish may help reduce levels of inflammatory proteins in the body. According to the Arthritis Foundation, fibres can also have this effect.

Types of Anti-Inflammatory Diets

Many popular diets have adhered to anti-inflammatory systems. For example, both the Mediterranean food and the DASH diet include fresh fruits and vegetables that are good for the heart, fish, whole grains, and fat. Inflammation seems to play a role in cardiovascular disease. Still, studies have shown that diet-based plant foods and a healthy Mediterranean diet of fats and oils can reduce the effects of inflammation on the cardiovascular system.

Can Anyone Help?

An anti-inflammatory diet can be used as a complementary therapy for many diseases that are exacerbated by chronic inflammation.

The following conditions involve inflammation:

- Rheumatoid arthritis
- Psoriasis
- Asthma
- Eosinophilic esophagitis
- Crohn's disease
- Colitis
- Inflammatory bowel disease
- Lupus
- Hashimoto's disease
- Metabolic syndrome

Metabolic syndrome refers to a series of illnesses that quickly occur at the same time, including type 2 diabetes, obesity, hypertension and cardiovascular diseases. Scientists believe that inflammation plays a role in all these factors. Therefore, an anti-inflammatory diet may help improve the health of patients with metabolic syndrome. A diet rich in an antioxidant may also help reduce the risk of certain cancers.

Food to Eat

An anti-inflammatory diet should combine the following multiple foods:

- Rich in nutrition
- Provide a variety of antioxidants
- Contains healthy fats

Foods that may help control inflammation include:

- Oily fish, such as tuna and salmon
- Fruits such as blueberries, blackberries, strawberries and cherries
- Vegetables including kale, spinach and broccoli
- Beans
- Nuts and seeds
- Olives and olive oil
- Fibre

The author of the 2017 article also suggested the following:

- Raw or moderately cooked vegetables
- Beans, such as lentils
- Spices such as ginger and turmeric
- Probiotics and prebiotics
- Tea
- Some herbs

It is worth remembering:

No food can improve human health. It is essential to include various healthy ingredients in the diet. Fresh, simple ingredients are the best. Processing changes the nutritional composition of the food. People should check the labels of prepared foods. For example, although cocoa is the right choice, cocoa-containing products usually also contain sugar and fat. The coloured plates will provide a range of antioxidants and other nutrients. Make sure to change the colour of fruits and vegetables.

Foods to Avoid

People who follow an anti-inflammatory diet should prevent or limit their intake:

- Manufactured food
- Foods with sugar or salt
- Unhealthy oil
- Processed carbohydrates, found in white bread, pasta and many baked goods
- Processed snack foods such as chips and biscuits
- Pre-made desserts such as cookies, sweets and ice cream
- Excessive alcohol

Also, people may find it helpful to limit intake of:

Gluten: Some people experience inflammation when they eat gluten. Gluten-free diets may have restrictions and are not suitable for everyone. However, if a person suspects that gluten will cause symptoms, they may want to consider eliminating it temporarily to see if their symptoms have improved.

Solanum: Plants belonging to the nightshade, such as tomatoes, eggplants, peppers, and potatoes, seem to cause a flare in some people with inflammatory diseases. There is limited evidence to confirm this effect, but one can try to reduce the symptoms of nightshade plants in the diet for 2 to 3 weeks to see if their symptoms have improved.

Carbohydrates: There is evidence that even if carbohydrates are wholesome, a high-carbohydrate diet may cause inflammation in some people. However, some carbohydrate-rich foods, such as sweet potatoes and whole grains, are excellent sources of antioxidants and other nutrients.

Can a Vegetarian Diet Reduce Inflammation?

For people who wish to reduce inflammation, vegetarianism is an option. The author of the 2019 review analyzed data from 40 studies. They concluded that people who follow a vegetarian diet might have lower levels of various inflammation markers. A 2017 study surveyed data from 268 people who followed a strict vegetarian diet, a milk-egg-vegetarian diet or a non-vegetarian diet. The outcomes of the research indicate that the consumption of animal products may increase the risk of systemic inflammation and insulin resistance. Early research in 2014 suggested that lower levels of inflammation may be the main benefit of a vegan diet.

Anti-Inflammatory Diet Tips

The transition to a new diet may be challenging, but the following tips may be helpful:

- Buy various fruits, vegetables and healthy snacks in the weekly shop.
- Gradually replace healthy meals with healthy homemade lunches.
- Use distilled water or soda instead of soda and other sugary drinks.

Other tips include:

- Discuss supplements with health professionals, such as cod liver oil or multivitamins.
- Add 30 minutes of moderate exercise to your daily activities.
- Maintain good sleep hygiene because lack of sleep can exacerbate inflammation.

Most Anti-Inflammatory Foods You Can Eat

Inflammation is both good and bad. On the one hand, it can help your body fight infections and injuries. On the other side, or chronic inflammation can lead to weight gain and disease. Stress, inflamed food and low levels of activity make this risk even more significant. However, research shows that certain foods can fight inflammation.

Berries

Berries are small fruits, rich in fibre, vitamins and minerals.

Although there are many variants, the most common ones include:

- Strawberry
- Blueberry
- Blueberry
- Blackberries

The berries contain an antioxidant called anthocyanin. These compounds have anti-inflammatory effects and can reduce the risk of illness. Your body produces natural killer cells (NK cells) that help keep the immune system functioning correctly. In a study of men, people who consumed blueberries daily delivered more NK cells than those who did not. In another study, overweight adults who ate strawberries were low in specific inflammation markers associated with heart disease.

Fatty Fish

Fatty fish is an essential source of protein and long-chain omega-3 fatty acids EPA and DHA.

Although all types of fish contain certain omega-3 fatty acids, these oily fish are one of the best sources:

- Salmon
- Sardine
- Herring
- Mackerel
- Anchovy

EPA and DHA can reduce inflammation, which leads to metabolic syndrome, heart disease, diabetes and kidney disease. Your body metabolizes these fatty acids into anti-inflammatory compounds called Resolvins and Protectin. Studies have discovered that people who consume salmon or EPA and DHA supplements have reduced inflammation marker C-reactive protein (CRP). However, in another study, people with irregular heart rhythms who took EPA and DHA daily had no difference in inflammation indicators compared to people who took a placebo.

Broccoli

Broccoli is very nutritious. It is a cruciferous vegetable, as well as cauliflower, brussels sprouts and kale. Studies have shown that eating more cruciferous vegetables is associated with a lower risk of heart disease and cancer.

This may be related to the anti-inflammatory effects of the antioxidants it contains. Broccoli is rich in sulforaphane, an antioxidant that fights inflammation by reducing the levels of cytokines and NF-kB that cause inflammation.

Avocado

Avocado is probably one of the few superfoods worth praising. They are rich in potassium, magnesium, fibre and monounsaturated fats that are good for heart health. They also contain carotenoids and tocopherols, which are associated with a reduced risk of cancer. In addition, a compound in avocado can reduce inflammation of young skin cells. In one study, when people ate a slice of avocado and hamburger, their inflammatory markers NF-kB and IL-6 were lower than those who ate burger alone.

Green Tea

You may have understood that green tea is one of the healthiest drinks you can drink. It reduces your risk of heart disease, cancer, Alzheimer's disease, obesity and other diseases. Many of its advantages are due to its antioxidant and anti-inflammatory properties; especially a substance called epigallocatechin-3-gallate (EGCG). EGCG suppresses inflammation by reducing the production of pro-inflammatory cytokines and destroying cellular fatty acids. You can buy green tea in most stores or online.

Chilli

Bell peppers and chilli peppers are rich in vitamin C and antioxidants and have powerful anti-inflammatory effects. Bell pepper provides antioxidant quercetin, a sign that can reduce the oxidative damage of sarcoidosis (an inflammatory disease). Chilli contains erucic acid and ferulic acid, which can reduce inflammation and lead to healthier ageing.

Mushroom

Although there are thousands of mushroom varieties all over the world, only a few are edible and can be grown commercially. These include truffles, Portobello mushrooms and shiitake mushrooms. Mushrooms have meagre calories and are rich in selenium, copper and all B vitamins. They also contain phenol and other antioxidants that provide anti-inflammatory protection. A particular mushroom called a lion's mane might reduce the low-grade inflammation associated with obesity. However, a study found that cooking mushrooms can significantly reduce their anti-inflammatory compounds. So, therefore, it is best to eat them raw or cooked.

Grapes

Grapes contain anthocyanins, which can reduce inflammation. In addition, they can reduce the risk of many diseases including heart disease, diabetes, obesity, Alzheimer's disease and eye diseases. Grapes are also one of the best sources of resveratrol, another compound with many health benefits.

In one study, inflammatory gene markers (including NF-kB) in heart disease patients who consumed grape extract daily decreased. More importantly, their adiponectin levels have increased. The low level of this hormone is associated with weight gain and an increased risk of cancer.

Turmeric

Turmeric is a spice with a strong earthy flavour, commonly used in curries and other Indian dishes. Curcumin is a potent anti-inflammatory nutrient, so it has received widespread attention. Turmeric can reduce inflammation associated with arthritis, diabetes and other diseases. In fact, daily consumption of 1 gram of curcumin combined with piperine in black pepper will cause a significant decrease in the CRP, an inflammation marker in patients with metabolic syndrome. However, it may be challenging to obtain enough curcumin to get noticeable effects from turmeric alone.

In one study, women who were overweight took 2.8 grams of turmeric daily, and their inflammation signs did not improve. It is more effective to take supplements containing isolated curcumin. Curcumin supplements are usually used in combination with piperine to increase curcumin absorption by 2,000%. If you are interested in using turmeric in cooking, you can find turmeric in most grocery stores or online.

Additional Virgin Olive Oil

Additional virgin olive oil is one of the best fats you can eat. It is rich in monounsaturated fats and the leading food in the Mediterranean diet and has many health benefits. Studies have shown that virgin olive oil can reduce the risk of heart disease, brain cancer and other severe health conditions.

In the study on the Mediterranean diet, people who consumed 1.7 ounces (50 ml) of olive oil daily had significantly lower CRP and other markers of inflammation. The action of olein, an antioxidant in olive oil, has been compared with anti-inflammatory drugs such as ibuprofen. Remember, extra virgin olive oil has a more potent anti-inflammatory effect than more refined olive oil. Extra virgin olive oil is easy to find in local grocery stores, but you can also buy it online.

Dark Chocolate and Cocoa

Dark chocolate is delicious and creamy, satisfying. It is also rich in antioxidants, which can reduce inflammation. These can reduce your risk of illness and lead to healthier ageing. Flavanol is responsible for the anti-inflammatory effect of chocolate and can keep the endothelial cells in the arteries healthy. In one study, smokers significantly improved endothelial function within 2 hours of consuming high-flavonol chocolate (65 sources).

However, make sure to choose dark chocolate with a cocoa content of at least 70%-a more significant percentage is even better-to obtain these anti-inflammatory effects. If you have forgotten this enjoyment during your last purchase, you can buy it online at any time.

Tomatoes

Tomato is a nutritional power. Tomatoes are productive in vitamin C, potassium and lycopene, which is an antioxidant with impressive anti-inflammatory properties. Lycopene may be particularly beneficial for reducing the pro-inflammatory compounds associated with several cancers.

One study determined that drinking tomato juice can significantly reduce the signs of inflammation in women who are overweight, while obese women cannot. Please note that cooking tomatoes with olive oil will maximize the absorption of lycopene. This is because lycopene is a carotenoid, a nutrient that can be better absorbed by fat.

Cherry

Cherries are delicious and rich in antioxidants, such as anthocyanins and catechins, which can fight inflammation. Although research on the health-promoting properties of tart cherries surpasses other varieties, sweet cherries also provide benefits. In one study, when people consumed 280 grams of cherries a day for one month, the level of CRP, an inflammation marker, decreased and remained low for 28 days after stopping cherries.

Inflammatory Food

In addition to adding nutritional and anti-inflammatory ingredients to the diet, it is essential to limit the consumption of foods that promote inflammation. For example, processed foods such as fast food, frozen foods and processed meat have been associated with higher levels of inflammatory markers (such as CRP). At the same time, fried foods and partially hydrogenated oils contain trans fat, which is an unsaturated fatty acid and is also associated with increased inflammation.

Other foods, such as sugar-sweetened beverages and refined carbohydrates, have also been shown to promote inflammation.

Here are some examples of foods related to increased inflammation:

- Junk food: fast food, light meals, potato chips, pretzels
- Refined carbohydrates: white bread, pasta, white rice, crackers, flour tortillas, crackers
- Fried food: French fries, doughnuts, fried chicken, mozzarella cheese sticks, egg rolls
- Sugary drinks: soda, sweet tea, energy drinks, sports drinks
- Processed meats: bacon, dried beef, canned pork, sausages, hot dogs, smoked meat
- Trans fats: shortening, partially hydrogenated vegetable oil, margarine

Can Diet Help with Inflammation?

Do you know that there may be a link between inflammation and increased risk of chronic diseases? Some studies have shown that heart disease, type 2 diabetes and obesity may be related to chronic inflammation. Inflammation is a healthy body reaction that promotes recovery. The inflammation indicates that the immune system is fighting infection. The infection may be related to bacteria, wounds, allergens or other causes.

Usually, we think the signs of inflammation are redness, swelling and pain. However, sometimes inflammation occurs in our bodies-patients with bronchitis have lung infections, which means that the lungs may become inflamed. This may indicate that their immune system is working hard to fight this infection. The signs of inflammation may not be visible. For others, chronic inflammation may be related to their immune system problems. Whatever the reason, chronic inflammation can damage the body's DNA and increase the risk of cancer.

What We Know and Don't Understand About Food and Inflammation

Promote various anti-inflammatory diets online. However, researchers are still figuring out how our diet affects inflammation. So far, it seems that eating a variety of nutritious foods may help reduce inflammation in the body. What we eat may help prevent and control chronic inflammation. Moreover, an overall healthy eating plan can provide nutrients that help maintain the normal functioning of the immune system:

- Fruits and vegetables contain natural ingredients called phytonutrients, which can help prevent inflammation.
- Healthy fats, such as monounsaturated fats and omega-3 fatty acids, may promote inflammation.

Foods high in saturated fat may exacerbate inflammation. In addition, highly processed foods and other foods containing trans fats may also cause inflammation.

Is there "Anti-Inflammatory Food"?

Dark chocolate (cocoa content over 70%), red wine, green tea, turmeric and ginger are believed to help reduce inflammation. However, many of the discoveries of the anti-inflammatory effects of these foods come from studies on laboratory animals. At present, we cannot conclude how these foods affect human inflammation. Moreover, it is not known how much and how long to eat "anti-inflammatory" food to eliminate inflammation. Currently, the best advice is to adopt a healthy diet.

Five diet methods can help reduce inflammation.

Step 1: Make fruits and vegetable half of the plate.

- Designed to include vegetables and fruits in every meal
- Eat a variety of brightly coloured vegetables and fruits
- All forms are included-including fresh, frozen, canned and dried. Just make sure to look for products without added sugar and lower sodium content.
- Pay attention to the vegetables in each subgroup every week, including dark green, red and orange vegetables, as well as beans and peas.

Step 2: Be Alert to Protein

- Five to six ounces of equivalents per day is appropriate for most moderately active people. Moreover, in terms of protein, fatty fish containing omega-3s should be selected several times a week.
- Enjoy a meat-free meal with beans such as tofu, bean temp and beans, peas and lentils.
- Choose foods with low protein content, such as thin pieces of skinless chicken or turkey or beef and pork.

- Includes low-fat or non-fat dairy products, such as skimmed milk and yoghurt, which have a low saturated fat content.
- Minimize highly processed foods such as deli meats, bacon and sausages.

Step 3: Choose Healthy Fats.

- Use monounsaturated fats, including olive oil, safflower, sunflower, canola, peanut and avocado oil.
- Eat more omega-3 rich foods
- Eat salmon or other fatty fish 2 to 3 times a week.
- Snack nuts, such as walnuts.
- Mix flax seeds, chia seeds and hemp seeds into salads and other dishes.
- Minimize highly processed foods containing partially hydrogenated oils and large amounts of saturated fats.

Step 4: Choose Whole Grains.

Always choose whole grain flour and cereals instead of refined flour.
It includes various coarse grains such as brown rice, quinoa, millet and wheat berries.

Step 5: Try Fresh Herbs and Spices.

- Add fresh herbs and add flavour to the dishes.
- Enrich your recipes by trying condiments.

Other lifestyle factors

Although the food you eat is essential, it is not the only factor affecting chronic inflammation. To stay healthy

- Get enough sleep-Both sleep quality and duration directly affect inflammation.
- Stay active-regular physical exercise has anti-inflammatory effects. On most days of the week, perform 30 to 60 minutes of moderate-intensity physical activity every day.
- Reach and maintain a healthy weight-too much fat in the body may exacerbate inflammation.

Need help designing an anti-inflammatory diet?

A registered dietitian nutritionist can help develop a diet plan that suits your unique lifestyle, taste preferences and medical needs.

Ways, the Vagus Nerve, can Relax You

`The vagus nerve is also known as the "wandering nerve" and can help you relax in an unprecedented way. This is a fascinating story in which a nerve appears, wandering from head to abdomen while relaxing all the body organs it visited on its way. But first, please see the picture above; this is the 2016 Supermoon. If you spend a few seconds staring at it, you will probably feel more relaxed.

When looking at the soft red moon, trees and flying birds under the blue-grey sky, you may take a deep breath unconsciously. If this is not the case and you don't feel very conscious, please take a deep breath. Try it now and take a deep breath. Once completed, you will find that it can almost relax you because slow deep breathing has always been done this way. We have this ability. This is through a physical process called vagus nerve stimulation.

Why is the Vagus Nerve?

The vagus nerve or "wandering nerve" is the longest autonomic nerve in the human body. It has come a long way as if it were wandering in its collection. It starts at the bottom of our brain, travels to the neck, and then further through the chest to the large intestine of the abdomen. In women, it is as low in the stomach as the cervix of the uterus.

The relaxation caused by deep breathing is due to the "wandering nerves" of our bodies. Scientists call it the vagus nerve and call it activation of the vagus nerve. Each side of our body has a vagus nerve. The vagus nerve, as part of the autonomic nervous system, controls body functions that you do not voluntarily control, such as heart rhythm. In addition to the beating heart, it also controls our bowel movements and sweating. It can also release tears, saliva and stomach acid. Although when something touches the back of our throat, it causes us to gag, and when a cotton swab tries to remove earwax, it makes us cough. Women with complete spinal cord injury experience orgasm through the vagus nerve.

Keep my heart beating: Our heart has a built-in pacemaker, the heart's natural pacemaker, called the sinus node (SAN). It regulates our heartbeat. In turn, the vagus nerve controls the pacemaker of our heart. The wandering nerve requires the SAN to instruct the heart to maintain its beat at a specific rate.

How important is the vagus nerve to our heart? Assuming the vagus nerve is removed, even if we relax in a hammock, our heart will beat about 100 times per minute. Any spirit that has been hitting all the time can quickly wear out our organs and ourselves. Therefore, a complete vagus nerve that is always alert can control our resting heart rate between 60 and 80 per minute. When we actively stimulate the vagus nerve, just like taking a deep breath to observe the super moon above, our hearts will relax.

What is Vagal Stimulation

Vagus nerve stimulation (VNS) is a surgical treatment used to treat uncontrolled epilepsy by transmitting a slight electrical pulse through the vagus nerve to the brain.

In surgical VNS, surgeons implant a device called a vagus nerve stimulator subcutaneously in the chest cavity to cause vagal nerve stimulation, which involves sending light electrical pulses through the vagus nerve. So, the US Food and Drug Administration has approved this device as a treatment option for the following people:

- Medically uncontrollable seizures, and
- Difficult to treat depression.
- Certain drugs can also stimulate the vagus nerve. This is chemical VNS.

How Important is the Vagus Nerve?

Christopher Bergland is a world-class endurance athlete and the ten authors of "The Way of Athletes: The Biology of Sweat and Bliss". The vagus nerve can relax you-gif once wrote: there is grace under pressure. "

The stimulated vagus nerve releases a bunch of anti-stress chemicals in our body, namely acetylcholine, prolactin, vasopressin and oxytocin. Among them, the neurochemical acetylcholine lowers our heart rate. We knew this as early as 1921 when German-born psychobiologist Otto Loewi showed that stimulation of the vagus nerve could slow the heartbeat of frogs. For this, he won the Nobel Prize in Physiology or Medicine in 1934.

In the midnight experiment of dreaming and dreaming midnight, Loewi took off two beating frog hearts and soaked them in a separate salt solution. Although he stimulated the vagus nerve of one of the centres, it slowed down that heart. Then, he took the saline from the slow-paced heart and put it into the second heart. This also caused the second heart to slow down. This proves that the vagus nerve releases a chemical substance, which slows down the heart rate.

A recent study showed that vagal nerve stimulation could help enhance our memory. This may open up a new world for Alzheimer's patients. The role of the vagus nerve in inhibiting human inflammation is also a promising research direction. Besides, patients with more robust vagal responses, that is, patients who are more affected by vagal stimulation, may recover better after stress events.

A study in January 2017 showed that vagus nerve stimulation therapy could help people overcome drug addiction by helping people learn new behaviours instead of drug-related behaviours.

No Drugs or Equipment.

Indeed, some indirect actions can stimulate the vagus nerve, but not as drastic as implant surgery, or what Loewi did in his initial experiment-cutting off the heart of a beating frog.

You can use the following ten simple methods to stimulate the "wandering nerves" to lower your heart rate and initiate the body's relaxation response:

Ways to Relax Through the Vagus Nerve

- Deep and slow breathing-abdominal breathing
- Hold your breath for a few seconds
- Splash your face with cold water
- Cough and throat
- Tighten abdominal muscles as if emptying the intestines downward
- Massage both sides of the neck-carotid sinus massage
- Eyeball
- Cheerful "joyful" laughter
- Meditation, especially loving meditation
- Sports and yoga

Vagus Exercises

What is the vagus nerve?

- Turn on neurogenesis and help our brain sprout new brain cells.
- Quickly eliminate stress, relaxation, and fight/escape by relaxing reactions.
- Enhance our memory.
- Resist inflammation.
- Help you fight high blood pressure.
- Prevents cortisol hormones and other oxidants from ageing and destroying the brain and body
- Prevent systemic (systemic) inflammation-the main factor leading to ageing and poor health.
- Help us overcome depression and anxiety.
- Help us sleep better.
- Raise the level of human growth hormone.
- Help us overcome insulin resistance.
- Refuse allergic reactions.
- Reduce the chance of stress and tension headaches.
- Help mitochondria multiply, and grow-this is the key to maintaining optimal energy levels without damaging our DNA and RNA.

- Affect our overall ability to live longer, healthier and more active lives.

How to Activate the Vagus Nerve on its Own?

Vagus nerve stimulation can be easily activated through a variety of breathing and relaxation techniques:

- Deep / slow abdominal breathing.
- 'OM' chanting
- Soak your face in cold water after exercise
- Fill your mouth with saliva and submerge your tongue to cause an over-relaxed vagal response.
- Drinking water loudly
- Sing loudly

To take a deep breath and inhale through your nose and exhale through your mouth, remember:

- Breathing is slow.
- Breathe deeply from the abdomen.
- The exhalation time is longer than the inhalation time.

Use the Breath to Relieve Pain.

You can learn to use breathing exercises to divert attention from pain to other places. Human thought Handle one thing at a time. If you focus on the rhythm of breathing, then you will not focus on the pain. When we feel pain, most of us stop breathing and hold our breath. Holding your breath will activate the fight/escape/freeze response; it will increase the pain, Stiffness, anxiety or fear.

You can follow these steps: inhale deeply into the abdomen (i.e., expand the diaphragm) fifth, stop and then exhale slowly through the small hole in the mouth. At rest, most people breathe 10 to 14 times per minute. Enter parasympathetic nerve / relax / the healing mode is ideal for reducing your breathing by 5 to 7 times per minute. Exhale through your mouth instead of the nose makes your breathing more conscious and helps you observe your breathing is easier.

When you reduce breathing every minute and enter parasympathetic mode, your muscles will relax, Eliminate your worries and anxieties. Increased oxygen supply to human cells, which helps Produce endorphins, good hormones for the human body. Tibetan monks have been practising "Breathing" has been for decades, but this is not mysterious. You can enhance your experience, Inspire love by imagining you and exhale thanks. These ancient technologies will also Improve memory, fight depression, lower blood pressure or heart rate, and boost immunity System-it's free!

'OM' Chanting

The International Yoga Magazine conducted an interesting study in 2011, in which "OM." Compare chanting with the pronunciation of "SSS" and rest status to determine if chanting it has a more stimulating effect on the vagus nerve. Studies have found that chanting is more effective instead of "sss" pronunciation or other states.

Effective "OM" recitation is related to the vibration around the ear and the whole body. It can be expected that this feeling will also pass the auricle branch of the vagus nerve will inactivate the margin (HPA axis).

How to Read it?

Press and hold the vowel (o) part of "OM" for 5 seconds, then continue to the consonant (m) part the next 10 seconds. Continue chanting for 10 minutes. Finally, take a deep breath and end with gratitude.

Cold Water

Physical exercise increases sympathetic nerve activity (HPA axis- fight / escape, stress response), with parasympathetic withdrawal (rest, digestion, rehabilitation, immune system), leading to higher heart rate (HR). Studies have found that it seems simple to soak cold water in your face

An effective method to reactivate the parasympathetic nerve immediately after exercise through accelerated exercise the vagus nerve stimulates a decrease in heart rate, bowel movements and opens the immune system. It is also effective to activate the vagus nerve in a non-motor environment.

In the cold-water face soak, the subject remained seated, bending his head forward into cold water. Immerse the face so that at least two-thirds of the forehead, eyes and cheeks were overwhelmed. The water temperature is maintained at 10-12 ° C.

Increased Saliva

The calmer the mind and the deeper the relaxation, the easier it will be to stimulate the saliva. When the mouth can produce a lot of salivae, you know the vagus nerve has been stimulated, the body is in a parasympathetic state.

To stimulate salivation, try relaxing and reclining on a chair, imagine a juicy lemon. Like your mouth full of saliva, just put your tongue in the bathtub (if this does not happen, just use a small amount of warm water will let your tongue bathe here. Just exercises to relax the will stimulate the secretion of saliva). Now relax further and feel the hands, feet, hips, behind the neck and let everything relax. Breathe this feeling deeply and stay here as long as possible.

Vagus Nerve Could Be Affecting Your Mood

Have you heard of the vagus nerve? If not, this may be the answer to your health question. Studies have shown that loud vagal tone (vagus nerve and active vagus nerve activity) can make the body better regulate blood sugar levels, thereby reducing the possibility of diabetes, stroke and cardiovascular disease. And the low vagal tone is associated with chronic inflammation. Enhancing vagal mood can help relieve brain fog, fatigue, anxiety, depression and indigestion.

The vagus nerve is composed of a pair of left and right nerves, extending from the sides of the brain stem behind the ear to the neck, neck, chest and abdomen. It is conceivable that it touches several main organs of the body-stomach and digestive tract, lung, heart, spleen, intestine, liver and kidney. Although specifically, it is part of the parasympathetic nervous system. This rest and digestive system can slow the heart rhythm, increase gastrointestinal and glandular activity and relax the gastrointestinal sphincter, thereby saving energy.

The vagus nerve is a component of the autonomic nerves of the nervous system. This is the side that happens without you having to think about or control it. So breathing, heart rate, digestion, and even how we absorb, process, and understand our experiences are all directly related to the vagus nerve.

Here is how to strengthen this essential element of the nervous system:

Cold Exposure

When the body adapts to the cold, the sympathetic system (fight or escape response) decreases, while the parasympathetic system increases, which is mediated by the vagus nerve. You can perform cold exposure experiments by washing cold water, trying cryotherapy, or even immersing your face in cold water.

Vitality Mike Perrine said: "There are many benefits, especially reducing inflammation, promoting metabolism and improving mood."

Meditation

Meditation has been shown to enhance the vagal activity, reduce sympathetic activity and increase vagal regulation. In one study, caring addicted meditators increased the tone of the vagus nerve, making them feel happier and more socially connected. Check out meditation apps such as "Headspace" and "Calm".

Yoga + Breathing Exercises

Yoga increases GABA (sedating neurotransmitters in the brain). The researchers believe that this is achieved by stimulating vagal afferent, which increases the activity of the parasympathetic nervous system. Yoga exercises such as pranayama, through specific techniques and practices to regulate breathing, will improve vagal tone. Ujjayi (sounds like the breath of the ocean) will increase parasympathetic nerve activity and heart rate variability, that is, the rhythm of the space between each heartbeat.

Try a yoga class in your area or practise breathing exercises at home. It is simple, for example, breathing through the nose four times, then exhaling slowly through the nose, while tightening the back of the throat-making a sea-like sound-the count is 6.

Probiotics

Certain probiotic strains, such as lactic acid bacteria, have been shown to increase GABA by stimulating the vagus nerve. So another study found that the probiotic strain Bifidobacterium longum works through the vagus nerve to normalize anxiety-like behaviour in mice. Buy high-quality, trusted probiotics now.

Sing and Change

Singing at the top of the lungs increases oxytocin and activates the muscles in the back of the throat connected to the vagus nerve, thereby enabling the vagus nerve. So, don't close singing in the shower!

Massage

You could manually stimulate the vagus nerve by massaging certain parts of the body. Neck massage along the carotid sinus (right side of the neck) can stimulate the vagus nerve. A foot massage can also increase the modulation of the vagus nerve and help lower blood pressure. Enjoy a massage or self-massage at home.

Fasting

It has been shown that fasting can stimulate the parasympathetic nervous system. Digestion consumes a lot of energy. Digesting food can give the body a little rest, and can provide extra energy for rebuilding the nervous system and relaxing the body. When completing the 21-day cleaning procedure, follow the twelve-hour agreement for the cleaning procedure. It is also a habit that is easy to develop after the process is concluded for a long time.

Laugh

Laughter tends to reduce sympathetic nervous system activity and increase parasympathetic nervous system activity. Although this may be caused by the diaphragm stimulating the vagus nerve, spending time with friends and family makes you feel good, and most importantly, laugh more!

How to Strengthen Your Vagus Nerve to Upgrade Your Whole Body

The vagus nerve pathway is a nervous system that connects outward from the brain and regulates many organs in the body- heart, lung, intestine, liver, etc. Modern medicine treats a single organ as a disease area and ignores the fact that the brain and nervous system tell the organ what to do. Your organ regularly sends status checks to your mind through the vagus nerve to report progress.

This is a two-way road. When all goes well, your brain will remain as it is. When the organ is struggling, it can send signals to the brain to obtain more resources. When your body starts to move, the vagus nerve transmits signals from the brain to the organs, thereby slowing down.

To ensure that the translation is not lost, the vagus nerve must be in a healthy state. Your brain and organs rely on vagal pathways to regulate things like:

- Hunger hormones and food intake

- inflammation
- Anxiety and escape
- immune response

The vagus nerve is essential because of its involvement. Please continue reading to learn how to support the vagus nerve through vagal tone.

It's Time, but Take a Deep Breath

There is a connection between breathing and heart rate, and the vagus nerve can regulate breathing. This is why the regular practice of yoga can reduce overall stress.

Yoga breathing and guided breathing exercises can calm your heart rhythm and lower blood pressure. The respiratory activity can increase vagal tone and effectively control the prehypertension of the experimental group. In one study, slow breathing exercises improved autonomic nerve function in healthy participants. Breathe quickly. That's because a quick breath makes your body think that it is escaping from a predator. That will trigger your body's alarm and trigger a stress response.

Box Breathing Towards S.O.S.

If you feel panic or want to blow a pad, try breathing.

- Take four breaths.
- Keep four numbers.
- The expiratory number is four.

- Wait for the number four.

Repeat the preceding steps until your hand is placed on the control again.

For the first few times, draw your fingers in a square pattern in the air. When you are confused, it can help you remember what to do.

The slow expansion of the lungs sends a signal to the heart, indicating that the soul is slowing down, which gives a feeling of calm throughout the nervous system. The vagus nerve connects all these signals and releases acetylcholine, a calming chemical that you can inject yourself at any time through relaxation techniques.

Chill Out, Literally

Adapting to the cold will slow the vagal response, thereby slowing down the activation of the sympathetic nervous system. Periodic cold air measurably reduces the pressure mark. Cold exposure helps relieve the symptoms of depression and anxiety, which may be regulated by the vagus nerve.

Stimulation of the vagal pathway stimulates digestion. When the rat's metabolism is slowed by anxiety, cold exposure reactivates the gastric nerve and returns everything to normal. All this happens through the vagus nerve pathway.

Keep Your Stomach, Happy.

Have you ever heard of the gut-brain axis? That means that the microorganisms in your digestive system communicate with the brain. Your microbiome is an ecosystem of friendly bacteria in the body and on the skin. Most commonly, when someone talks about the microbiome, they are talking about microorganisms in the gut and colon.

As the science of microbiome develops, the scientific community is exploring ways in which more and more microbiomes affect your entire body. Research on the link between the microbiome and emotions is expanding, and the communication between the gut and the brain depends on the vagus nerve.

Research on animal models and humans supports the idea that a booming microbiome can suppress anxiety and improve your mood. Some studies have examined this effect with or without a complete vagus nerve to understand whether the vagal pathway is involved. Rodents supplemented with specific probiotic strains showed reduced anxiety and depression indicators, but not in animals that had vagus nerves cut off before the experiment.

The researchers discovered the beneficial effects of probiotics on human emotions. Healthy women who have eaten fermented food for four weeks show positive changes in brain activity, especially in the part of the brain that controls emotions and feelings. From animal studies and scientists' understanding of the vagus nerve, you can make a reliable guess that the intestinal-brain communication here occurs through the vagus nerve.

The best way to support the intestinal flora is to conduct a comprehensive microbiome test, such as Viome. Viome is a home test kit that can be used to quickly analyze the microbiome and then get personalized dietary recommendations to restore balance.

Find Your Safety Tips.

Dr Stephen Porges, a vagal expert, established the Polyvagal theory (more on bullet-proof broadcasting), which proposes a decision process for deciding whether to activate combat or flight. You are not aware of this process-it all happens in the background, and different branches of the vagus nerve will be activated according to different situations.

When you encounter terrifying stimuli, the first layer to pass is the level of response to social communication-speech, body language, vocals and other nonverbal cues. If the incentive is too strong to reason, the brain will activate the "fight or escape" response. When it fails, the most primal fear reaction is to play with possums-feeling frozen. When you know that your fears are unreasonable, you can use security tips to stop panic at the first level and prevent the brain from falling into a fight or runaway response. You can try the following methods.

Use a Soothing Voice.

In an interview with Bulletproof Radio, Stephen Porges explained a way in which this phenomenon is hardwired in children.

Rhythm (singing) speech (also called "mother") can calm children. Waldorf school training teachers use this tone to maintain a calm and happy classroom. If you visit the nearby playground in the early morning, then you have seen its operation.

Changing your intonation also applies to adults. Meditation directed in person or by recording uses a slow, rhythmic tone of speech. Using voice as a reminder to relax can make your brain enter a relaxed state at a faster rate than normal conversation sounds.

Train Yourself in Safety Tips

With a little practice and you can train your mood to feel safe. Safety tips can avoid your fear and anxiety reactions. One way is to create "safe places" or "happy places" while staying calm. For this reason, you imagine yourself in a place of complete relaxation and feel contented and peaceful. Use sensory information as much as possible-imagine attractions, smells, sounds, etc.

Practice this visualization often. This way, when you start to feel fear or anger, you can start a "safe place" effortlessly. It's there when needed.

Take Care of Your Myelin.

Your vagus nerve is myelinated, which means it is covered with a layer of protective fat that can isolate it and help the signal spread effectively. When myelin on any nerve breaks down, the nerve will not work.

Surgical Implantable Electronic Vagus Nerve Stimulator

When you fight against something, the vagus nerve activates the immune system. Doctors use this knowledge to treat inflammatory diseases by stimulating the vagus nerve with electricity and drugs. For patients with severe epilepsy or depression, doctors surgically implant a vagus nerve stimulator because it suppresses the inflammatory response.

You can Adjust Your Baby's Vagus Nerve

The baby's vagal emotion is related to many factors. The vagal tone of infants born too premature babies or mothers with depression and anxiety during pregnancy is low.

If you have experienced something during pregnancy, don't worry. You can help improve your baby's vagal pathway through normal bonding behaviour and care.

Washing cold water should probably wait until the junior student agrees. During infancy, baby massage and kangaroo care (to keep the baby's skin to skin) help the baby's vagus nerve form. If your child has passed infancy, you can work with them to mobilize the vagus nerve in some mature ways, such as breathing techniques and cold wind in the shower.

Considering that the benefits of vagal conditioning extend to the main organs and back of the body, a massage, yoga class and a few minutes of chicken skin ump may be worthwhile. For more ways to support the entire system from head to toe, please pop up your information in the box below to avoid losing anything.

Massage for Vagus Nerve Stimulation

Massage is one of the simplest (and most sensory) ways to increase vagal tone. We have developed a unique blend of aromatic oils-our new vagal nerve oil-with precious flavours of juniper, chamomile, lavender and jojoba. When gently massage the neck, this essential oil can stimulate enthusiasm and physical and mental health. In order to enhance the massage experience of the vagus nerve, we have developed illustrated self-massage instructions (and the use of vagus nerve oil) for your relaxation and enjoyment.

Massage Technique to Increase Vagus Nerve

Manually massage the neck and focus along the sinuses to stimulate vagal nerve oil. In this order:

Step 1: Pump the two-handed vagal nerve oil into your hands, then knead them together

Step 2: Put your hand on the nose and suck deeply.

Step 3: Starting from the collarbone, gently massage upwards along the left side of the neck.

Step 4: Repeat along the right side of the neck.

Step 5: Wipe gently behind the earlobe with two fingers.

Step 6: Place your hands on your chest and stagger your fingers.

Step 7: Place the interlaced fingers behind the head, keeping the head straight, but move the line of sight entirely to the right. Stay until you feel like swallowing, sighing or yawning.

Step 8: Repeat with the other side.

This will put your autonomic nervous system (vagus nerve) into the parasympathetic or relaxation state.

CPSIA information can be obtained
at www.ICGtesting.com
Printed in the USA
LVHW021842031120
670613LV00032B/1344